MAN&MOTOR the 20th century love affair

MAN&MOTOR the 20th century love affair

edited by Derek Jewell●designed by Michael Rand/David Hillma

Library of Congress catalog card number: 67-13128
Printed and bound in Great Britain

MAN & MOTOR
the 20th century love affair

photographic adviser Christopher Angeloglou ● technical adviser Maxwell Boyd

 WALKER AND COMPANY, NEW YORK

Introduction: the evidence

People have not always loved the motor-car. A man driving a car across Tower Bridge in 1896 was faced with a crowd who had to be restrained from dumping him, and his machine, into the Thames below.

There were similar scenes in most countries which the motor-car invaded, though fewer perhaps in the United States. This may have been a reflection of that well-known American frontier feeling for freedom and experimentalism; maybe it was just that Americans had more room.

The anger against cars was understandable. They were noisy and dangerous. They frightened people and horses; and many countries, like Britain, were horsy. They also smelt; and on most roads they would churn up a fog of dust behind them that besmirched the landscape for a full 15 minutes afterwards. So restrictive were the early laws against them, and so anxious were the public to help the police enforce them, that pioneer motorists must have felt like hunted animals. The police boxed pretty dirty, too. Their evidence against a man summoned for "furiously driving a car" at Croydon in 1901 estimated his speeds variously between 16 to 153 miles an hour.

There was certainly little sign then that in later days names like Panhard, Benz, Lanchester, Levassor, de Dion, Royce and Rolls would form a new hagiology. Jean-Joseph-Etienne Lenoir, who in 1862 drove a vehicle that used petroleum spirit vapour and electric ignition through the streets of Paris, was cursed rather than canonised.

Society's ostracism did not last. The motor-car was too useful, too exciting and, for some, too profitable to be kept down for long. By 1901 there were over 300 different makes of car being manufactured throughout the world. The love affair was beginning.

"Love" may seem a strong word. But it is not misused. There are good commercial reasons why man should tolerate the motor-car — sniff its noxious fumes, allow it to dictate the shape of our cities and landscapes, see it kill tens of thousands of people each year. It is an indispensable part of twentieth century living, for business or pleasure. Without the automobile-making industry, the economies of great nations might collapse. In America, for instance, one out of every six businesses — and one in every seven salaried workers — is connected in one way or another with the motor-car business.

But modern man's feeling for the car has deeper roots. He has become enamoured of it. No other inanimate object has in our century inspired such a close and involved relationship. The car has become both part of man's personality and an expression of it.

Psychiatrists say they know all about this: that through the car men fulfil their desire for freedom, for power, for superiority, for virility above the norm. It has become almost a cliche that the car is a symbol of sexual prowess. Phallic symbols litter the advertisements for petrol and oil and automobiles.

Stirling Moss once said there are two things no man will admit he can't do well: drive and make love. "If I had a big enough front door," said Les Leston, another racing driver, of his Ferrari, "I'd take it into the house with me and up to bed." A man cleaning his car on the Roehampton council estate near London was asked why he did it. "I'm clean in body," he said. "I have to dress reasonably smart, so I don't think there's any good of dressing smart and having a dirty car."

Because the car is a much-loved thing (has it not become the most common status symbol of urban society?) people like to beautify it. They will clean and polish it with dire regularity and thoroughness; in extreme cases they will not take it out thereafter if it rains. They will decorate it after their fashion – with woodrim steering wheels or phoney exhaust pipes, with plastic flowers or venetian blinds. "Bolt-on goodies" the trade calls all this. It is like hanging jewellery on the object of your passion. Or buying toys for a rather spoilt member of the family. Well, isn't it like a member of the family? Doesn't it get its own room?

For some their car becomes the symbol of their

(Published) — 1968

fantasy life, for others an extension of their home. It is, of course, well known as the auxiliary bed-room, or front parlour, of our days. It can also be a portable living-room or office; a portable seat at the movies (America has 4,000 drive-in theatres); and a portable pew.

This needs further explanation. In California, the most extreme of all car-cult areas, there are now open-air, drive-in churches. "We had", an American cleric was saying on TV one night, "a great big dream of building a chain of walk-in, drive-in churches. From San Francisco to San Diego." He was speaking, by microphone, and with patent pride, at one such drive-in sanctuary at the time. "By the time this service is over, 10,000 people will have streamed in and out of this place, worshipping in the privacy of their family cars." There is, too, a temple erected in many countries to the automobile itself. It is called a Motor Show. And even this is only half of it. The motor-car is inextricably intertwined with the creative arts as well as the crafts, the business, the routine, the worship, of the twentieth century.

Great engineers, and designers, devote their waking and sleeping hours to it. Young, and not-so-young men of almost superhuman skills give their lives for it on racing tracks everywhere. Millions of words are written about it, and by this I do not mean only the columns of motoring journalism. Our finest novelists and essayists have made it part of their work, often treating it in careful, obsessive detail. There are also ad-men (if you regard them as creative artists) who spend long hours discovering what our dreams are and then shoot them back at us in the shape of cars. Why else do they always show their cars in mountains, in fields, by lakes, by beaches, with never another exhaust pipe in sight? Never, of course, in a traffic jam.

Poets, it's true - though not all of them - have largely ignored the car, but the lyric-writers of popular songs have not, neither have painters and sculptors. There are sculptors today who use parts of the automobile, or crushed car bodies, as their staple material. There is also a woman in Buckinghamshire who so loved her 1932 Austin that she could not bear the thought of anyone else owning it. She had it crushed into a column of metal, first to be an ornament in her garden, then to act as the headstone for her grave.

It is quite common for people to burst into tears when, finally, they deliver up their old cars to the breakers. That's the death of the loved one, of course, and the money people spend trying to keep their cars from death's door is phenomenal. In the United States the figure for car repairs is considerably higher than the annual six billion dollars spent on doctors' bills for human beings. Thunderbird, Imp, Sting Ray, Cresta, Princess: the very names imply the romance and the worship of the motor-car. There was also a vogue once for giving cars pet names (one of the first great marques was, indeed, named after a girl: Mercedes) and though this tradition has faded, cars are still treated as if they were people.

"I feel a bit of a heel getting rid of it. It's part of me," said Ewen Solon, an actor, of a car which had come to the end of its useful life. "That car is looking at me now and saying 'You stinker. After all I've done for you, you're going to put me in the knacker's yard.'"

The point need not be laboured further. People love cars, even though in mid-century, as increasingly they dominate our lives, our feeling for them may be more like a love-hate relationship. In a sense it is the love affair of the twentieth century. That is what this book is about.

DEREK JEWELL

5

Contents

Among the photographers whose work is represented in this book are Christopher Angeloglou (Page 77, 200-201 — Brailey, King car-crusher), Alan Ballard (35, 43, 188 — Braden), Horst Baumann (28, 93, 157), Maxwell Boyd (48-49, 51), Gerry Cranham (54-55), Robert Daley (39, 63), Duffy (45, 112-113, 188 — Shrimpton), Graham Finlayson (78-80, 100, 172-173, 175-176), Henry Groshinsky (199), Frank Herrmann (166-167), Rayment Kirby (158), David Montgomery (200 — Aggio), Denis Rolfe (97), Lord Snowdon (41), Michael Ward (8-9), Patrick Ward (25-27, 66-67, 140-141), Bryan Wharton (30-31, 47, 98-99, 142-143), Ian Yeomans (106-107)

Wrapper and cover designs by David Hillman and Michael Rand; jacket and cover photographs by Ian Yeomans
End-paper design by François Dallegret
Commentaries, introductions and captions are, except where otherwise indicated, by the editor

1 The racers

Above: *the pace of Grand Prix racing. This was the 1966 Cooper-Maserati, testing at Goodwood, with Roy Salvadori driving.*

It begins with going fast. Speed is perhaps the most important single reason why human beings are enamoured of cars. Love of speed seems almost instinctive and basic in twentieth-century man. Aldous Huxley said it provides the only genuinely modern pleasure, though people also like to say he believed speed to be the only new sin of our age.

Anyone can go fast in a car. But that is not the same as motor racing, which at summit level is arguably the most exciting and dangerous competitive sport in the world. Some men say it is beautiful as well as thril-

ling. Certainly it is also a business. Success on the track sells cars off it.

Very, very few men indeed possess the skills, the reflexes, the temperament, the competitive instinct to become Grand Prix drivers. This is why such men have become the folk-heroes of our time. A terrible pro-portion even of the best of them get killed or crippled. Because the game they play is the ultimate expression of our fascination with the speed of the automobile, the first section of this book is devoted to it.

Above: *the power of Grand Prix racing. In 1966 Formula I cars leapt to 3 litres. This was the Cooper-Maserati engine.*

9

Barrier-breakers: the men, the machines by Bill Boddy

Every few years since 1900, a new racing car has arrived to push the limits of speed, performance — and safety — significantly further. And each car has tended to find the driver who seemed perfectly mated with it. Here the editor of the magazine 'Motor Sport' chooses the eleven most important machines and men in racing history. Temperamentally, Bill Boddy, now in his fifties, is in direct line of descent from those early motoring pioneers who banded together like conspirators to outwit police and hostile public. Unbendingly, this shy and diffident man has spent a lifetime championing what he sees as the rights of motorists; his personal contribution to each monthly issue of his magazine, each piece discreetly signed 'W.B.', numbers 15,000 words.

"So", said 'Motor Sport' after a woman had been praised in court for reporting an incident of dangerous driving, "present-day Hitlerites have a happy hunting ground in car-packed Britain, with official approval for Gestapo actions. St Christopher, deliver us!"

Levassor: Panhard-Levassor 1895

Almost as soon as there were motor-cars, there was motor racing. The sport that later was to charge the imagination of millions of people around the world began in France. On June 11, 1895.

There had been a reliability trial, sponsored by a newspaper, *Le Petit Journal*, the previous year. This took place between Paris and Rouen, a distance of 78¾ miles, and attracted an entry of 102 vehicles, propelled not only by petrol, steam and electricity but by such optimistic methods as pedals, a system of levers, hydraulics, compressed air, the weight of the passengers or just gravity. The Comte de Dion's steam tractor, towing a carriage, made best time, but the first prize of 500 francs was divided between Panhard and Peugeot petrol cars since these were regarded as more practical machines.

This was not a true race. But the first three horseless carriages home averaged better than 11 m.p.h., a pace so prodigious that the French newspaper refused to support another similar contest.

Thirsting for a proper race, the Comte de Dion and Baron Zuylen collected supporters and nearly £2,800 prize money and devised a cruel marathon, requiring competitors to drive from Paris to Bordeaux and back, over 732 miles of narrow dusty roads never previously traversed by mechanically-propelled vehicles locked in combat.

For this pioneer race Emil Levassor (left in our lower picture) constructed a crude Phenix-engined Panhard developing about 4 h.p. at 800 r.p.m. (top picture). Perched on this solid-tyred carriage with his engineer, Playade (right in picture), beside him, he steered by tiller, pressing on so well that he reached the town of Ruffec before his co-driver was out of bed. It was a great feat by the man who was the mechanical genius behind the Panhard marque, in a car as top-heavy as it was long. We are told that "driving through the night at top speed (perhaps 18½ m.p.h.) with the inefficient oil lamps was no easy task"— surely a classic understatement.

Nevertheless, Levassor continued to Bordeaux and then set off on the long journey back to Paris, refusing on the return leg to hand over to his now wide-awake co-driver at Ruffec in case he lost his formidable lead. At Tours he was 4½ hours ahead of the Peugeot opposition. Every 100 kilometres he stopped for supplies, but rested for only 22 minutes on a drive occupying 48 hours 48 minutes. This 15 m.p.h. average for two days and nights is an epic of motor racing.

But although Levassor won 12,600 francs and a monument at Porte Maillot, he lost the premier award because his car (its number, 5, can be clearly seen in the picture) only had two seats!

Gabriel:
Paris–Madrid Mors 1903

After that first Paris—Bordeaux race the new sport boomed. Race followed race along the ruler-straight, tree-lined roads of Europe. Be-goggled, dust-coated adventurers fought primitive but powerful automobiles in these pioneer marathons. They raced from Paris to Bordeaux again, from Paris to Amsterdam and back, to Toulouse, to Berlin, to Vienna. And all the time they were learning valuable lessons about electric ignition, pneumatic tyres, wheel-steering. Engines grew ever larger, speeds rose, and racing between determined men seeking to publicise various makes of car was firmly established. By 1903 the racing light cars could do nearly 90 m.p.h.

Then came Paris—Madrid, with 3 million spectators milling about the open-road course. Two hundred vehicles, motor-cycles included, tore off in the direction of Bordeaux.

Tragedy followed. In their wake they left dead and injured spectators (though the numbers were at first exaggerated) and authority stepped in. The race was stopped. Horses tugged the cars to Bordeaux station. Open-road racing was *mort*.

But one man made Bordeaux. Gabriel. In his 70 h.p. Mors (above), with one of the first streamlined bodies, he overtook 79 opponents and achieved an average of 65.3 m.p.h. over 342 of the most hazardous, havoc-struck miles in racing history. One car came close to Gabriel's: Louis Renault's light racer, which made 62.3 m.p.h. But his brother Marcel had crashed and died.

Gabriel's was the epic of courage, though. In his big machine that looked like an upturned boat he steered down the narrow roads by the line of the tree-tops as he plunged blind into the dust-clouds of slower cars.

Boillot:
Peugeot 1912

The demise of racing across the unguarded roads of Europe sent cars to closed circuits. Speeds rose over good surfaces, round courses free from roaming onlookers, where drivers could practice assiduously. Brakes, road-holding and steering were heavily taxed on the many corners. Engines remained enormous, but science was coming in.

The French Grand Prix had become the premier annual race, although after Mercedes won it in 1908 the French sulked and it was abandoned until 1912. By this time the Peugeot racing drivers Zuccarelli, Boillot and Goux had persuaded Swiss engineer Ernest Henry to build them cars using his advanced twin-overhead-camshaft inclined multiple-valve engines. At Dieppe in 1912 (where the picture shows Georges Boillot, darling of an incredulous public, in action) these comparatively small 7.6-litre Peugeots were more than a

match for the gigantic 14-litre Fiat and 15-litre Lorraine-Dietrich cars. They raced for two days and 956 miles, and Boillot, wearing his familiar woollen hat (above right), won at 68.4 m.p.h.

Today we regard a 7½-litre engine as enormous. But before the Kaiser war it was thought fantastic that the Peugeots were so fast. The car, and Boillot's phenomenal driving, made the small-engined racer 'in', especially as 3-litre side-valve Sunbeams had run home third, fourth and fifth.

Engine-size came down still further in the 1913 Grand Prix. Peugeot had 5.6-litre cars and Boillot's came first, Goux's second. Boillot was, moreover, something of an inventor; eared, quick-change hub caps were his idea. And Henry's famous valve gear became accepted practice for racing engines after 1918. You find it in Jaguars, Aston Martins and Alfa Romeos even today.

Lautenschlager: Mercedes 1914

The 1912 Peugeot engine designed by Henry was to revolutionise racing, but in 1914 Mercedes and others still relied on a single-overhead-camshaft engine. Racing, though, continued to improve performance and safety. Front-wheel brakes were taken up by Peugeot and Delage for the 1914 French Grand Prix at Lyons. Tyres that would about last out a tough road race had appeared two years earlier.

Germany announced, via Mercedes, that she intended to win the last great contest in Europe before she went to war. Her team of white four-cylinder 4½-litre Mercedes was meticulously prepared and its drivers—Christian Lautenschlager, Salzer, Wagner, Seiler and Pilette—came early to France, plotting gear ratios and studying the course. Mercedes may not have had Henry valve gear or front-wheel brakes, but they had discarded chain drive and their cars poked out 115 h.p.

With the shadow of calamity creeping over Europe, there was a feeling of nationalism more intense even than usual about the contest. To fight the menacing Mercedes, whose engines resembled those in the fighter planes the Kaiser was even then building, France still relied on Boillot and the Peugeot. The Frenchman never drove better—but new factors were entering motor racing. First, the Peugeots were outnumbered, five against three; second, team tactics had arrived. One Mercedes would go all out, drawing on the French cars until they broke up.

Round the 23-mile circuit they battled, the Mercedes matching in balance, speed and acceleration the better stopping power of the Peugeots. Towards the end Boillot led, but still the phlegmatic Lautenschlager (above, in the victorious car), who was controlled from the pits with military precision, waited for the Peugeot to break.

After six hours' racing, two laps from the end, Lautenschlager took the lead. On the last desperate lap, as Boillot strained to catch the German, the back axle of his Peugeot expired. It coasted to rest, as twenty-five other retired competitors had done. Mercedes went on to come 1, 2, 3. One month later Germany was at war with France and Boillot was to be shot down over French soil in aerial combat. It was the end of an era.

14

Murphy: Duesenberg 1921

Ernest Henry continued to be a power in the design field even after the war. He took his twin-cam Peugeot engine further forward by using the straight-eight cylinder form, much influenced by the war-time Bugatti aero-engines on which he worked.

The straight-eight theme was tried out successfully at Indianapolis in 1920 during the 500-mile track race, but the winning Monroe was similar to Henry's 1913 four-cylinder Peugeot. Then came the first post-war French Grand Prix, run at Le Mans, in 1921. For this there was a 3-litre limit, a move instituted to stimulate progress in engine design still further. Henry's imprint was on many of the entrants.

Sunbeam and Ballot had straight-eight engines, the former a copy of Henry's Ballot lay-out. Fiat, too, had eight cylinders in line, but they departed from Henry's ideas by copying the pre-war Mercedes. The notable new contenders, however, were the Americans, making their first European racing entry since 1908. Their cars were straight-eight Duesenbergs, also influenced by Bugatti aero-engines, which would run up to 5,000 r.p.m., gave as much power as the 4½-litre Mercedes of 1914, and had hydraulic four-wheel brakes for the first time. They also had a fine driver: Jimmy Murphy (left, and above in his Duesenberg).

One Duesenberg threw a rod, another was held back by clutch slip, but over a stone-strewn course Murphy proved supreme, despite finishing without coolant, a pebble having punctured his radiator. He was the first, and thus far the last, American driving an American car to win a major European G.P. He covered the 322 miles at 78.1 m.p.h. Another American, Ralph de Palma, was second in a straight-eight Ballot.

Nazzaro:
Fiat 1922

As engineering advancement was relentlessly pursued, a 2-litre limit was introduced for the 1922 Grand Prix season. This was soon to be countered by the supercharger, a pump which could force mixture into the engine and thus give it an artificial capacity and power well above its norm. But not yet. For a time, leading makes continued with the usual atmospheric induction for their engines and Fiat, with their 1922 G.P. cars, set a fashion in body style and specification that was to dominate 2-litre racing.

Strasbourg was the venue for the French Grand Prix that year. The Fiats, with six-cylinder, roller-bearing engines giving 92 b.h.p. at 4,500 r.p.m., were lightened to the extreme. They scaled 13 cwt. unladen. It may have been this, or inferior material, which made them

somewhat unsafe. During the race, back axles broke on two of them, killing Biagio Nazarro, nephew of veteran Felice Nazarro (seen above both inside and out of his car), who came first at over 79 m.p.h. and took the lap record to 87¾ m.p.h.

Nazarro had won this great contest for Fiat in 1907, when he was the debonair darling of the ladies. The lower picture on the opposite page shows Nazarro as he was around that time. He is at the wheel of the mighty 300 h.p. Fiat SB4-190 of 1908 which he tested prior to its attacking—unsuccessfully—the land speed record in 1914. The Fiat was left at Ostend at the outbreak of war and vanished along with its Russian owner.

By 1923, the supercharger was 'in'. Not that it was a new idea. Chadwick had tried it in 1908, Mercedes in 1921. Now most racing engines began to use it, with Fiat in the lead. They had an awful fiasco in the 1923 200-mile race at Brooklands, from which Malcolm Campbell and Carlo Salamano both retired dramatically, but they won the 1923 Italian G.P. using a Rootes-blown straight-eight, the first supercharged car to win a G.P.

The 2-litre rule forced the pace. Sunbeam supercharged their six-cylinder engine and won at San Sebastian. In 1924 it was Alfa Romeo's turn to dominate racing with their beautiful straight-eight P2 cars. In 1925 Delage swept all before them, using twelve tiny cylinders in their dual-blower, 190 b.h.p. engines. And speeds kept on increasing. These two-seater racers could hit 135 m.p.h.

Nuvolari:
Alfa Romeo 1935

NUVOLARI

After the days of supercharged Fiats and Sunbeams, racing underwent considerable change. The 2-litre limit was replaced by a 1½-litre formula, which was dominated by the complicated Lory-designed blown straight-eight Delage cars. Speeds rose so dangerously that riding mechanics were barred. By 1927 a team of 1,500 c.c., 130 m.p.h. G.P. cars cost over £40,000 in current currency to build. These highly-specialised machines, burning odd fuels, were far removed from everyday cars.

Depleted fields resulted and led to a low-ebb period of racing. But politics were moving in. Before the mid-Thirties, Mussolini and Hitler saw in international motor racing a useful propaganda medium. In 1931 racing revived under no-holds-barred rules, and because mechanics were not allowed, single-seater cars appeared, while long races called for changes of drivers.

Under these rules the Alfa Romeo Tipo B single-seater was evolved from the Monza two-seater. At first it had a 2·6-litre, twin-cam, straight-eight engine, but this was later enlarged to 2·9, 3·2 and eventually to 3·8 litres. With its slim chassis, this Alfa Romeo

18

was the first true single-seater to run in European Grands Prix.

Alfa Romeo withdrew from racing in 1933, but Enzo Ferrari took over the Vittorio Jano-designed Tipo Bs. With the larger engine size and Dubonnet independent front suspension, these Scuderia Ferrari Alfas were still a match for the new German Mercedes racers, especially with Tazio Nuvolari at the wheel.

Nuvolari is considered by many authorities to have been the greatest driver of all time. Slight, wiry, excitable, the little Italian knew how to 'tiger'. He was the first to exploit four-wheel-drift cornering to compensate for tired brakes. He became idolised enough to appear on postcards (opposite page), with the inevitable laurel wreath. In the photograph above he is cornering in an Alfa at Montlhery during the 1935 French Grand Prix. A month later he beat the Germans on their home ground at Nurburgring.

Thereafter motor racing was to become a fantastic contest of technical prowess between the Auto-Union and Mercedes-Benz teams driving under the banner of the Nazi regime.

Caracciola:
Mercedes-Benz 1937

The political propaganda which prompted the racing of 1934-39 produced the most enthralling spectacle of all time.

Enormously powerful German cars drifted the corners, accelerated out of bends with wheels spinning and black burnt rubber streaked on the road. Along the straights they howled at not far short of 200 m.p.h.

Aghast, the officials tried to curb high performance with a maximum weight limit of 750 kilograms. But with no check on financial expenditure, the engineers of Stuttgart created light-alloy power units developing 600 b.h.p. from 5·6-litres for these 16½ cwt cars. Suspension developments, using soft springing and de Dion back axles in conjunction with a stiff, tubular chassis, gave drivers some measure of control in these over-steering titans.

The difficulty was to find drivers capable of extending them. Alfred Neubauer, the Mercedes racing manager, had hawk's eyes as a talent spotter, but he had to bring in Dick Seaman from England to eke out his all-German team, led by Caracciola (left) who drove the fabulous W.125 Mercedes-Benz (above). Alfa Romeo snatched a few victories still, but Mercedes were mainly opposed by rear-engined Auto-Unions. They were exceedingly tricky jobs to handle and only Nuvolari and Rosemeyer truly mastered them. The season of 1937 was the last of this battle of the giants; Mercedes won 9 races, Auto-Union 6.

Ascari:
Ferrari 1951

The titanic years of Grand Prix motor racing died with World War II. But racing blossomed again, as always. By 1951 it was contested in Formula I events between supercharged 1½-litre cars and non-supercharged cars of up to 4½-litres.

Alfa Romeo, thanks to outside support, had been able to field a team of very fast, blown 1½-litres which at first beat everything. But they were delicate machines, which needed stripping and overhaul after every race. Behind them breathed Enzo Ferrari—with fewer resources but immense ambition. His designer, Aurelio Lampredi, favoured the less-stressed big engine, without forced induction.

The Tipo 159 Alfa Romeos had been improved by seasons of development, and their saloon-car-sized engines ran up to 9,000 r.p.m., delivering over 380 b.h.p. But the V12 Ferraris, built in a hurry, caught the Alfettes before the 1951 season was over. It was a fascinating technical battle. With the Ferraris giving a relatively easy 380 b.h.p. at 7,500 r.p.m., Alfa replied with more like 400-plus at over 10,000 r.p.m. But their engines had to burn very rich alcohol mixtures to cool the valves, and they did only 1½ miles to the gallon. This meant frequent refuelling, or starting with heavy loads of fuel which upset the handling. The supercharger had never caught on for production cars, so the atmospherically-fed engines were closer to family-car techniques.

Under these circumstances Ferrari forged ahead in races which showed how much road-holding had improved since before the war. Their best driver was plump, full-breasted Alberto Ascari (left, characteristically wearing peak-less helmet, and above in 4½-litre V12 Ferrari).

21

Fangio:
Mercedes-Benz 1954

Daimler-Benz of Stuttgart use motor racing for research—and for the publicity value of success. They have made a habit of dominating periods of racing, then retiring all-conquering at the end of a given Formula.

In 1903, although their team cars were lost in a factory fire, they borrowed touring Sixty Mercedes from enamoured customers and won the Gordon Bennett Trophy in Ireland. Mercedes had such a convincing victory in the 1908 French Grand Prix that French manufacturers refused to support their own race for three years. On the eve of World War I a team of white Mercedes dominated this same race and vanquished the French Peugeots. In the age of Hitler, they won the Grands Prix of the late Thirties with gloriously large, powerful and dangerous cars.

After World War II, racing was won by science, not brute force. But Mercedes-Benz continued to beat all opponents. So far as Grand Prix racing was concerned the Stuttgart company returned to the circuits in 1954, having roused their racing department—which veteran Alfred Neubauer still headed—with the competitive 300SL sports cars. Again they produced a technical triumph.

The supercharged 2½-litre engine was the vogue, and Mercedes built a straight-eight with fuel injection, desmodromic mechanically-closed valves, torsion-bar all-round independent springing, swing-axle rear suspension, and a five-speed all-synchromesh gearbox. The car was so effective that it was soon to out-race every rival.

On their first appearance, in the French G.P., these new W196 Mercedes finished first and second. But there was one snag. They were equipped with all-enveloping bodywork, which proved a handicap at Silverstone in the British G.P., where Juan Manuel Fangio—a very great driver indeed—took the practice lap record (he is seen doing it above) but lost the race to the Italians. His enclosed front wheels spoiled the precision of his cornering. So the bodies on the frames were changed, and this new version of the W196 was all-conquering. Fangio gained the World Driver's Championship in 1954 and 1955, and the champagne reward of victory (left) became a common occurrence for the rugged, calm man from the Argentine.

Stirling Moss followed in the wheel-tracks of Fangio during these two successful seasons and was to win the 1955 Mille Miglia, last of the great open-road contests, in a 300SLR sports Mercedes-Benz closely related to the victorious Grand Prix cars. One day Mercedes-Benz will return.

Clark: Lotus 1965

Jim Clark and Lotus symbolise the dominance of British cars and drivers from the late 1950s onwards. Connaught, H.W.M. and B.R.M. had tried in the Fifties without success, but retired millionaire industrialist Tony Vandervell at last won the World Manufacturers' Championship for Britain in 1958 with his Vanwall cars, even though his top driver, Stirling Moss, was just pipped for the Drivers' Championship by Mike Hawthorn.

Power was toned down by changing the Formula I limit to unblown 1½-litre engines from 1961, but lap speeds still rose as chassis design improved. Costs were rising too. Soon only Ferrari and B.R.M. could afford to build their own engines. Smaller firms like Cooper and Lotus found their salvation in the Coventry-Climax engine, adapted from a fire-pump power unit!

Under the 1½-litre formula the whole concept of the racing car changed. The Cooper Company (see page 62) had started the trend, designing small, light, rear-engined cars: they won the World Championship, with Jack Brabham from Australia driving, in 1959 and 1960. Then Colin Chapman joined in. His Lotus designs incorporated still more scientific ideas, especially for road-holding. Suspensions were set up for different circuits; and fantastic new tyres gave superb 'cling' in all weathers.

By now, drivers lay almost fully reclined in cramped cockpits. Lotus brought in the very stiff monocoque form, and engine poke was enhanced by fuel injection and electronic ignition. Clark (above, in cockpit, with Chapman)

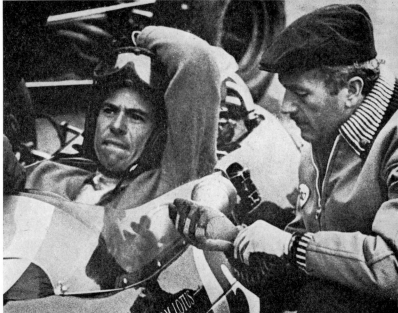

dominated the Lotus victories, taking the World Championship in 1963 and 1965. Graham Hill also won the Championship (1962) with B.R.M., and in 1965 Chapman applied G.P. techniques to a Ford-powered Lotus (top picture) to win the Indianapolis 500 Mile Race, with Clark driving. Hill won it in a Lola-Ford, with Clark second, in 1966.

Brabham and Honda now made their own cars for a scene which science had rendered rather dull but very desperate. The safety factor of modern racing had, however, rubbed off on production models. The authorities upped Formula I engines to 3 litres for 1966 without too many misgivings.

23

The driver's world

1 Not so much a circus, more a travelling monastery

Hunter Davies was born in 1936. Since leaving Durham University he has been a newspaper reporter and gossip-columnist, most notably as Atticus of 'The Sunday Times'. The film rights of his first novel, 'Here We Go, Round the Mulberry Bush', were quickly sold in 1965. He is, in relation to motor racing, an outsider. He is not particularly enamoured of it, nor has he seen much of it. His reportage after following some of the leading drivers around is all the cooler, and perhaps more revealing, because of that.

Jim Clark and Jackie Stewart, while sharing the same suite at a hotel near Goodwood, received a telegram congratulating them on their marriage to each other. They found out that some girls had sent it, so they broke into their room, put sugar in their beds and hid their underwear. Jackie Stewart then found confetti in his bedroom and a month's supply of the Pill in his car (his wife was expecting their first baby soon after).

On one transatlantic flight, about a dozen British drivers were all on the same plane. To while away the long hours, they had a whip-round just to see if they could tempt the air hostess to strip off. They started at a pound a head and got it up to five pounds. They never actually persuaded her, although the pilot agreed and chipped in five shillings.

On the night before one important race, a well-known British driver, whose wife wasn't with him, woke up in his hotel bedroom to find a naked strip-tease girl in bed beside him. All very satirical, so the other drivers thought. They'd paid and planted her. Drivers who are staying in hotels with their wives are used to having managers barging in on them. The trick is for some joker to tell the hotel manager that a sex maniac has locked himself in that room with a chambermaid.

The best-known risible anecdote of them all, still told on most circuits with great glee, concerns Harry Schell, the French-American driver. At Rheims one year he left his Goggomobil outside his hotel. The other drivers got together, carried it upstairs and put it in the reading room on the first floor. They then took every piece of furniture out of his bedroom. When he arrived with his girl friend, the bedroom was bare, except for a bowl of flowers in the middle of the floor.

Harry Schell was killed on May 13, 1960, while doing a practice run at the Silverstone circuit. He was just 39 years old.

Racing drivers are not sex maniacs. In fact most of them seem less interested in sex than any other group of sportsmen (if you look upon racing as a sport) and far less than any other group of show business personalities (if you look upon racing as show business).

Any sex element in their japes is purely a development of the undergraduate chamber-pot-on-tower joke. They are adults in physique, will-power and financial resources, but they still have a schoolboy streak in them.

This is because racing drivers live a private, enclosed life. In this confined state, part of their persona has been put under a magnifying glass and blown up and enlarged. Their powers of concentration and their control over their mental and physical reactions are developed to an intense degree. But other parts of their development often tend to be left behind; like their sense of humour.

This weakness for pranks exists, but it is the last, and minor relic of the old cavalier-gentleman image of the racing driver.

To meet them in civvies, with their discreet suits and well-scrubbed faces, they radiate about as much excitement as accountants. Socially, they now come from all backgrounds.

In Britain especially, it has become a classless sport, with perhaps more opportunities to get into it than in any other country. In the last decade, drivers have been coming down the range, from upper to middle class, and now to lower middle class.

Jim Clark went to Loretto, the Scottish public school. Jackie Stewart, his fellow Scot, went to the local secondary school and left at 15. There are very few working-class lads around yet, but they shouldn't be long arriving in force.

Sir John Whitmore is one of the dwindling band of aristocratic types still around, and he is a sports car rather than Grand Prix driver. He was the European saloon car champion of 1965.

He went to Eton and all that and his father was Lord-Lieutenant of Essex. But to me he seemed more of a beatnik than a blue blood. He wore a wispy beard and dressed like a Rocker when I called. He said: "I haven't got one friend from my old school.

"When I inherited the title, all my friends were amazed and said where did you get that from, then? I'm not sure why my father got it. For being a bloody good chap, I suppose."

I spent a lot of time at one track trying to find Lady Whitmore (Sir John was already in bed, as it was after nine o'clock). She is Swedish, very Mod in dress. She was wearing huge square spectacles which covered the whole of her forehead and nose. "Some people wear make-up," she said. "I wear glasses."

But John Whitmore is an exception. The more glamorous, dare-devil type of driver (Mike Hawthorn and Stirling Moss both had more than a touch of this image) has virtually disappeared. Before the war racing drivers really were all gentlemen trying to be mechanics. Today, racing drivers are mechanics trying to be gentlemen. Perhaps *engineers* rather than mechanics, although it spoils the aphorism. Mechanics in motor racing tend to be a lesser breed, as far as status goes. They are the men. Drivers are the officers.

So today the Grand Prix driver is a highly skilled engineer (super-mechanic, if you like), much sought after, who flies all over the world to perform difficult feats which only a dozen people in the world have the skill, knowledge and daring to do anything like as well.

The minute his job is done, his first thought is to get back home, to the wife and kids and the quiet respectability of suburbia. They still talk about the racing drivers' 'circus', which makes it sound very gay indeed. But apart from the occasional schoolboy stunts, the mad, dare-devil days are over. When Jack Brabham (a quiet man, nicknamed 'Chatty Jack') became in 1966 the first driver to win a Championship Grand Prix in a car he had made himself, it symbolised the change in racing.

Racing drivers, as they move round the world, are now more like a travelling monastery than a circus, each with his self-imposed vows of chastity (at least outside marriage), obedience and temperance.

The motor journalists are about the only part of the racing circus with any atmosphere. Unlike many other specialist journalists, they are all on good and intimate terms with the drivers. They know all their private lives and worries, although they never write about them. (You rarely get political correspondents, or sports writers, on such friendly and social terms with their subjects. At the bottom of the scale, you get gossip columnists, who know least about their subject yet tell the most.)

The motoring journalists eat and live with the drivers. In fact they do more eating and living than the drivers, who always pack up early. Racing drivers themselves don't drink or smoke or stay up late or eat huge meals or live it up in any way whatsoever. Unless you happen to be a car fanatic, more than a couple of hours with any driver is a pretty boring experience.

It's hard to think of exceptions to these generalisations. Innes Ireland does drink, admittedly. But he actually tells you he drinks, which somehow makes it a bit of a boast. You know that really he's averagely sober.

Racing drivers tend to be small to medium height, with muscular shoulders and forearms. They like wearing short-sleeved shirts which show off their arms. They tend to be rather selfish, though not in a nasty way. It's just that they are so geared to winning that in their private life everything has to revolve round them.

At home, on the rare occasions that drivers are home, they live well, but nondescriptly. They like to try new gadgets, but hardly have time to use them. In the main they are all completely uninterested in any cultural affairs, have not much knowledge of current events, have no time for religion and vote Conservative.

29

They go to each others' parties, but apart from that they stay in their own homes and see little of each other. Most are married and most have children. Their wives, who often travel from race to race keeping lap charts, maybe feeling very bored or very frightened, never ask their husbands to give up racing. In most cases they know it would be pointless. They tolerate it.

Drivers tend to keep up with their friends from their pre-famous days. This makes them different from show business people, who tend to change their friends as they change the size of their billings.

Racing drivers are single-minded in everything. Even casually playing squash or ping-pong for relaxation, they can't stop themselves taking it seriously. They're determined to beat their opponents out of sight.

At the peak of their concentration, they can be very tense indeed. Before a big race, everyone else goes in fear and trembling of an outburst, and every driver quite understood Colin Chapman's incident with the police at the 1965 Dutch Grand Prix.

Racing drivers tend to be British; in fact Britain has developed a virtual monopoly. In most seasons of the 1960s the top three or four drivers in the World Championship table have been British (no one dare say English, with so many good Scotsmen around). There has been the odd American, Australian or Italian.

This wasn't really brought home to me, till I found myself, lost, in a little village about 30 miles from Le Mans. On the walls of a bar the locals had

pinned up photographs, torn out of magazines and newspapers. Out of nineteen pictures of racing stars, fifteen were British. Many I'd never heard of.

It's hard luck being British unless you're brilliant; you can be nobody, comparatively speaking, at home, yet a folk hero abroad.

Racing drivers, as everybody knows, can make a lot of money. A good deal comes from the oil and component firms. They finance motor racing. They put a lot in and expect, and get, absolute dedication and professionalism. In fact, if it wasn't for them, there wouldn't be much big-time racing.

They put money in to get prestige and publicity. Jaguars owe a lot of their international reputation to winning successive Le Mans in the 1950s and Ford of Detroit are gaining from racing now. But it is also a testing ground for new brakes, new engines and new ideas.

British drivers don't talk about the money they get. It's just not done. But it's been estimated that any World Champion will make about £40,000 in his championship year. Other top-class drivers have little trouble in making from £7,000 to £20,000 a year.

The money comes from many sources. Firstly, and most important, there is the retaining money and bonuses from the oil, motor and associated firms. Clark, World Champion in 1963 and 1965, gets annual retainers from several of them: like Lotus, Dunlop or Firestone, Girling, Ford, Ferodo and Esso.

Secondly, starting money. Because of his status, a champion such as Clark gets £500 for each Grand Prix he appears in.

Above: the race, the sport's raison d'etre. Here Jim Clark's Lotus leads the field at Brands Hatch. A top Grand Prix driver will cover 15,000 miles a year racing round tracks like this. "You try," said Graham Hill, "not to drive at ten-tenths, but just near it. At ten-tenths you make mistakes, because it's really over the limit."

31

Prize money is by comparison hardly worth racing for. Apart from the special case of the great American race at Indianapolis (Clark's total prize money for this race in 1965, which he shared with Lotus, was around £55,000, and Graham Hill got a similar reward in 1966) the usual prize for a Grand Prix winner is not much over £500–£1,000.

As well as these three sources, there are of course all the fringe benefits: advertising everything from clothes and food to driving schools; writing books and newspaper articles and using your name and knowledge to start your own garage business.

But Grand Prix drivers have to work very hard for all their money. They are lucky to get more than four weekends at home during the whole year. They often spend long winter periods out of the country; maybe racing in Australia.

There's an inevitability about their week during the summer—when most World Championship races are held—which hardly varies. It goes something like this:

Tuesday is usually their one day off. They spend it at home, in theory catching up with domestic life, but in practice dealing with letters and contracts.

On Wednesday they usually have business commitments—looking after their garage, or whatever it is they're trying to run on the side, usually as an investment for the future.

Thursday they spend travelling to wherever the next race is going to be. If this is a long way away, or if it is going to be a lengthy meeting, they often start travelling on the Wednesday.

Friday and Saturday are the main practice days. Sunday there's the race. On Monday they travel home.

In a year, they go round the world many times—flying up to 150,000 miles, driving about 25,000 miles. They take part in about forty races a year. They race in all about 15,000 miles.

All Grand Prix drivers say that the tensest part of their work is waiting for the race to begin. This usually happens about three o'clock on the Sunday afternoon.

Most drivers try to stay in bed at their hotel as long as possible, avoiding everybody. They eat little if at all. After a light breakfast they try to read some thriller or light novel, just to keep themselves in bed longer. They then get dressed for the race, even

though there is probably still four hours to go. They put on their flameproof underpants and vest and then their driving overalls. It's too much trouble to get changed twice before a race.

They drive to the track and sit around the paddock behind the pits. Race officials like to see them there at least an hour before the start, just to be sure.

Last-minute minor checks are being made on the car by the mechanics. The drivers sit around, getting tense. This is when Jim Clark, an habitual nail-biter, finds himself biting his nails.

They move into the pits about 20 minutes before the start. The crowd has been there for hours, perhaps days if they've been watching the practices.

The murmur from the crowd opposite the pits comes to a crescendo. If by chance they spot a favourite, they break into cheers and shouting. Most drivers show themselves in front of the pits at least once. Not out of vanity, just that they feel the crowds deserve something for their devotion. After all, they won't see much of the drivers once the race begins. They wave a hand, modestly, in recognition, then disappear back into the pits.

In the pits the cars are being warmed up. In such a confined space, the noise is overwhelming. Nobody can hear anybody else, even shouting. The drivers start putting in their ear plugs. About 15 minutes before the off the cars are wheeled out on to the starting grid.

The drivers put on their helmets, wipe their goggles, then go out to their cars. In recent years Surtees, Clark and Bandini have usually been about the first out. Graham Hill is always last. Bonnier walks out carrying a bottle of Vichy water. In his car, he takes a final swig. Hill usually takes a swig as well. Jackie Stewart always has a mechanic bring him some Coke.

As they are buried deep and tightly in their cars, only their helmets can be seen. These give a clue to their character.

Graham Hill has the London Rowing Club colours on his. Jackie Stewart has the Royal Stewart tartan, being a proud Scot. Jim Clark wears the dark blue helmet of his old club, the Border Reivers, being a proud Borderer. John Surtees, a tough, quiet, grey character, has always favoured a greyish helmet with a blue stripe.

The 5-minute signal is held up on a

board for all the drivers to see, then the 4-minute, then the 3-minute. All the drivers must now be in their cars. At the 2-minute signal, engines are started and the starting grid is cleared of all photographers. At one minute, the cars roll forward from the dummy starting grid to the proper start, so that anyone in trouble is left behind, out of the way.

At the half-minute signal, all drivers start watching the starter. His flag goes up at 5 seconds.

When the flag falls, the circuit erupts. The cars are off with the speed and passion of space ships. Twenty bits of machinery and twenty men with the power of 8,000 horses, all catapulted into hell.

They've gone. The crowd, which has been straining forward and up, now visibly subsides. In the pits, the loudest noise is the ticking of the stop-watches.

Gently the crowd rises up again, craning for the first noise and the first sight of the leading car. Sometimes, you can spot a helicopter, fluttering miles out in the country, following the ribbon of the track, keeping up with cars, as if at any minute it might pounce on the leader.

Grand Prix drivers don't try to kill themselves on the first lap, the way lesser drivers do. They know there's a long way to go. But there's usually still a fight.

You hear the noise first. The rising scream of the engine—even louder than it used to be since they replaced 1½-litre engines with 3-litre for the 1966 season—with the driver blipping the throttle as he works down through the gears, from top to second, for the last 60 m.p.h. curve. Then the raging roar as the throttle is opened and the car snarls past the pits at 160, 170 or 180 miles an hour.

Despite the noise and the excitement, the drivers are at last settling down. Jim Clark says the only time he relaxes is when he gets behind the wheel.

They don't worry about death. They know the risks, but they know exactly what they can and can't do. If Jim Clark says, which he does, that he is going to take a certain corner at 135 m.p.h. and leave a 6-inch gap, then he does.

If, off the track, you try to push them into talking about death, they say: "Well, you can just as easily be killed in the street by a bus, can't you?" They really believe the risk is not much different, so confident are they in their own skills. On the track, death is a subject they've put to the bottom of their consciousness. Off the track, they admit it exists and take out huge insurance policies. Then forget it.

They have their own jargon, their own shorthand, to describe how they're driving in a certain race. Driving at ten-tenths means flat and completely out. The mind and muscles are stretched to the limit and so is the car. "You try not to drive at ten-tenths, but just near it," says Graham Hill. "At ten-tenths you make mistakes, because it's really over the limit."

In a race like the 24-hour Le Mans, which is for sports cars, each driver aims to drive at seven-tenths, because endurance is what is needed. In a two-or-three-hour Grand Prix, for racing cars, the winner might for a moment touch ten-tenths, but what's needed is to drive all the time at nine-tenths. Especially those select few G.P. races which count towards the World Championship.

They are oblivious of the crowds. They hear no noise. Now and again, almost by a freak, they suddenly recognise a photographer's face. Then they steel themselves. The sin of recognition can lose a second's concentration. But their sense of smell is intense. They can scent the difference between a faulty clutch and faulty brakes.

As the race progresses, the neck stiffens and the shoulders tire. The helmet begins to feel like lead. If they haven't kept their mouth shut, their throat will be sore from the dryness and the epiglottis will start to swell. New drivers have to train themselves to stop their mouths from opening, the body's natural reaction to excitement. Jackie Stewart says he still consciously has to clamp tight his jaws.

By the end of the race, they will have lost 5 lbs. in sweat, they will have blisters on one hand from gear changing and they will be literally unable to take the other hand off the wheel. So tightly has it been held there that for a few moments it can be impossible to move.

Sometimes the winning driver, on his triumphal tour of the track after the race, finds it difficult to raise his hand to the crowd.

The driver's world

2 Private view

When racing is so risky, why do men do it?
What kind of people are they; what do
they feel? Here are six of the greatest
Grand Prix drivers talking—and one wife.

Stirling Moss

*b. September 17, 1929, Bayswater, London:
probably rivalled only by Juan Fangio,
who was his model, as the greatest post-
war driver. Yet Moss was never World
Champion, partly because, at a time when
British cars were not the fastest in the
world, he chose to drive, as often as he
could, privately-owned cars made in
Britain. He was still five times second in
the World Championship, and third three
times. He raced for sixteen seasons, which
was far longer than any of his contem-
poraries. He won 194 races, including
sixteen World Championship Grands Prix,
which was an incredible 40 per cent-plus of
of all those he entered. Most of his rivals
had to be content with perhaps a score, or
less, of victories. He survived, and re-
covered swiftly from, a bad crash in 1960
at Spa, Belgium, which broke both his legs.
But he crashed again, even more disas-
trously, on April 23, 1962, at Goodwood.
He did not race for a year. Then he returned
to Goodwood to test himself, alone. By his
standards, and those of others, his reactions were no longer quick enough. There
was no choice but retirement. These words
were spoken partly before, partly after,
he gave up. They come from 'All But My
Life', a book produced with Ken Purdy.*

It's odd how many commonly held
ideas are all wrong. The notion that you
need a lot of raw courage to race, for
instance. Actually I don't think courage
is any advantage at all except in certain
special circumstances. It's a disadvan-
tage. If a driver has too much courage
it's difficult for him to discover his
limitations until perhaps it's too late.
... Enzo Ferrari told me that he believes
that the accidents happen before the
man gets into the car. In many cases
I'm inclined to agree with him. Attitude
of mind and mental condition and
knowing when you're dropping off in

effectiveness; physical fatigue comes on
slowly, slowly, it could be measured
with a micrometer; you're giving energy
gradually but continually, and then
quite suddenly you're into your reserve,
you're a fifth-second slow in reacting to
something, and perhaps that's when you
leave us.

Fear is always there and we must
control it. For example, I will not sit on
the pit-counter, and look at my car
standing on the grid, and say to myself,
that front wheel hub-nut might be loose,
so I shall just stroll over and tap it with
a hammer. Once I start doing that I shall
have to strip the car myself, before
every race. .... You've got to have faith
in your mechanics, in the people who
are with you, and you've got to have
faith in yourself. When I get into my
car I don't think I have ever in my life
consciously considered the point of
being killed. If you asked me if it was a
dangerous sport, I'd say yes, obviously.
But not for me. I would say the only
danger to me is if something falls off or
somebody spins in front of me where I
can't help hitting him, or if I hit oil on
the road. But if you asked me didn't I
think it dangerous to the point where I
might overdrive and go off the road, I'd
be insulted. I mean, boy, it's as simple
as that.

It doesn't frighten me to go over the
blind brow of a hill at 160 or 170 miles an
hour. I know I shall make it. I say to
myself, if I say anything, that I know
how to do this, this is what I have spent
my life learning, the chance of anything
happening is next to nil, and I'll do it.

What's the point of living if one's not
able to do at least *one* thing?

If you habitually go through the
corners one-fifth of a second slower than
your maximum, you can make a reputation, you can earn a living, you can
even win a race now and then—but you
are no racing driver.

Nothing is sillier than this notion
that drivers have a death-wish. Most of
them enjoy life infinitely more than the

Right: *Moss in
1965. "I took a
very great deal
out of motor
racing, but I put
a lot back too. I
do feel that I
gave it all but
my life."*

average man, and it's nothing to do with eat, drink and be merry for tomorrow we die, either. I've been accused of living a 20-hour day and I plead guilty, with pleasure. I live for the day.

You could say it's an odd life, but it's like a story I remember about the man who was told the roulette game was crooked, and he said: 'Yes, I know—but it's the only game in town.'

In the end one has one's work—the only game in town. I wouldn't want any other work. Obviously the major satisfaction in my life is racing, and I enjoy it even when I'm frustrated, sometimes I think maybe *most* when I'm frustrated; I think, I can't damn well win, I've lost five laps in the pit, it's impossible to win now, mathematically impossible, but then I began to think, well, my God, even if I can't win I'm going to damned well go, and then I can really enjoy fast motoring, for the exhilaration of it and because I'm trying to prove something to myself; they may have five laps on me, but I'm going to take one back, and the lap record is always there to be broken.

To go flat-out through a bend that is surrounded by level lawn is one thing, but to go flat-out through a bend that has a stone wall on one side and a precipice on the other—that's an *achievement!*

You go through a corner absolutely flat out, right on the ragged edge, but absolutely in control, on your own line to an inch, the car just hanging there, the tyres as good as geared to the road, locked to it, and yet you know that if you ask one more mile an hour of the car, if you put another 5 pounds of side-thrust on it, you'll lose the whole flaming vehicle as surely as if someone had smeared the road with 6 inches of grease; so you stay just this side of that fraction of extra speed, that fraction of extra weight that could ruin everything, and perhaps kill you to boot, you're on top of it all, and the exhilaration, the thrill is tremendous, you say to yourself, all right, you bastards, top that one, match it, even, and you feel like a painter who has just put the last brushstroke on a canvas, after years of trying to catch a certain expression—it's rewarding. And you must grant that it's not monotonous. No art can be monotonous, and I believe that driving, as

practised by some very few people in the world, is an art-form, and is related to ballet. Driving is certainly like ballet in that it is all discipline, rhythm, movement. I've had people tell me it's a mad thing to say that driving can be an art. After all, we can all of us drive, can't we? Of course, and we can all sing, and write, and most of us can dance, and draw some kind of picture, but some do it a little better than others, that's all. . . .

Racing is rather like painting to me: the car is only the instrument, as paints are to a painter. All right, one car is better than another, fine, and one kind of paint is better than another, very well, but it really doesn't matter, the painter creates with whatever he has at hand, and if he hasn't anything better he'll use a child's set of crayons. Give Picasso a broken two-shilling set of crayons and he'll give you something worth two thousand pounds. After all, I think driving is an art. I really do maintain that.

People ask: 'Aren't you upset about not being World Champion? Doesn't it bother you, that you were runner-up five times?' And the answer is, in honesty, that the first year I was pretty much upset, it would be correct to say, very much upset. But the disappointment got less each time. Partially it was just conditioning, a second disappointment is easier to bear than the first, a third is easier than the second. Partially it was something else, even now I'm not sure what it was, but I might say it was the realisation that while having the championship would mean perhaps a lot to Stirling Moss Limited, it might not mean much to Stirling Moss. . . . I'd rather go down in history as the man who never won the championship than as the man who won it once. If I won it once, what of that? . . . Winning it six times won't make me *as* good a driver as Juan Manuel Fangio, and winning it ten times wouldn't make me a better driver, because I am not. Fangio was better than I was, and that's that.

I think a pit's all the better for a bit of crumpet, somebody to wave to, somebody to take your mind off things, if just by chance you come in half a lap ahead, and the transmission in bits. . . , I used to discipline myself so severely.

Left: *Moss in 1955. Driving a Mercedes 300 SLR sports car he had just won the Mille Miglia, regarded till then as an Italian monopoly. He was the first Englishman to win this greatest of road races. His co-driver over the incredibly punishing* 1,000 *miles was Denis Jenkinson. Moss developed so much confidence in his co-driver's intimate knowledge of the route that, if Jenkinson signalled the road ahead was straight after a blind brow, he would take it at* 170 *m.p.h. Moss did the* 1,000 *miles in* 10 *hours* 7 *minutes 48 seconds, sometimes overtaking low-flying aeroplanes.*

C

I would not have intercourse for five days before a race. Later, I began to think, that was going pretty far, who needs to live at all, allowing oneself sex two days out of seven? I believed that if I had made love the night before a race, I would be physically just that little bit weaker when I drove, and that belief was enough for me. Then one night before a race at Brands Hatch I was with a girl. We were fond of each other, and I abandoned my rule. Next day I had seven races, quite a few really, only short ones, but seven, and I won the lot! I was really swinging, I was on great form.

That day didn't altogether change my mind, though. After all, they were short races, I had intervals of rest. The night before a really hard race, Le Mans, Sebring, the Mille Miglia, or a G.P. race—no.

An odd fact, while I don't get a conscious sexual stimulation from driving, I do get a tremendous stimulation, I think of it as intellectual, that's not the right word, but it's a non-*physical* sensation, and it produces a tranquillity that is very like the tranquillity that follows a deep relationship. Driving does that to me. My mind is calm, but very active, and I feel at peace.

I remember a time I think Masten (Gregory) would like to have run over me. It was in Havana, the year the Castro people kidnapped Fangio. There was a lot of oil on the circuit, and I let Masten past into first place, pretty heartlessly, rather like you'd send someone ahead of a squad of soldiers with a mine-detector. Let old Masten find the oil, I said to myself. Then there was a bad accident after a bit and a marshal put out a red flag. Masten stood on everything and slowed right down. I started to slow down, but then I ran through the regulations in my mind and remembered that a red flag, which meant everybody come to a grinding halt the race is over sort of thing, a red flag has no validity except when shown by the clerk of the course, usually at the finish-line. So I stuck it into second gear and jumped on the throttle and ran past Masten to win. That had been my intention anyway. But Masten was sore. He said he reckoned that he had really won the race, and that I had cheated him out of it. I said: 'If you don't know the regs, Masten, you must expect to be beaten by somebody who

does.' But then I told him I'd split first prize money with him if he'd split second with me, so we came out dead even, and then he felt better.

I don't mind anyone talking to me before a start. I don't care in the least. If I'm sitting in the car, a boy can ask me for an autograph. I'm happy to talk about anything, a play I saw the night before, a girl, up to the moment I start the engine, I couldn't care less. I've done my practice, I reckon I know the course, I reckon the car to be ready, I can't make a plan, I can't foresee what's to happen when fifteen of us pile into the first corner, so why should I bother thinking about it?

For me it has to be in a motor car, in contact with the earth, if not by much, and a man using his hands, his feet, his eyes, his brain to balance inertia and momentum and gravity and centrifugal force in an equation that changes ten times a second; in a vehicle, if you like, that represents the best efforts of the most skilful specialist designers in the world, and a beautiful thing, too—you must admit, there have been very few ugly racing-cars; *that* is living, and in the company, if you like, of the dozen or fifteen men in the world who can do what you're doing, and, let's say, on a real circuit like the Nurburgring, *that* is motor racing, and when you think of it in that fashion, as it really is, you realise that it's absurd to compare it with any other sport. I'm not being provincial, I am not narrow-minded, I hope I'm not, but I really do believe that: there is nothing in life so satisfying. Caracciola said it years ago, that it was the most intoxicating sensation in life, something like that. And it is! . . .

I took a very great deal out of motor racing, but I put a lot back, too. I do feel that I gave it all but my life.

Phil Hill

b. April 20, 1927, Florida: World Champion, 1961, driving for Ferrari. In the race that clinched the Championship his Ferrari team-mate, Count Wolfgang von Trips, plunged into the crowd at Monza, killed himself, and fifteen others. Hill was 34, a nervous and perceptive man. Before that day he had raced exclusively with Ferrari for eight years. Apart from Grand Prix wins, he had three times come first in the great Le Mans 24 Hours sports car race. But in 1962, the World Champion no longer raced as fast. He and Ferrari parted. In 1964 he drove for the British Cooper works team, again not fast enough. These words were spoken both before and not long after he won the Championship.

❝I'm in the wrong business. I don't want to beat anybody, I don't want to be the big hero. I'm a peace-loving man basically. . . .

How can you be friends with a racing driver? You try to beat them all day on the circuit, and then at night you're supposed to forget all that? I think all racing drivers secretly hate each other.

Racing brings out the worst in me. I don't know what would have become of me if I hadn't become a race driver, as a person, I mean, but I'm not sure I like the person I am now. Racing makes me selfish, irritable, defensive. There are thirty other guys trying to get where I am. I have to be on my guard all the time. I even have to hang around the cars when I could be doing something useful, in order to make sure the mechanics are doing what I have asked them to do. We're not allowed to touch the cars! I don't hang around the cars all the time because I like to, but to protect my interests. If I could get out of this sport with any ego left, I would.

Life is a struggle whatever work you do, but at least in any other business you don't have to risk your life. . . . It depends how much glorification your ego needs. Some drivers need so much that the danger of what they are doing goes right out of the window. They don't even think of it.

There was a very fine ethical line which both of us (Clark and I) recognised. Certain tactics were okay. Others were too dangerous. Some drivers would not have recognised this ethical line.

There is one driver, for instance, who has a reputation for imprudence and who now uses this reputation as a weapon to scare other drivers out of his way. I think that's evil.

It is always the same. I'm asleep in a warm bed, the sun is shining in the window and I start to wake up and I'm lying there all warm and secure. And then I start to think: this is not just any day. This is a very special day. This is race day. Then in an instant all the warmth and security is gone, the bed is cold, and I sit up wide awake. . . .

I would so love to get out of this unbent. I have a horror of cripples. Even when I was a little boy I couldn't bear to look at anyone who was deformed, could not bear to see them suffering. I guess I've always worried about ending up that way myself. I want to get out of this in one piece. Do you know, I've never been hurt in an accident.

I no longer have as much need to race, to win. I don't have as much hunger any more. I am no longer willing to risk killing myself.❞

Left: *Robert Daley took this photograph of Phil Hill as he climbed from his car after coming second in the 1962 Monaco Grand Prix. Few pictures show so cruelly the strain of modern motor racing: heat, fumes, noise, wind and the constant concentration needed all contrive to exhaust a driver utterly in the space of a couple of hours.*

39

Jim Clark

b. March 4, 1936, Fife, Scotland: World Champion 1963 and 1965, driving for Lotus works team, and without doubt the leading Grand Prix driver of the mid-1960s. Raised on a farm, to which he has said he will return as soon as he feels he can no longer drive at the summit. Colin Chapman's brilliant monocoque designs—like a bed on wheels, Clark called the first—were crucial to his successes, which have included a world record of seven Grand Prix wins in the 1963 season, and six successive Grand Prix victories in 1965. In the same year he became the first non-American since 1916 to win the Indianapolis 500, the greatest motor racing event in the U.S. calendar; he was the first Briton ever to win it.

❛It was terribly hot and the surface was almost molten tar. This brought two problems, one, that the car would slide on the tar as though on ice, and also that the gravel would break loose and come flying into your face if you slipstreamed anyone . . . When we got to the braking area at the end of the straight, it was like flying into shrapnel. A hail of stones of all shapes and sizes peppered the cars and the drivers. The noise of stones on metal was fantastic, but the worst noise of all was the dull thud of the occasional boulder hitting you on the bridge of the nose. I made the mistake —but only once—of baring my clenched teeth in agony, and nearly had half of them knocked out. The stones stripped the paint from my helmet, and some of the skin off my face.

Finally the goggles fell to pieces under the battering, leaving my eyes unprotected, until I could slip on the spare pair which most drivers always carry round their necks. Unfortunately, in doing this I lost too much ground and dropped out of the slipstream of the other cars. Two laps from the end Bonnier retired with engine trouble, leaving Gurney and Baghetti to fight it out to a tremendous finish with Baghetti winning by no more than a car's length. Aching and bruised, I trundled in third, and only after the race did I realise that I had also burnt my foot on the overheated pedals. I couldn't wear a shoe on it for more than a week. Physically, it was one of my most gruelling races ever.

One driver in particular used to get his wife to stand on the corner at the end of the straight at Snetterton. He would go out practising and his wife would hold a stone in her hand. Every lap he would wave her farther down nearer the corner as he began to get used to his braking limits, until finally he would give her the signal and she would put the stone down as a marker. Later in the evening, this driver would go out and paint the stone white.

However, some of the drivers got to know about this and one day one of them moved the stone about 50 yards back up the road away from the corner. Well, of course, the advantage of having your braking point marked was that when everyone else in the race was settling down you could rush up to the corners and brake at planned points and steal quite a march on the opposition. This time, though, the driver took off like a bat and gained the lead. He sped down the straight to his white marker stone and braked hard. But as it was now 50 yards further up the track, he was still braking when the first half dozen in the field swept past him to the true braking point. So his little game was foiled.

It was great stuff driving the Lister north and I'll never forget an incident on that trip. I was somewhere near Huntingdon where all those American Air Force bases are, when I noticed a Ford Thunderbird in the distance. I was bashing on fairly fast, but there was no speedometer on the Lister, yet I realised that he must have been going at around 120 m.p.h. I found that I wasn't catching him so I got faster and faster and in the end I was doing 5,500 r.p.m. in top in the Lister which was about 150 m.p.h. or so and I came screaming up behind him and just tore past . . .

The driver obviously had no idea that I was coming up behind him. It was a Sunday morning and there was no other traffic on the road. He wouldn't have expected anyone to pass him at the speed he was going. He must have got such a hell of a fright for the Lister's exhaust pipes were on his side of the car. I didn't just ease past him. I really blasted past and I'd love to have seen his face.❜

Right: this was Jim Clark away from the racing circuits, photographed by Lord Snowdon in 1966. It was not a season which went well for him, for Lotus were awaiting their new 3-litre engine, and only very skilful driving kept him and others, like Graham Hill and Jackie Stewart, in competition at all with the more powerful machinery run by Jack Brabham. Clark, indeed, missed the French G.P. altogether after being hit in the face by a partridge during practice. Those who meet him are often surprised by his modesty. He is a quiet, relaxed and very pleasant man, who likes—as do most other racing drivers—open-air sports like water-skiing. But he claims to be a very nervous person: "I bite my nails all the way down. I fidget all the time." And he once said: "I had to be coaxed into my first Grand Prix car. In 1959, Reg Parnell, who was then team manager for Aston Martin, offered me a car for 1960. I sort of shuddered and cried 'help'. I told him I didn't think I could handle it."

Peter Arundell

b. November 8, 1933, Ilford, Essex: came to the fore in Grand Prix racing the hard way, and late. Mechanic first, then driver. In 1957 was entering sports car races and working in his father's garage: "Six hundred quid a year—that was fifty quid for my fags, and the rest went on the car." In 1959 he married a German girl, Ricarda. In 1964 he was No. 2 to Jim Clark in the Lotus Formula I team and lying third in the World Championship. Then, on July 5, he crashed at Rheims at 130 m.p.h., flew 300 ft. through the air and landed on his head. Eighteen months of agony and frustration later he returned to racing. Virtually no one in history has made the top league again after so shattering an accident. In his first comeback race, the South African G.P. in January, 1966, he came third, and said he was furious he hadn't done better; his exhaust pipe had fallen off. This is what he said a few days before that race:

❝Don't you say I nearly died. I was nowhere near death. I want to do it again because, well, it's just my life. It's a bit of a problem as a family man, but when I married Rikki I was already motor racing. I suppose she realises life would be unbearable if I wasn't racing. She's always the one who's said that. I think she'd sooner I didn't, but this would apply to any driver's wife. I do miss it when I can't race. It's something that gets built into you. It's no more dangerous to me than a man wielding a hammer every day. He may hit himself, and I—well, I do think about having a shunt, but never about losing my life. I may get nervy, but once the race starts you don't think about anything except the man in front. That's the way it will be again. I haven't changed physically or mentally. I have the same thoughts I used to have. I can still drive a car pretty fast. I'll need time, of course. To get a race-winning performance you have to know the car, the mechanics—everything. I've got to get back into the swing of it. . . .

What pleases me no end is knowing you can win and picking your moment. I always plan as I drive. I never just go at it hammer and tongs. If you can't leave everybody, then you must sit and plan it. Most cars are evenly matched these days, therefore it's a question of who can outfumble who at the crucial moments. . . . And of who is lucky. That's important to a racing driver. I was lucky in 1963 at the Solitude—that's a track near Stuttgart. I was then No. 3 in the Formula I team for Lotus to Jimmy (Clark) and Trevor (Taylor), and I didn't get much of a look in in those days. Well, my car had been going better than Trevor's in practice, so I offered it to him. He took it and then expired, and so did Jimmy. I lasted in Trevor's car and came second to Brabham. I always seem to be saying Trevor had bad luck. His life's a story of that. . . .

I'm just 32 now, and judging by my young friend Mr. Graham Hill I reckon I've at least five years at the top if I play it right. I know all that stuff about never coming back, but it *can* be done. Innes made the effort, but he came back too quickly. So did Henry Taylor . . . and they found themselves in the middle of it again, and the second bad one put them off. If I had a second one too quickly I daresay it would put me off. But it won't if I can help it. There's nothing wrong with me. I just need a bit more muscle in the legs.

People say there's a bit of tiger about my driving, a bit of hate. I suppose that's right, but though I go fast I never thrash it. Plenty of people go faster than me on the road. I think they're bloody mad. I'm not in love with cars in that situation. They just get me from A to B.

Mark you, now I'm coming back I'm going to make more than a living out of it. People don't seem to realise you don't necessarily make a fortune out of racing. Only a living. You give your life to a firm and something happens and puts you out of it all and you're forgotten. That's it—finished, forgotten. Well, that's got to change. This time I've got to have good insurance provided and more financial rewards.

A motoring journalist, he slated me once as a novice. He wrote about how I spun it 'as he has often done before'. I felt like saying to him 'Come and do it yourself, and we'll pick you out of the bank and bury you'.

Trevor had a nasty shunt at Enna. Bandini dropped a wheel over the edge

Right: *Arundell cleans his road car, a Ford Cortina G.T. Of his track driving, Colin Chapman of Lotus said: "He has this tremendous determination to win. This simply isn't true of most drivers. It's the quality that marks out the potentially great racing driver from the rest." During the greater part of the 1966 season, however, he had little chance to show his quality because Lotuses were underpowered compared with the 3-litre cars of Brabham, Cooper and other marques.*

and showered up stones and muck that blinded him. At 150, that was, and he lost it in a big way, though he only got nasty bruising. It took me five laps to get over this. I was very upset—you get that way with someone you've had a close relationship with—because I didn't know what had happened to him. All I could see was the ambulance roaring round. But then I got a board with TREVOR on it from the pits and a thumbs-up, and I thought, well, you're still here, mate—so I had a gorgeous go for ten laps until finally I outfumbled Bandini. I came second to Surtees.

I don't have any of that. Not courage. I get butterflies. So does anyone. Listen, no driver gets to the top unless he does have fear, because otherwise he doesn't live long enough. Just write that down. . . .

Neil, my son, he's mad about cars, and later on if he wanted to I would let him race them. I know how it feels, wanting to. There isn't any substitute for motor racing, you see. I don't know why. Perhaps it's that my natural abilities are never properly used except on a racing circuit.

Graham Hill

b. February 15, 1929, Hampstead, London: World Champion in 1962, driving a B.R.M. He and younger man, Jackie Stewart, have made a very effective B.R.M.team. An oarsman (stroking London Rowing Club first eight at Henley) before he became a racing driver; his wife Bette also rowed —for England. Parents were comfortably middle-class, but Hill, unusually, entered racing via being a mechanic. Now noted for the amount of time he still spends in garage over preparation of cars. Took racing lessons—5s a lap—at Brands Hatch in 1953 and spent five more years reaching the top. By 1965 had a £15,000 house, three children, one nanny, one char—and life insurance costing him £20 a week. In 1966 became only the second British driver, following Jim Clark in 1965, to win the Indianapolis 500.

❝I knew I just couldn't be an engineer for the rest of my life, nine to five, just another cog in industry. I'm happy now. I still can't get over the fact that I get paid, and well paid, for something I enjoy doing so much.

What I enjoy is the feeling of control over the car. The feeling of power. I like trying to drive to perfection. I am a perfectionist. I can't suffer fools. I know I tend to be a bit short-tempered.

I wouldn't say I'm fulfilled. Racing is a means of self-expression, but you don't express emotions, the way an artist does. I'm envious of those who can.

The self-expression in driving comes out on the roads in every country. The French drive as if they couldn't care less. The Germans tend to be a bit arrogant. The Italians are very competitive. The English are a bit self-righteous, but I'd say they're the best drivers in the world.

Racing drivers' characters come through in their driving. I have a mental card index where I file their behaviour. If you really understand the other driver, you should be able to anticipate what he is going to do, and cut down the risks.

It is the underlying danger which unites drivers. We're not sloppy about each other, but we're all good friends. Because of the common risk, we have a mutual respect for each other. At some time or other, we put our life in the hands of other drivers.

People are always moaning about racing not being such fun as it was in the old days. Well, all I can say is that it's no different from any other sport. Everything is a very serious business, isn't it? As standards get higher, you have to be that bit more professional, more dedicated, more intense. To be a racing driver nowadays, it depends how badly you want to win. I'm enjoying myself in trying to win. And the time I spend in the garage isn't a chore. I don't regret not being able to sit beside the pool with a large gin and tonic. If people say it's not like the old days, they've already accepted the fact they're not going to win.

Don't ask me to analyse *exactly* why I enjoy it. But it's powerful enough to make me do it, all the money apart. I get frightened, certainly. But that's part of it. It's probably happened 20,000 times, so you learn to live with it.❞

Mrs Graham Hill

❝Only once in our married life have I ever mentioned what might happen. It was just a few years ago. I suddenly said to him: 'What do I do if you get killed?' He said: 'Don't you worry about a thing. It's all arranged. Just leave it to your old Dad.'

We've never discussed it since. I know he prefers me not to think about it. I don't really worry, except from time to time when something happens and you see an ambulance racing off. Then you worry who it is. . . .

But when your man's O.K., then you get back to the race and you never worry again, until something else happens. . . .

He has changed since I first met him. Life is more serious. He has more responsibilities. He's a known personality now.

We owe a lot to racing. We would never have had all this house, all this life, but for racing.❞

Left: *Hill at home in Mill Hill, London, with wife Bette and two of his three children, Brigitte and Damon. He is one of the few men to whom racing has brought big rewards, including around £50,000-plus from the Indianapolis 500 of 1966. "But when the starting flag goes down," said Hill, "you don't care a damn about money."*

John Surtees

b. February 11, 1934, Tatsfield, Surrey: World Champion, 1964, driving for Ferrari. First man to reach top rank both as motor-cyclist and Grand Prix racing driver; won World Championship in motor-cycle racing seven times before he switched to four wheels in 1960. "I don't believe in marking time," he said of the change-over. "I think you have to carry on trying to get higher. If you don't you start going down." Utterly dedicated man, quiet and introspective, the professional par excellence: non-smoker and non-drinker. His wife, Pat (they married in 1962), has followed him around the world acting as part-time secretary, navigator, time-keeper, even co-driver. "You never get over fear," she said once. "You just learn to work with it." Trained in his youth as a mechanic, and has spent much time helping build and prepare cars, even with Ferrari, with whom his relations have often been uneasy. In September, 1965, badly injured in 100 m.p.h. crash while practising at Mossport circuit near Toronto for Canadian Grand Prix; suffered spine fractures, broken pelvis, ruptured kidney. He came back for the 1966 World Championship season, won the Belgian Grand Prix at Spa for Enzo Ferrari—then quit the Italian marque after a long period of friction with race-team manager Eugenio Dragoni.

❝I think racing has changed. It's bound to have changed, because before the war you had to have very large capital backing before you were involved in motor racing, except on the Continent. An English rider had to have very large family backing. The people who began to set the trend were the Germans. Since the war, with motor racing becoming more commercialised and with the extra backing, fuel companies and such-like, and with the advent of the Formula Junior cars, it does allow people to start with rather limited resources, and if you can drive a car you get the opportunity. And this is why I think a slightly different person has come about. And basically it becomes more serious, because if you're racing against somebody with ability who's serious, well then you've got to be serious to beat them.

I think a person who has not experienced fear and does not realise the dangers involved in it should not be in motor racing. I think the impression that someone goes into motor racing surrounded by a guardian angel is entirely wrong. I had two or three accidents with broken steering. Well there, honestly and truly, there's no question of my skill getting me out of these problems, it was just lucky the car didn't turn over, didn't catch fire. It was in somebody else's hands.

I have learned to take calculated risks. You work it all out beforehand. Exactly what your car is capable of, what you believe you yourself are capable of. I won't say that between races I haven't got into a smouldering mood sometimes, when there seemed to be a hoodoo on my car, but once I am at the starting point I make myself go deadly calm. It is the only way to win races.

Of course you must have fire in your belly. But you must never lose your temper on the track. Hating your rivals once the race has started can blur your judgment as much as alcohol. That's why I never drink spirits. It must be your own fire in your belly. And no alibis afterwards. Keep your mouth shut.

I need lots of sleep. Fortunately I sleep easily. I don't think you could survive at this game if you had nightmares every night. I had one once. I found myself on the floor, with my arms outstretched and locked as though I was driving. I've had a crash, I told myself, still half asleep. The next day I really had one. I'm glad to say I haven't had that kind of nightmare since.

Motor racing has many political pitfalls. There are a lot of characters on the fringe—men who don't know the meaning of the word sport—gunning for you, particularly when you're successful.❞

2 The makers

General Motors of America—which makes Chevrolet, Oldsmobile, Buick, Pontiac, and Cadillac cars—is the world's largest manufacturer. Not of motor-cars only; of anything. One staggering General Motors' statistic makes the point: their net income increase in 1965—£139 million—was over twice the total profits of Britain's biggest (and highly diversified) company, Imperial Chemical Industries. The automobile has created vast fortunes in most of the world's industrialised nations. But there are forces other than the profit-motive which spur men to build cars. Especially fast cars. To create the perfect machine, which excels in speed and performance, can become a dream, an obsession, a kind of loving. The second section of this book reflects some aspects of the making game.

Above: *Sir William Lyons, the founder of Jaguar. His genius has lain in creating very fast, very beautiful cars at a price low enough to boost sales.*

49

Five great marques

Ferrari: never break down with honour
by Robert Daley

**"Sensual, emotional, highly-strung things";
the writer, Eric Dymock, was talking about
Ferraris. Of all modern cars that go very
fast, Ferraris have the greatest glamour, are
cocooned in the most melodramatic mystique. Robert Daley, an American journalist,
underlined this when he wrote about the
marque and its enigmatic creator in his
classic study of motor racing, 'The Cruel
Sport'. This was a controversial book – but
it was praised, despite their reservations,
by drivers like Moss, Clark and Graham
Hill. It was called "one of the epic books"
by Phil Hill. Here are the words set down
by Daley about Ferrari in 1964. Some of the
statistics may date with the years: the
essence of what he said, and the power
with which he said it, will not.**

There are no roads where cars are raced
which have not known the banshee wail
and frightening agility of Ferrari race
cars.

Ferraris have sped to victory in Florida,
Venezuela and Australia, through the
soundless forests of West Germany, the
chic and haughty streets of Monte
Carlo, the mountains of Mexico, the
deserts of North Africa. They have won
races lasting two hours. They have won
races lasting seven days. Ferrari drivers
have won five World Championships
since 1952; in the nine seasons that the
sports car World Championship existed,
Ferrari won it seven times.

No other marque can match the record
in victories of the blood-red cars. Nor
their record in death.

In 1953 in Argentina, a Ferrari slewed
into the mob, slaughtered about fifteen
people and maimed many more.

In Italy during the 1957 Mille Miglia, a
Ferrari rocketed off the road and struck
down eleven.

In Cuba during the 1958 Gran Premio,
a Ferrari killed seven.

At Monza, Italy, during the 1961 Grand
Prix, a Ferrari killed sixteen.

Six drivers under contract to the
Ferrari factory, skilled professionals,
have crashed to their deaths since 1955.

The man whose cars bring glory and
death to so many is a mysterious
figure—a recluse who never goes to
races, who is rarely seen in public, who
appears to suffer intensely each time a
driver is killed, who seems to love his
drivers like sons, but then sends his
cars out the next week anyway.

Enzo Ferrari, in his late sixties, is a
stern, unapproachable man. All who
come in contact with him defer to him.
No one sits down until he does. He has
no intimates. He is addressed only as
Commendatore, the rank to which he
was raised by the Italian King before
the war, in recognition of the glorious
victories he had won for Italy.

Commendatore Ferrari grew up in
Carpi, a village nine miles north of
Modena, present capital of the Ferrari
kingdom. He was a mule-shoer in the
Italian army during World War I. After
the war he had a short, undistinguished
career as a race driver, taking over
about 1925 as team manager for Alfa
Romeo. When the Alfas quit racing,
Ferrari bought the team of cars and
raced them under his own name. Most
of the great drivers of that epoch worked
for him: Nuvolari, Varzi, Campari and
others.

In 1939 Ferrari came to Modena to
build his own cars. War began. Worried
about possible bombings, Ferrari moved
the factory to Maranello, 10 miles west,
and spent the war making machine
tools.

The first Ferrari cars appeared after
the war. It is said that the transition
from tool-making to cars was made
thanks to the devotion of workers who
laboured on the cars after hours. This is
part of the legend which surrounds
Ferrari.

Today Ferrari's factory domain
covers an area equivalent to two city
blocks, and no one enters it without a
pass.

Right: *Ferrari
mechanics work
on a Formula I
car at Monza in
1964; Enzo
Ferrari strides
by, forbidding
and alone. This,
the second day of
practice for the
Italian Grand
Prix, is the soli-
tary occasion of
the year that he
is to be seen at a
racing circuit.
Once the
practice was over
he went away,
as usual, and
missed the race,
even though this
was one of the
very good Ferrari
years, when his
No. 1 driver,
John Surtees,
became World
Champion.
Maxwell Boyd
was the photog-
rapher.*

Ferrari produces and sells about 600 luxury convertibles and coupés a year at prices ranging from 9,300 dollars (if bought in lire at the factory) to nearly 15,000 dollars (if delivered to a James Stewart or William Holden in Hollywood). At Christmas, 1962, Ferrari claimed that every car he would build in 1963 had already been ordered.

To produce 600 cars a year Ferrari employs about 300 men. And to produce a dozen racers a year he employs forty more, which gives a fair idea of how the man thinks and what he really loves. Each racing car must cost Ferrari at least 40,000 dollars.

He is no philanthropist. He does not lose money. The cost of racing is met partly by starting and prize money, partly by a subsidy paid Ferrari by the Italian automobile industry; and part of it can be written off as advertising for the luxury models.

The Ferrari marque has been the most successful that has ever raced, and it is the only one that has gone on and on in every type of racing, year after year, without stopping.

Other marques (Mercedes, Alfa Romeo, Maserati and the rest) always withdrew from time to time for lack of manpower or money or simply because they had no real need to keep racing. Enzo Ferrari has always seen to it that the manpower and money were there. The need he has supplied from deep inside himself: racing is rooted in his soul. The perfection of the racing automobile, the perfection of the breed, is all he lives for.

He is an autocratic man. Things must be done his way, or not at all. Harry Schell once called him "an impossible man to work for". The designers and engineers Ferrari employs rarely last more than a year or two. Team managers seldom last longer.

The cars are true Ferrari cars. They mirror Ferrari, and no one else. Ferrari's engines are always more powerful than other marques can mount. Ferrari is not an engineer, but he knows engines. He has insights. He forces his ideas on his engineers and if one engineer quits, he gets another. And his engines stay more powerful than anyone else's.

His cars are tougher, stronger than others, and break down far less. "My cars must be beautiful," says Ferrari. "But more than that, they must not stop out on the circuit. For then people will say, 'what a pity, it was so pretty'." And his voice is tinged with disgust. He can lose with honour, provided it does not happen too often; he can never break down with honour. Because Ferrari cars are stronger, they are also inherently safer. All drivers recognise this, and admire it, even if they cannot admire Ferrari personally.

Ferrari is an arch-conservative. He won't change anything until it gets defeated in race after race. His cars are bigger and heavier than the others, and he does not care. "They have more horsepower," Ferrari says stubbornly, "and they don't break down."

He rarely pays any attention to what drivers say. Their suggested improvements are ignored. He appears to love his drivers, but no one believes he really does, and many who worked for him in the past despise him.

The central fact of Enzo Ferrari's life is death. But not the death of drivers. It was the death in 1956 of his son, Alfredo, called Dino, of leukemia at the age of 25. The boy had been bedridden part of every year from the age of 16. He kept asking his father why his body was so feeble when his mind was so alert, so eager to live. Ferrari had no answer. He had had much experience in death, but death had never been personal until now.

Ferrari had planned that the boy should be the greatest automotive engineer of all time, that his own name would be perpetuated by the greatness he had left behind in his son. This was his dream, all bound up in the son he worshipped and knew was going to die.

Ferrari has not accustomed himself to Dino's death. He keeps Dino's memory alive in every possible way, even ordering the boy's name embossed on the engine blocks of the race cars.

Every day he is in Modena, Ferrari visits Dino's tomb, locks himself inside and broods. Associates say he goes there when drivers are killed, too.

Ferrari's life has become his cars. He works twelve to fifteen hours a day, Sundays included. "A man has no need of entertainment," he told me. "Entertainment only distracts from his duty. If a man has his duty, that is enough."

Ferrari is said to be wealthy, but all the money goes back into his cars. He lives with his wife and three dogs in a five-room apartment over the warehouse in Modena, and when he goes to the factory in Maranello he drives a Fiat. His two offices are starkly furnished. The only ornament in Maranello is a big, black-bordered picture of Dino with votive lights burning under it. In Modena there is a similar funereal picture of Dino and, standing in a row on a shelf, photos of his six contract drivers for the year. The snapshots and the men are impermanent. Any errant breeze or any minute error of judgment at 150 miles per hour could blow one over.

Ferrari will not negotiate with drivers. They take what he offers, or they leave—and the pay is less than elsewhere. At the end of one season, Phil Hill and Dan Gurney asked for raises. Ferrari fired Gurney. Wanting to keep Hill, he then announced that Hill was retiring from the sport, and would not drive a Ferrari in the United States Grand Prix the next month. Hill did in fact drive a Ferrari in that race. "Ferrari decided to give me one last chance," Hill said glumly. "And I took it." He did not get the raise.

Ferrari makes little effort to sign the best drivers each year. The best drivers sign with factories which offer the best terms; with Ferrari there is no question of terms. Ferrari's drivers usually have a flaw, and usually it is the same flaw: a need to drive faster than is, for them, safe. Ferrari's drivers are usually men who crash a great deal: Musso, Portago, Castellotti, Trips, Behra, Rodriguez. And currently, Willy Mairesse. Such men are nervous, inaccurate, nonprudent men. They drive very fast; they have tremendous desire to excel. Never mind the peril.

They appeal to something in Ferrari.

Ferrari also hired Tony Brooks—for a year. And he kept Phil Hill and Oliver Gendebien for many years, always, it seemed, against his better judgment.

The primary reason Ferraris have crashed more than other marques is that so many Ferrari drivers have had this temperamental flaw. The secondary reason is that Ferrari would always hire six drivers for three cars—the regulars had to push to the limit to stay ahead of the reserves. Nor would Ferrari name a team leader as all other marques always did. He left the drivers to settle for themselves upon a team leader. If this meant a dog-fight for first place during a race, Ferrari would watch from Modena with an amused glint in his eye. In 1961 Hill and Trips were virtually tied for the World Championship. The Ferrari cars were so strong that year that one or the other had to win each race—nothing else could challenge. Both drivers desperately wanted Ferrari to name a team leader; it is dangerous to race it out in identical cars. But Ferrari never said a word.

Finally in the next to last race, the Italian Grand Prix, Trips stalled at the start. Hill got off to a big lead. As Trips hurried to catch up, he must have thought: this is the break that will settle the World Championship, a bad break for me; I must hold my foot down, hold my foot down.

If Ferrari had named a team leader one way or the other, Trips would not have driven those first two frantic laps in such a heavy-footed panic. They were the last laps of his life.

The next year Hill hardly even tried. The Ferrari was again somewhat slower than other cars, but probably not as slow as Hill made it look.

At the factory in Maranello, men watched Ferrari, and then publicly expressed Ferrari's thoughts. Hill has lost his enthusiasm, they said.

Hill said: "They think I should go out there in an inferior car and sacrifice myself to the honour and glory of Ferrari. There have been too many sacrifices already. I won't be another. I won't be one of their sacrifices."

Overleaf: *one of the rear wheels springs from the ground as John Surtees hurtles on his way during the German Grand Prix at Nurburgring in 1965. Gerry Cranham's picture captures perfectly the "banshee wail and frightening agility" of the Ferraris. It also points to the fearful punishment racing cars take. This is a tough and sometimes cruel business for both machines and men. Even so dominating a figure as Enzo Ferrari has found it so. In 1966, for example, his best driver, John Surtees, broke with him after winning the Belgian Grand Prix. Then Ferrari had to miss the next G.P. —the British— because of strikes at his Modena factory.*

D

Ford: how Lizzie changed the world by Ralph Stein

Ferrari is special; Ford is for everyone. But it's likely that the intensity of feeling for the automobile was just as powerful inside Henry Ford, the father of modern mass production, as it has been inside the Commendatore. This account of the Model T was written by Ralph Stein for his 'Treasury of the Automobile', arguably one of the two or three most beautiful books on cars. He is American and a long-time car-addict, who began in 1932 with an Alfa Romeo and has since owned and driven, among other things, a 1907 Welch, an Alfa Zagato, a Type 51 Bugatti and a 1935 P-2 Continental Rolls-Royce.

Of all the automobiles ever built, none did more to change the world than Henry Ford's Tin Lizzie.

Its life span almost exactly paralleled that of Henry Royce's Silver Ghost—from 1908 to 1927—but while only a few thousand Rolls-Royces were made in those nineteen years, 15,456,868 Model T Fords rattled their way off the assembly lines. On one busy day, October 31, 1925, an amazing 9,109 flivvers were built. Between 1917 and 1927 Ford made half the cars produced in the United States.

Like a million other farm boys of the Eighties, Henry Ford was crazy about mechanisms. At first he tinkered with clocks and watches, but by the early Nineties, when he had a job with the Detroit Edison Company, he was desperately involved with an automobile. In 1896 he finally got it running.

This brakeless, reverseless, two-cylinder buckboard wasn't much of a machine compared to the fairly sophisticated automobiles already running in Europe, but it was good enough to get some friends of Ford's to advance him a little money to go on experimenting. By 1899 he had built a much better machine, quit his job with the electric light company and become superintendent of the Detroit Automobile Company, one of the myriad little outfits rushing into the car business.

Ford already had his mind on a cheap car almost anyone could afford, but he wasn't the boss, and the Detroit Automobile Company went under while trying to sell the few dull and expen-

ST CAR

Left: *Henry Ford in his first car, built in 1896. If it wasn't exactly lovable (Stein calls it a buckboard) it was good enough to get him the cash, as an advance, that built an empire.*

57

sive machines it succeeded in building.

Now, to make his name known, Ford began to build racing cars. With spectacular success he beat the great Alexander Winton's 70 h.p. machine and almost immediately new money became available to start the Ford Motor Company, first as a partnership with Alexander Malcolmson, a Detroit coal dealer, in 1902, and then as a corporation in 1903. In the five years or so until he hit the jackpot with the Model T, Ford brought out a series of fairly successful light cars and, at the insistence of his partners, one fancy lemon, the Model K. This was not at all the sort of machine Henry wanted to manufacture. It was big, it had a fuel-hungry six-cylinder engine, and it was expensive. Even at the high price of 2,800 dollars, the company lost money on it. Further, it had a too-flimsy planetary transmission, which was most likely Ford's fault (he just loved planetaries and later put one in the Model T).

By 1906, Ford was building the Model N and was approaching his ideal of "the universal car", as he called it. This Model N was the direct ancestor of the T—it even looked like a T in the shape of its radiator and its transverse front spring.

But although thousands of Ns and its de luxe versions, the Models R and S, were sold at quite low prices (the N cost a mere 600 dollars), they had not acquired that stamp of pure genius which was to make Ford the best-known car name in the world.

On October 1, 1908, the most maligned and the most praised, the most reliable and the most cantankerous, the ugliest and the most functional of all cars was born—the Model T.

It was about as beautiful as a kitchen coal-store precariously balanced on the cat's cradle of springs and rods above four impossibly skinny wheels. Its huge top, which ballooned aloft over the passengers, may have offered protection from the elements, but it looked monstrous.

Contrary to that oft-quoted remark of Henry Ford's, "They can have any colour they like as long as it's black" (which he very likely never said), the early Ford T touring cars were dark Brewster green with red striping. There were even very early Ts with *red* bodies!

But looks meant little to tough old Henry. When someone asked him how far behind the front seats the back seats were to be placed, he said: "Far enough for a farmer to get his milk cans on the floor." And with the farmer in mind again, the T was hardly more complicated than a plough. Baling wire, pliers, a screwdriver could keep one going, and in later years you could buy parts for Ford Ts in the dime store.

With all its simplicity, the Model T was full of innovations:

Its 2·9-litre, 22-h.p., four-cylinder engine was cast in one piece, but it had a detachable cylinder head in a day when such a convenience was unheard of. Although the very earliest European machines' heads had been made separately because of casting problems, most manufacturers fought shy of having to make a water-tight, gas-tight joint at such a crucial point in their engines.

The narrow chassis sat on transverse springs fore and aft which made for steering of phenomenal lock—a T could turn on an Indian-head penny.

The driver sat on the left where he belonged in a right-side-of-the-road country. The early Autocar was first with the notion, but Ford made it stick. In a few years most U.S. car builders had followed suit.

The Model T made its own electricity from a magneto built into the flywheel. (I can remember very well playing with the greasy horseshoe magnets we pried out of the derelict Fords with which the junk-yards of my youth abounded.) The English Lanchester had a similar magneto and might well have given Ford the idea.

The engine, clutch, transmission, flywheel, and universal joint all shared a common oil chamber: when you poured oil into the crankcase every part was certain to get some.

Although the last days of the T slightly antedated my debut as a driver, I can well remember the oddities of control necessary when managing one. The T, of course, had no hand gearshift. Its two speeds and reverse were controlled by means of three foot pedals, which tightened the brake bands of the planetary transmission and that of the foot brake inside the gearbox. A hand lever operated the tiny brakes on the rear wheels. There was no accelerator. To vary engine speed you diddled with a lever on the steering column, where also lived the spark-control lever. Once the

58

engine was started—until 1919, by hand cranking—you pressed the left-hand pedal halfway down, which put the gears in neutral. Then you released the hand-brake, which had kept the gears in neutral while you cranked. To get moving, you tramped all the way down on the same left-hand pedal, meanwhile opening the hand throttle. You were now in low. At about eight miles an hour you eased the throttle a bit and took your foot right off the pedal. With a neck-snapping bound and a mournful howl from the transmission the flivver catapulted ahead. You were now in high, in which speed you could do 40 m.p.h. if all was well with the engine.

If you wanted to back up, you pushed the left pedal down again halfway, into neutral, and trod on the middle pedal. You could if you liked use this middle pedal as a brake. (The instruction book recommended this to equalise band wear). Being able to bound back and forth like a rubber ball on elastic was one of youth's joys in a T.

To stop you tramped on everything. It didn't matter which two pedals your feet hit.

T drivers became expert at driving rearward, for even in low, due to chronically worn bands, smallish hills were sometimes unclimbable. Undaunted, drivers went up backwards. But there was another reason for being a virtuoso in reverse. The full tank was under the front seat and fed the carburettor by gravity. With a near-empty tank on a hill the petrol was unable to climb up to the carburettor. Going up backwards raised the tank above the carburettor.

With all its little foibles, the T was nearly unbreakable, mostly because it was made of superlative materials, better than many of the more expensive machines of its day. In 1905, Henry Ford was at a speed trial on a Florida beach when a French car wrecked itself. Impressed by its stamina before the debacle he quietly put a bit of metal from its engine in his pocket. Back in Detroit, Ford had a metallurgist analyse the fragment and discovered that it was chrome-vanadium steel. From then on every Ford car had some of this steel in its construction, made in a small steel mill built by Ford.

As the farmers realised that here, at last, was a cheap, reliable machine to lift them out of the mud, to set them free from the horse, and to end their isolation, production zoomed and prices went down.

In 1909, when the first Ts reached their owners, the price was 850 dollars. By 1912, it was 600 dollars; by 1918, 450 dollars. In 1924 it reached its all-time low of 290 dollars. Just before it went out of production in 1926 it cost 380 dollars. But by now it had electric starting and lighting and detachable wire wheels with balloon tyres.

Of course, it was mass production that made these incredibly low prices possible. And although Ford had certainly not invented mass production, he was the first to use it on such a colossal scale. In August, 1913, it took twelve-and-a-half man-hours to build a chassis. But as the technique of the assembly line was perfected the time dropped. By December, 1913, it was two hours and thirty-eight minutes, by January, 1914, one hour and thirty-three minutes. After that the factory remained silent on how few man-hours it took to whip out a Tin Lizzie.

Although the Model T gave way to the Model A in 1927, it still lives on. For it is the most popular (especially the brass-radiatored, wooden-dashboard examples of pre-1915) of all the machines treasured by antique-car collectors.

Everyman's transport: a gallery of Fords by Bill Boddy

Since the Model T it has been a virtually unbroken success story. Ford of America — and of Britain, Germany and France — is the second largest producer of motor vehicles in the world, specialising in dependable transport for Everyman. But apart from utility cars and commercial vehicles, Ford has raced (and by 1966 had a ragingly-active competition programme), has built a luxury car (the Lincoln) that rivalled Cadillac and Packard, and is conscientiously concerned with inbuilt safety in its automobiles. Henry Ford was obviously a mechanical genius. Not only did he pioneer mass-production; before that he tried for the land speed record, flirted with the quality car market. These are some of the machines, American and British, in the historic progress he instigated.

1896: Henry Ford's first auto-buggy which he built by hand and drove to a cool reception at his father's farm near Dearborn, Michigan. It raised 200 dollars, but Ford bought it back. Today, restored, it is in the Greenfield Village Museum.

1904: the year when Henry Ford (standing, right) achieved an unrecognised Land Speed Record of 91.4 m.p.h. on the ice with one of his celebrated racers. Tiller-steered, its gigantic cylinders measured '7" × '7".

1908: Model T. Its production run lasted till 1927. Technically unaltered during that span, its appearance was modernised with reluctance. When it ceased production, up to 10 million were still in use, so spares were made for years after—

1903: Model A, the Ford Motor Company's first production. A neat little run-about, it had a side-cranked horizontal 2-cylinder engine. Transmission was planetary and fool-proof, as on the later Model T. It cost 850 dollars, did 30 m.p.h.

1904: Model B, with four vertical cylinders. Made to carry four people at 40 m.p.h. — if you had 2,000 dollars to spare. Battery ignition and epicyclic gears persisted — and there were still only two forward speeds.

Model A replaced Model T. Speculation was intense as the world waited for its specification. When it arrived in December, 1927, crowds stopped New York traffic to get a glimpse. They saw four cylinders, crash gearbox—a new step for Ford.

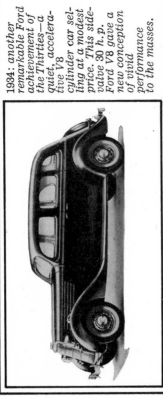

1934: another remarkable Ford achievement of the Thirties—a quiet, accelerative V8 cylinder car selling at a modest price. This side-valve 30 h.p. Ford V8 gave a new conception of vivid performance to the masses.

1959: post-war traffic conditions called for a nippy small saloon, and good sales depended on stylish lines. This was achieved by British Ford with their Anglia, seen here in its 1959 guise. It is still raced and rallied.

1966: still onwards . . . this big V6 Zephyr is stuffed with urge, bristles with practical features, and has many safety factors. Striving to follow Stuttgart in road-holding if not in top speed there is, at last, all-round independent suspension.

luxury, Henry Ford brought out this big 60 m.p.h., 6-cylinder Model K. It was fast, but lost money at the selling price of 2,800 dollars. Shown here in sporting roadster form, even this one had planetary cogs.

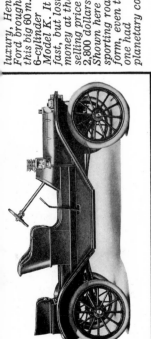

1935: at last, the £100 car. Ford of Dagenham succeeded where others had failed with this 8 h.p. Popular saloon. It had big-car lines, a conventional specification, with Ford's transverse springing. A better-equipped version nevertheless outsold it.

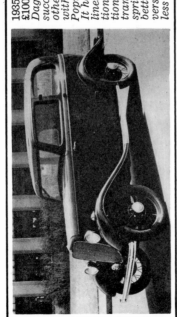

1946: reliable, economical transport typical of British Ford products between and after two world wars was provided by this 10 h.p. Prefect. They can still be counted on the roads, proof of their honest construction.

1965: up-to-the-minute lines, Aeroflow ventilation of high efficiency enabling windows to be kept shut—hence fixed quarter-lights—and a powerful V4 power unit make this Ford Corsair de luxe a Dagenham best-seller.

Cooper: blacksmith in the pits
by Derek Jewell

There are men with pots of money who love making cars. There are also those who chalk out designs on garage floors, then use bits of old air-raid shelters and motor-bike engines to achieve their dream. Charles and John Cooper are of the latter kind. No man has done more for modern Grand Prix racing – or for young bloods without money who want to move fast – than John Cooper.

John Cooper likes turning forward somersaults in public. In 1959 and 1960 he was doing it all the time around the race circuits of the world. Whenever Jack Brabham or Roy Salvadori or Bruce McLaren won for him in a Grand Prix, he would go head-over-heels on the tarmac by the pits: and they were doing a lot of winning.

Those were the golden days for the Cooper Car Company of Surbiton, Surrey, England, and later of Byfleet, in the same county. Brabham, their works driver, was World Champion in two successive seasons. Twice their Formula I car won the World Manufacturers' Championship, which no British car had done before. It was an astonishing achievement for a small family company taking on the big-money giants like Ferrari and Maserati. It put the seal on the emergence of Britain for the first time as the premier motor racing nation of the world. That was mostly Cooper's doing.

"I suppose Surbiton made a song and dance about it all?"

"They put our rates up."

"No, honestly?"

"And we had crowds of people at the garage shouting and screaming about our all-night sessions getting cars ready for races."

"And that's all?"

"Well," said John Newton Cooper, "our local baker did make us a cake."

Cooper, in his forties, is a large, rumpled man, with a square, Jack Hawkins kind of face. His hands, which have helped build so many winners, and have poked into their works from Indianapolis to Nurburgring, are rarely in repose. He seems not to hold it against Surbiton that the town, one of those archetypes of respectable commuterdom, virtually ignored him and his father, Charles, nor that motor racing has given him grievous disappointments as well as sweet triumphs. Between 1960 and 1966, in which year the old Formula I engine limit of 1½ litres leapt to 3 litres, the big British name in Grand Prix racing was not Cooper but the firm's long-time rival Lotus, based in another London suburb, Hornsey, and fired by the brilliant designing of Colin Chapman and the driving of Jim Clark.

Not that the years immediately after 1960 were exactly *unsuccessful* for Coopers. The Mini-Cooper alone ensured that. The idea of the box-car, with no frills outside and a lot of room inside, was that of Alec Issigonis, the British Motor Corporation's chief designer and engineer. The idea of putting more horses inside it was John Cooper's.

"I'd known Alec for a long time, you see. Only the second race I was in, back in 1947, I beat him. We've been friends ever since. He let me have one of the early test Minis, and I couldn't believe it I was so impressed.

"I took one to Italy, and Lampredi—he was chief designer for Ferrari then—saw me with it at Monza. After he'd tried it out he said: 'If that car didn't look so bloody awful, I'd shoot myself.'

"Soon all the G.P. drivers and their mates had got Minis and were tuning them a bit. I suggested to Issigonis that we should build a good one for the boys. So we converted one—pushed up the engine size from 850 c.c. to 1000 c.c., put on disc brakes, tarted it up generally. Then we and B.M.C. did further development together. After that we raced them and they rallied them."

It was originally intended that a dozen or so Mini-Coopers should be made for a few special people. By the mid-Sixties production had exceeded 60,000. The car dominated the Monte Carlo, the Tulip, the Alpine—every

62

major rally in the world. In saloon car racing it won both the British and European championships. The royalties the car brought from B.M.C. to Coopers did much to keep the company solvent, for Formula I racing is an expensive business.

But the Mini alone could not be enough for John Cooper. He wanted to turn forward somersaults again. Grand Prix racing and Formula I remains the summit, and this is where he has always wanted to be.

"We all know it. This is what *really* gets him. He'll only be satisfied if he builds cars that win the most important prizes in the world." This is Duggie Johnson talking, and he should know. He joined Coopers when he was 15 and has stayed for over a quarter of a century. He has probably built more racing cars—well over a thousand—than any other man in the world, all of them Coopers.

"Where racing cars are concerned," says Roy Salvadori, ex-Cooper driver, who became the marque's racing manager, "John Cooper is the most excitable man I know. He *feels* for those cars.

"In the pits suddenly he'll start fidgeting with a pencil or something. Then he'll go walking round the car. Round and round and round. Popping questions. Have you done this? Have you done that? Worrying. He's too experienced ever to tell a driver to go faster. He'll be at the side of the track muttering, 'Now's the time to go slow. Now's the time not to stress the car.'

"You want to know what he's really like? We were at Silverstone once practising. John says, 'Well, everything's wonderful. The sun's shining, the car's handling O.K., the brakes are fine, the gearbox is fine. There's only

one thing wrong. We're two seconds bloody slower than the opposition.'

"In this game everyone suffers from nerves. John hides it most of the time. But you watch him. He loves cars, and he can hate them too. So much so he'll kick a car if it behaves badly. He wants to win G.P.s all right."

The reasons why go back a long way.

The Cooper Car Company only stopped being a father-and-son business in 1964 when Charles Cooper died. He gave the company its image of practical, down-to-earth engineering. He was an apprentice at Napiers, the engineering and racing car firm, then chief mechanic to Kaye Don, one of the great early racers, and later opened his own general garage at Ewell Road, Surbiton, in 1933. He was one of the first to build himself the miniature Flying Flea plane in the Thirties.

When John Cooper was eight, his father gave him his first car (maximum speed 40 m.p.h.) which he drove around the paddock at Brooklands, the great British racing circuit of the first half of the century. At 12 he had another car, with a pepped-up Austin 7 engine. He drove that at Brooklands too, on the circuit, at 87 m.p.h.—until the authorities found out.

He left Surbiton County Grammar School at 15, and the idea that he should be a racing driver never left him—throughout his apprenticeship at Coopers and with a toolmaker; during his war service (four years on secret work including one-man subs); or later when he was in the R.A.F. Nor, it seems, did the idea of the small racing car.

Not a madly expensive car, though, like the Formula I and II models, whose engines then ranged up to 4½ litres—much bigger than the most powerful family saloons. These would cost thousands. Only Formula III—up to 500 c.c., motor-cycle size—could be small enough. John Cooper wanted, above all, cheapness.

Before the war, motor racing was a rich man's sport. In 1947 the Coopers, father and son, changed all that. They chalked out a rough design on the floor of their garage at Surbiton and set to work. Quite *why* they built their first car John Cooper now can't precisely explain. They knew there was a rising tide of interest among the impecunious who wanted to go fast, but they had at that time no commercial ambitions. It was just something they wanted to do.

It was a bits-and-pieces model. The chassis came from a Fiat Topolino. There were Ford universal joints and a motor-cycle clutch and gearbox. Because steel was short, the frame uprights were made from bits of a derelict Morrison air-raid shelter. The 500 c.c. single-cylinder J.A.P. dirt-track engine was placed behind the driver for better traction and weight-saving. That rear-mounted engine was important, both for Cooper cars and the whole future of racing. It set a trend.

It took only five weeks to create this car, but John Cooper soon began to win sprints and hill-climbs. A second model was made for another driver, Eric Brandon, who, in his schooldays, had raced motor-bikes against John. He began winning too. There were more orders. Coopers decided to lay down a batch of a dozen cars. They had, almost accidentally, become a car-manufacturing company.

One of those first dozen cars, cream-coloured, was taken over by a teenager named Stirling Moss. He was the first of a long string of drivers who were to sharpen their skills on Coopers of all sizes: Peter Collins, Mike Hawthorn, Stuart Lewis-Evans, Harry Schell, Ivor Bueb, Les Leston, Ken Wharton, Jack Brabham, Roy Salvadori.

Motor-racing journalists have tended to say that Cooper cars are good blacksmith's jobs. The image stands for strength. And that was true from the beginning. Fragile as the cars looked, they did not sacrifice strength or rigidity for lightness. It was one of Charles Cooper's principles. "If I see anybody shunt one of my motor cars," he said once, "I like to see them get up and walk away." Drivers usually did.

In one 500 c.c. race at the Avus circuit in Berlin, John Cooper crashed into a wall to avoid ramming two cars which had already collided. He then pushed his car 150 yards to get it started—and still won the race, at over 93 m.p.h., at that time a record.

At Blandford Camp, Dorset, in 1949, a Cooper ran into some trees and catapulted on to the guardroom roof. The driver, Major Peter Braid, who was tipped out as the car landed, couldn't push it anywhere. But astonishingly he stayed in one piece, and so did the car.

Ironically, he died six years later—in a rail crash at Barnes.

By the early 1950s, Coopers had almost killed 500 c.c. racing. They won so often that the sense of contest diminished. John Cooper had also scooped up international speed trial records with a streamlined 500, and the firm were now building sports cars as well as racing cars. There was only one direction in which Coopers could move. Upwards—into the world of Formula I and II.

Their search for a more powerful, and winning, racing car lasted for most of the Fifties. It was a considerable gamble, for soon a new competitor was breathing hot behind them—the Lotus Car Company and Colin Chapman. The single-mindedness of Coopers in this period lost them their lead in sports cars to Chapman but, ironically, it was a sports car they used in 1955 to help them make the first breakthrough towards their Grand Prix ambitions.

Into it they put a new power unit, the Coventry-Climax 1100 c.c. (developed, improbably, from a fire-pump engine) which in the next few years was to be bored out again and again to force its

Above: Cooper cars are tough. This bizarre accident happened in 1949 to a 500 c.c. Cooper—the car on which a generation of drivers, including Stirling Moss, learned their trade. During a race the car hit some trees and catapulted on to this roof. Both it and the driver suffered comparatively minor damage.

size nearer 2000 c.c. The car was revolutionary, the forerunner of all today's Formula I designs.

It was small and light. It had a rear engine, the first time one had been used with conventional transmission in a fast car since German experiments pre-war. And it had a sawn-off back. Some people called it a Manx tail, others a 'spoiler'.

"That car was way ahead of its time," says Roy Salvadori. "So quick, so stable—the perfect streamlining. That sawn-off back created a pressure in the air stream that kept the rear-end on the deck.

"The story got around that John had chopped off the tail because he couldn't get two of the cars in the transporter. Do you believe that? Well, I'm still not sure. He likes to be light-hearted about it. So it's a mystery."

It seems not quite such a mystery to Owen Maddock. He was fifteen years with Coopers (people usually are long-stayers with them) before he left in 1963 with a yen to design hovercraft, and he did all the drawings for Cooper cars in the Fifties. "The chopped-off tail was a bit more scientific than that—but, all right, yes it did help in the transporters." Somehow Cooper people don't like confessing there's too much slide-rule in their business.

Because that 1955 sports car was a commercial success, Coopers had the cash to transform it into a racing car. At once they began winning Formula II races—and selling the car in a big way. Their works is the only place you *can* buy a Cooper. This firm, which buys engines and the usual list of accessories (tyres, brakes and so on) ready-made, but manufactures everything else on the spot, offers no dealerships. By 1957, with an engine beefed up to 1900 c.c. and Jack Brabham to drive the car, Coopers were crowding even the big Formula I machines.

The sixth place won by Jack Brabham (the world's best driver and development tester *combined* during the Fifties and Sixties, according to Cooper) at Monaco in 1957 was one pointer. And the victory gained by Stirling Moss driving a Rob Walker-owned Cooper in the Argentine G.P. of 1958 was the most staggering *grande épreuve* result since before the war. He beat the far more powerful Ferraris and Maseratis of Fangio, Hawthorn and Musso. He did it

with the white canvas of his heavily-punished tyres showing through for the last eight laps.

Not only was this the first G.P. win for a Cooper—with an engine half a litre under the permitted size. This car cost less than £3,000; its rivals cost ten times as much. Coopers finished that 1958 season third in the Manufacturers' Championship (Formula I) behind Vanwall and Ferrari.

It was a remarkable performance for a small family firm of strictly limited resources against the heavier machinery of far wealthier concerns. Both Brabham and Salvadori, the other works driver, had instructions to avoid excessive risks (crashes resulting in car write-offs, as had happened to Ferrari, would have put Coopers out of the racing business) and even to limit their engine revs to 6,000—at least 1,000 below their known maximum—to lessen the chance of an engine blow-up.

"John had to worry too much about finance," Salvadori remembers. "Whenever we got edgy with each other—which wasn't often—it was because he didn't want to practice as much as I did, to keep down the chances of a shunt. At Nurburgring once I'd been going very fast in the wet in practice. He told me not to push it. But I took the car out again and went even quicker. I came off the road and ploughed through hedges and trees for 300 yards.

"It really damaged the car, but when John saw it he just said, 'O.K. A very minor shunt.' And you know, it was in terribly bad shape. He must have been eating his guts out. But he worked all night on it, and never said another damn thing. I still finished third. That's the way he works."

But Coopers knew they were now very close to their goal. At the end of 1958, John Cooper, Brabham and Owen Maddock sat down to plan again. "We just said, 'Right, let's build an even tinier motor car, engine at the back—that's the way to win G.P.s. Let's run next year's car now.' Until we did that," says Cooper, "G.P. cars were twice the size they are today. We set the style that everyone's copied."

The car they designed was slim, low and looked incredibly fragile. The legend still persists that John Cooper once more chalked it out on the floor. "Coopers," says Les Leston, another former driver on their works team,

Previous page: John Cooper in 1965, with stripped-down Formula I racing car. "He is," according to Stirling Moss, "a mechanic who works with his mechanics." Between 1948 and 1965, in the small workshops attached to a suburban garage, his firm turned out more racing cars than any other maker in the world. The photograph is by Patrick Ward.

"tend to go in for knife and fork methods."

Coventry-Climax produced a new engine for it from the drawing board in three months flat—at last, the full-sized Formula I specification, at that time 2½ litres—and Coopers proceeded to hammer the world. That year, 1959, they took the Manufacturers' Championships in Formula I, II and III. Brabham was World Champion—though he only clinched it when he pushed home at Sebring for fourth place and collapsed by the car.

He made it seem easier the next year. The car he drove then seemed even lower and narrower, tapered like a flat cigar. And there was a completely new 5-speed gearbox. "That was how we kept in front of the rest," says Cooper. "They'd got the message of our 1959 car, but that year everybody was in gearbox trouble and we weren't."

The advantage was crucial. In a dazzling sequence, Brabham came first in the G.P.s at Zandvoort, Spa, Rheims, Silverstone and Oporto. He was World Champion once more, and again Coopers had won the manufacturers' titles for all three formulas. The sum of what they had given to world racing by now was probably unparalleled.

They had opened up the sport to people without much money and their cars had trained a whole generation of drivers. They had set the trend for small, rear-engined Formula I cars. They had been first with magnesium wheels (they are lighter, yet don't whip under stress), with double wishbone suspension all round, with effective use of disc brakes.

That the marque should have declined in the great races of the world during the early Sixties after reaching that peak may seem surprising. There are many explanations, most of them intrinsically bound up with the continuing rise of Colin Chapman's Lotus. John Cooper, who seems self-critical enough to admit mistakes as well as to claim successes, set out some of them in the summer of 1965.

"There was the Mini in 1961 to concern us. But what reduced us to mere plodding was that we lost Jack Brabham. He wanted to race his own cars. For several years we simply hadn't got a driver of his calibre.

"I thought that with us, Bruce McLaren could make a World Champion, and we put all our eggs in that basket. I was wrong, that's all. I rate Clark, Surtees" (this was before Surtees was badly injured in Canada), "Stewart, Gurney, Hill and Brabham as the best six in the world right now—in that order. And Bruce is the best No. 2 driver in the world.

"Then there's the car. In 1959 and 1960 we had a car a year ahead of its time. After that everyone had basically the same kit of parts—with better drivers. Lotus did more development than we did—in a sense they had more incentive to develop. They had Jim Clark, who got better and better. And Colin Chapman has added a deal more science to the ideas we introduced.

"To win G.P.s you need three things: a great chassis, a great engine, and a great driver. And they go together. If you don't have a great driver, then somehow when your engine goes back to the makers for overhaul, they don't put so much into it. It's a vicious circle, hard to break—and all the time team morale goes down if you're not winning.

"There were other things, too. In 1963 I had a bad crash at over a hundred on the Kingston by-pass in a Mini I'd designed, with engines front and rear. They say I nearly died. That affected me for a year—and I still get headaches. Perhaps it's slowed me down a bit. Then my father was ill for a long time before he died in '64."

Others told a similar story in that same year, sometimes changing the emphasis. . . .

Roy Salvadori: "Every organisation has a bad time sometimes—a relaxing period that can be fatal. I suppose John didn't show much interest in design because he felt he hadn't got the drivers. So the cars he turned out weren't the greatest."

Stirling Moss: "Racing simply became more scientific. Lotus made the racing car an artistic piece of work—by using science. John's more a fundamentalist—a terribly talented blacksmith who's done as much as Lotus, maybe more, in a different way."

Maxwell Boyd: "In 1962 Chapman brought out this great idea of the monocoque car, body and frame combined, with the metal outer covering carrying the stresses. That's where Chapman's slide-rule-and-theory scored over John Cooper's practical-engineer

E

69

approach. Lotuses were just that bit lighter.''

Les Leston: "Chapman's way is to drive a car to the limit and if it doesn't break he'll lighten it till it does break. Then he'll go back a stage, and there's the car—as light as it *can* be. John Cooper hates to break a car. Perhaps he's too much of a nice chap for motor racing now—too easy.''

It all added up: to a *grande épreuve* decline, but not yet to a fall. For in 1965 things were changing again for Coopers. In April of that year they ensured their survival in Formula I racing by merging, for £250,000, with the Chipstead Motor Group, headed by Jonathan Sieff, son of one of the directors of the superbly successful Marks and Spencer store chain, and a racing driver himself until he was badly injured in a crash at Le Mans in 1960.

"I was getting to the stage when I knew we'd have to give up motor racing because of the cost,'' said Cooper. "Jonathan Sieff saved us really. He had the money. So the deal was done.'' It left Cooper as managing director of his company, with Roy Salvadori as racing manager.

The new deal also meant a modification of part of the old corner-shop Cooper mystique. For the racing section of the company moved to more spacious Chipstead premises at Byfleet. The Surbiton garage was left solely as a Mini-Cooper servicing station.

That garage, though, still sums up the essence of the operation which established the name of its founder in international motor racing. It looks like any medium-sized suburban petrol station; except that in pre-1966 days there would often be racing cars lying by the pumps. To inexpert eyes they looked very small, like abandoned toys.

It stands on a corner. There is an old building—white and 1930s marine-style —and beside it a new addition with a sweeping curved front and a lot of glass. Behind the glass are the small workshops where over 2,000 racing and sports cars were made between 1948 and 1965 by a mere couple of dozen men.

It was a ridiculously tiny place in which to create world-beating cars. It always looked crowded—skeleton cars in jigs hard against piles of bright magnesium; men with spanners stepping over stray pieces of glass-fibre

superstructure to delve in stripped-down cars with huge springs, wide fat tyres, and steering wheels so small they looked ridiculous. "People used to come here,'' said one mechanic, "and say 'Where's the factory, then?' ''

Compare this pocket-handkerchief set-up, which took months to produce a racing car, with the vast Ferrari operation, which once replaced four wrecked G.P. cars with new ones in a few days. Compare, in fact, almost any aspect of Cooper with Ferrari. John Cooper works closely with his drivers, who help put the cars together and are usually his friends. Most Ferrari drivers are scarcely allowed to touch their machines except on the track.

"He's a very approachable bloke,'' says Stirling Moss. "When I was racing he'd always give you a hand to change an engine. And he's very open-minded. I liked him because he was prepared to let me juggle with his cars. I'd bore holes anywhere he'd say was okay—in the pedals, the brackets, all over the place—to make the car lighter. He's a mechanic who works with his mechanics.'' Enzo Ferrari, by contrast, buys the best talent and then stands aloof.

Cooper doesn't spend as much time as many managing directors in his office— a rather bare room, both at Surbiton and later at Byfleet, containing only a few trophies. When he *is* there, the phone rings continually; he seems to be constantly under pressure. "Let's try,'' he was saying into the phone, "to make that bracket much stronger and bolt on all four bolts. I think it'll help, cock.''

Not that the conversation is always so technical. There's a young and ingenuous quality to Cooper.

Salvadori was on the other end of a different phone call, talking about the South African Grand Prix. Cooper's end went like this: "Well, I'm going. I don't know about you . . . I want a week's water-skiing, mate. . . . Never mind about the programme. We'll only be away a week. . . . It's the last race the old cars will do. Let's get some money.''

Then he was up, out of the chair, moving round the works at speed. Poking his nose into every corner of it, asking questions, advising.

The men he talks with are almost invariably long at the game, and long with Coopers. "He'll be very interested in detail at the prototype stage,'' says

Duggie Johnson. "He'll change things, ask for a slightly heavier gauge material—that sort of thing. Once the prototype's finished he never worries us."

Cooper loves talking about cars; sometimes, he says, he thinks he likes talking about them more than actually watching them race. There is passion in it either way.

"He gets worked up fairly easily," says Owen Maddock. "Especially if anything's getting in the way of making his cars. He's very impatient with British industry. Once he went to a German firm to get a crown wheel and pinion because delivery here was six times as long. For ever afterwards he was threatening other British firms he'd go abroad for the bits they made for us.

"Getting impassioned is the way he gets things done. Once he slammed a phone down so hard he broke it. The mechanics had a motto for him: 'When in doubt, scream and shout!' "

But there is one aspect of the sport of motor racing about which he does not scream and shout; and his quiet intensity is all the more revealing. By 1965, something seemed to have gone out of racing for John Cooper.

"It isn't quite what it was, though, is it? Take Fangio. *That* was driving. Tyre-smoke, opposite lock on the corners, all that. Driving on the seat of his pants. But now Jim Clark, he lies in the car and he looks like he's going at half-speed it's so smooth. It's more like driving a plane. You go into a corner at certain revs and you come out at certain revs. Scientific driving. It's brilliant all right, but it doesn't *look* anything. And racing is suffering because it doesn't.

"It's a different game on the inside, too. In the old days it was good fun. People did it because they liked it. Now, it's a business. Just that."

Racing has changed; the Cooper Car Company has changed. With the start of the new 3-litre specification for Formula I cars in 1966, even the engines inside Cooper's designs had to change. Coventry-Climax, the old stand-bys for British cars, withdrew from this too-expensive game. Cooper turned to an Italian engine, Maserati.

The year was especially critical for Cooper. He started the 1966 Grand Prix season with more 3-litre cars ready for the circuits than anyone else, with more resources behind him than ever before, knowing he must prove he could head a scientific company in an age of scientific motoring; that the Chapman formula of slide-rule plus co-ordinating flair hadn't left Coopers behind for ever. Ironically it was Cooper's ex-driver, Brabham, now running his own cars, who soon began to set the World Championship pace.

"Mark you," Cooper had said before the start of the 1966 season, "whatever happens, everyone has got to find himself a driver capable of staying on the road and not killing himself."

He made that sound very, very important. Of the sixteen men who lined up for the Monaco G.P. in 1958, seven were dead by 1965 (Stuart Lewis-Evans, Collins, Musso, Schell, Behra, von Trips and Hawthorn) and three so badly injured that they had not raced again. In a sport so dangerous the Cooper record was impressive. In all their years of racing they had, as Cooper spoke, never lost a team driver.

"Nothing," as Salvadori says, "ever falls off a Cooper. It means a lot, that, having faith your car won't come apart."

It sounds like a testimonial to the Coopers, Charles and John. There is a postscript.

"A Mini-Cooper—well, you can pick one up second-hand for three or four hundred and go racing with it. Racing couldn't be much cheaper, could it?" John Cooper sounds excited when he says that, and why shouldn't he? World championships aren't everything. It has been something to be the leader of a revolution.

Rolls-Royce:
whatsoever rightly done is noble
by Peter Dunn

Is Rolls-Royce the best-loved car in the world? Certainly no car name has such in-built depth of meaning. It infers luxury, money, power, snobbisme, specialness. There's also a touch of the old-fashioned to it; even today it is redolent of the past glories of the English aristocracy. Peter Dunn, who wrote this account of Rolls-Roycery, is a special correspondent for 'The Sunday Times Magazine'. Previously he was industrial writer with 'The Observer'.

People are always searching out the symbolism in the Best Car in the World. Some people take it seriously: an American art historian recently produced a paper entitled 'The Ideological Antecedents of the Rolls-Royce Radiator' in which he said that (together with the mascot known to chauffeurs as Emily or Phyllis) it symbolises "the profound and clashing passions of the British spirit". To everybody else, the Rolls-Royce symbolises the pampered life of the English milord.

Frank and fearless questions have been asked about whether in fact the Rolls-Royce is the Best Car in the World. The answer, almost invariably, is yes. It is probably also the best-loved car in the world. One of the extraordinary things about it is the fact that anyone who has a new Rolls employs somebody else to drive it, though in fact the cars are deliberately designed for owner-drivers.

The radiator grille remains the distinguishing feature. The Bentley T is exactly the same as the Silver Shadow introduced in 1965 apart from the radiator and the price, which is a few score pounds lower. The radiator is hand-built from 80 different parts in a tin shed with a high roof at Crewe, Cheshire, England, called The Chapel. Each surface is slightly convex to give the impression of even greater solidarity.

Its design has remained unchanged since the century began. The only alteration came when Sir Henry Royce died in 1933 and the interlocking Rs were painted black instead of red; they have stayed black ever since. The com-

pany once sued a French millionaire who tried to fit a different grille. It won its case. There have been problems with non-R-R owners fitting R-R radiators to Cadillacs and suchlike. As they discovered when it came to the Silver Shadow, the R-R radiator can be styled into almost any shape or body.

For all its elegance in such areas as *The Power Game* (this TV series borrowed a Silver Shadow for Sir John Wilder), Rolls-Royce seems geared to a distant era. The plush innards of the car are still called its "interior appointments". The dignity and aloofness of the company, its deliberate non-involvment in stormy publicity, all add to the overall image of the aristocrat holding his own in a hostile world.

Behind the barrier of mystery, however, there is a beaver-like activity. The Silver Shadow, when it was introduced at the 1965 Paris Motor Show, created something of a sensation with its advanced electronics and engineering. It nearly appeared as the Silver Mist, but the name was hurriedly changed when it was discovered that 'mist' translated into German means: "Dung, manure, excrement; dung-heap; dirt; fog (Naut)." Much of the Shadow's success is due to the Rolls director of engineering, Mr. Harry Grylls.

Mr. Grylls, son of a Cornish J.P. who invented the 'rapid cinema' (a sort of high-speed camera) which he donated to the Admiralty during the First World War out of patriotism, joined Rolls-Royce directly he came down from Cambridge.

"In a Rolls," he said, "you isolate yourself from the noise of the world.

I'd like to say that we're glad there still exists the clientele who appreciate the difference between our car and everyone else's. These professionally successful men really appreciate the car. They don't *just* buy it because it's got a Rolls-Royce radiator."

Its lack of gimmickry is one of the great points about the Rolls. Different systems are tried, but are not incorporated in production models until the company is quite certain that they are genuine improvements: "We first put disc brakes on one of our experimental cars 12 years ago," said Mr. Grylls. "But we found you could wear them out between Crewe and London without even touching the brake pedal because in bad weather grit formed a crust on the discs. So we had to do a lot more

work on them." The Shadow now has disc brakes. "We've led the way in electric light equipment," continued Mr. Grylls. "If an R-R headlamp fails, the lamps come on again with a circuit which is already waiting. Automatic headlamp dippers don't work in England. There are far too many corners on the roads and far too many walls, which *worries* an automatic dipper with reflections of itself."

There is a small touch of cloak-and-dagger about Rolls-Royce: "We've always got funny-looking cars going in and out of these gates here," said an R-R man. "We've always got production cars minus their radiators and bumpers and cars with strange-looking bodies. A new experimental car carefully left dirty and unpolished in that

Opposite page: *front view of Silver Shadow, the new-look Rolls-Royce introduced in* 1965. *It was almost called the Silver Mist: for the reason why it wasn't, read Mr. Dunn . . .*

Left: *before Rolls joined Royce* (1906), *the latter was building cars on his own account. This one is vintage-1904— 10 h.p. two-cylinder, and one of the first three cars Sir Henry Royce produced. On the wall, in Cooke Street, Manchester, can be seen the firm's name plate.*

Overleaf: *one of the great classic Rolls of the 1920s, a Phantom tourer— with, of course, a chauffeur. Few people actually drive their own R-R.*

73

lot doesn't show up. They look like wrecks actually.''

The company buys models of other manufacturers' cars and sifts through the dissected parts for good ideas—but then other manufacturers buy Rolls for the same reason: "We're always looking at everyone else's ideas," said Mr. Grylls. "Much more than anyone else. I'd say we never hesitate to copy anything that we liked. Some manufacturers say, 'We can't do that, because someone else has done it,' but not us. Synchromesh was the first one. We were the first to adapt it when it was only American. We immediately improved on it and fitted it.''

The Rolls-Royce factory at Crewe (in which town British Rail also bottles its wine) is reached by a long, winding rural road; the works are big and clean but don't look at all ostentatious. The engines and chassis are built here, as are the standard cars. Coachbuilt cars, however, are made in London.

There are two outstanding democratic traditions at Rolls-Royce. The first is that R-R staff are all called by their initials, which prevents confusion as to who should be called 'sir' and who 'hey you'. "It just sort of happens when you arrive," said MWm (Miller-Williams, the chief Press officer speaking). Thus Royce was 'R' and Rolls 'CSR'; Lord Hives the retired Chairman was 'Hs'; the chief executive, Sir Denning Pearson, 'Psn'; and Dr. Llewellyn Smith, managing director of the motor car division, 'LS'.

Executives at Crewe eat in a plain brick building which has the air of an old A.R.P. headquarters. They sit for meals at a round table so that, theoretically at least, nobody can sit at the head; "Don't let that fool you," said one R-R man. The senior executive present usually sits with his back to the light streaming in through the window. The table talk is general and sometimes people sound suspicious of wild London orgy life.

It takes between eight and ten weeks to build a Rolls: about a week of assembly, three weeks on the interior appointments (all the veneer in one car is taken from the same walnut log), at least two weeks' road testing, and about another week in the final finish. During that time, 272 feet of pipes go into the car. There are sixteen standard colours of which silver is the most popular, but one woman sent a sample of her nail varnish to the works and got that colour.

The Scottish Co-operative Wholesale Society uses Rolls-Royces as hearses and when they ordered 30 new cars they asked for a special rebate since they didn't feel that their customers would appreciate heaters or radios. Dr. Nkrumah, while he was still in power in Ghana, had a fleet of five Rolls which were scattered throughout Accra so that nobody could be quite sure where the Doctor himself was.

Bullet-proof windows are not so much in demand now as they were just after the war, and no armour-plating has been done for more than a dozen years. "You can still make a good job of armour plating one seat of the motor car," said Rolls-Royce. "The difficult thing is to do it for all types of attack."

Hundreds of stories circulate about stiff-upper-lipped after-sales service. There is one famous story over which debate is always breaking out in the papers. Is it apocryphal or isn't it? Two engineers are said to have been flown to Switzerland to mend a broken crankshaft; after some time the owner wrote to the firm and asked for a bill. The only answer he got was that "Rolls-Royce crankshafts do not break." Rolls-Royce said later: "We've done this sort of thing where the local man's not up to doing the job. If the car's under guarantee, he probably wouldn't get a bill. But he'd get a thumping great one if he was out of guarantee."

Everyone who works at Rolls-Royce is aware that it's the quality of the thing that matters, which is demonstrated by the fact that there have only been 51,000 Rolls and Bentleys "since the year dot." In the front entrance hall at Crewe is the legend: "Quiduis Recte Factum Quamuis Humile Praeclarum"—Whatsoever rightly done, however humble, is noble.

Right: Rolls-Royces are made for lasting—and this Silver Ghost first saw the road in 1911. It is still used regularly for racing, rallies, and workaday journeys. Owner John Bolster, technical editor of 'Autosport' and frequent broadcaster on motoring, found it in 1945 in a stable where it had mouldered since 1923. Bolster, who says he likes Rolls-Royces because "they're put together about right", drove the car off almost immediately he bought it, pausing only to cut off the perished tyres and fit new ones. There was even fuel (benzol) in the tank. His deerstalker hat dates from his first TV appearance: "The producer liked it and said keep it." His driving experience dates from age 12 ("I used to tell the chauffeur to move over") and culminated in race-driving. He had to give this up after he broke his neck while driving an E.R.A. in the British Grand Prix of 1948.

Aston Martin: going lyrical at £5 an hour
by Elisabeth Woolley

It was always rather special: the associations with James Bond have only made it more so. The Aston Martin today disputes with Ferrari the honour of being the ultimate in desirability, glitter, sexuality, loveability. Graham Finlayson's pictures, below and overleaf, suggest some of the reasons for this. It is a very carefully hand-made automobile: one man will follow through the making of one car. The aluminium body will be shaped with scrupulous care, using shears. The pistons and rods (centre of top row) are specially balanced. Pieces of the engine (see bottom row) are even lovingly polished by hand. Elisabeth Woolley fills in some of the details about the Aston mystique overleaf.

It may seem inevitable now—though it wasn't before—that an Aston Martin should have been chosen to be the all-systems-go (and incidentally all-British) James Bond car in *Goldfinger* and *Thunderball*. It has always had glamour. But Bond added a dimension, giving it the sort of mystique that stops small boys in their tracks and makes girls at traffic lights peer to see whether the driver lives up to his car's promise.

The DB5 used in *Goldfinger*, with its oil slip, smokescreen, ejector seat and all, cost £15,000 to build. A standard Aston Martin DB6 costs around £5,000, which, considering the skill and the loving care lavished on the construction of Astons, is regarded by many people as not expensive.

The same kind of painstaking precision goes into the making of an Aston as into a Balenciaga dress. The 750 employees at David Brown's factory in Newport Pagnell, Bedfordshire, turn out no more than about a dozen cars a week. One thousand man-hours (which, with materials, works out at £5 per hour) go into each car. The aluminium Superleggera body is sculpted by hand and fitted over the tubular steel framework; the rough edges are trimmed off with shears. Each coat of paint is hand-polished before the next layer is applied; the seats in each car are covered with five hides.

The DB6 is designed very much on Italian lines with fastback and spoiler tail which reduces wind resistance. The top gear—fifth—is virtually overdrive and allows a maximum speed of 150 m.p.h., but an Aston cruises effortlessly at 120.

One of the points which is often raised by Aston devotees is the space—both for rear-seat passengers and in the boot. Both models—the saloon and the coupé, dashingly called the Volante—are full four-seaters. The dashboard is arranged to look rather like an aircraft control panel.

Each four-litre engine is assembled by one engineer—a sort of one man-one motor system. The pistons and rods are specially balanced—a light piston against a correspondingly heavy rod so that the engine is capable of taking the power. It's much the same sort of process as the tuning-up of a less powerful engine.

The kind of things that make an Aston worthwhile are the details: the electrically-heated rear window, the air-conditioning, the little device that reduces the intensity of the indicators at night. It's like knowing that your clothes don't need safety pins to hold them together.

Aston Martin started manufacturing cars before the first world war. The Martin part of the name derives from one of the men involved in the initial design. The Aston bit was worked in because of the firm's success on the Aston Clinton hill-climb in Buckinghamshire. When the massive David Brown Corporation took over in 1947, the racing tradition continued, culminating in a win at Le Mans in 1959.

After this great success, Aston Martin pulled out of the racing community, mainly because of the enormous expense involved, and concentrated on the production of high-luxury, high-performance cars. Since then, the DB generations have been in a pretty well constant state of development and refinement, but, in essentials, the DB6 is based on the earlier Aston racing models.

How much the James Bond and Aston Martin booms are coincidental, and how much the one is responsible for the other, is a debatable point. The fact remains that during the early part of the 1960s Aston's export market grew at an unprecedented rate.

Perfection, of course, cannot be 100 per cent guaranteed, even with the minute care that is taken over Astons. It is possibly the precision and fine but vulnerable balance of the whole machine which accounts for some of its defects. A company director in Newcastle bought one and several repairs were necessary—some of them electrical, some engineering. In his case, the major problem was the gearbox.

Astons admitted in early 1966 that they had had trouble with gearboxes, but they then set about fitting a more robust version able to cope with the big 282 b.h.p. engine. Any recurring complaints—water penetration has been one—are minutely investigated.

The vast majority of Aston owners, however, develop a lyrical style when talking about the car in their lives, and even the company director in Newcastle has owned a string of Astons, not wanting to branch out. To almost everyone, and especially to the stringback-gloved brigade, it is the ultimate automobile, perhaps even more so than the Rolls.

Making the loved one

It is, perhaps, easy to love an Aston Martin. But the astonishing thing is that as much affection may be lavished on a car turned out at the rate of 1,000 a day. This is how the mass-made object is created, and how long it takes. Drawings by David Frankland and Peter Sullivan.

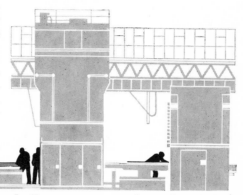

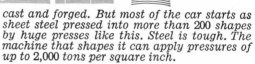

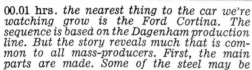

00.01 hrs. *the nearest thing to the car we're watching grow is the Ford Cortina. The sequence is based on the Dagenham production line. But the story reveals much that is common to all mass-producers. First, the main parts are made. Some of the steel may be* cast and forged. But most of the car starts as sheet steel pressed into more than 200 shapes by huge presses like this. Steel is tough. The machine that shapes it can apply pressures of up to 2,000 tons per square inch.

04.00 hrs: *the preliminaries are over. The embryo moves to the main production line. First, it needs extra muscle; all major panel joints are gas-welded to give greater strength under cornering stress. Then it gets some extra organs and limbs. Doors, bonnet and boot* covers all swinging in ready-made on an overhead monorail are fitted, bolted on to hinges with pneumatic spanners. Finally, its makers ensure its skin will be without blemish. Scratches and welding marks are polished smooth to make the body fit for painting.

15.30 hrs: *this is the time for the car to get its quota of individuality—in the trim shops. Here it becomes basic or de luxe, floor-change geared or steering-column geared, and so on. The permutations a maker offers run into thousands. At the final painting stage a teleprinter had indicated what top-coat colours were to be used. Now a teleprinter taps out trim variants for the car: the details end up on a card on its* bonnet. The build-up goes further. Scores of components stacked beside the production line are fitted: electric wiring, lights, grill, head-lining, windscreen, door windows.

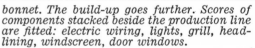

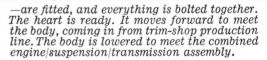

18.50 hrs: *enter the heart—the engine. It arrives complete with carburettors, exhaust manifold, etc. and is then mated to the clutch/gearbox unit. Drive-shaft, rear axle, front and rear suspensions—including hubs and brakes* —are fitted, and everything is bolted together. The heart is ready. It moves forward to meet the body, coming in from trim-shop production line. The body is lowered to meet the combined engine/suspension/transmission assembly.

20.20 hrs: *the car comes down in the world to have its wheels put on. Five matching wheels drop from a slot and are bolted on. For the first time the car is standing on its own four feet. All that's needed now is the elixir of life: petrol. That goes into the tank when the car again moves on to a raised line to enable work to take place at two levels. No one wants to drive a car standing up. So the seats (the last* item of all) are put in. Checkers watch as the engine idles. There's a lot of checking at this stage. When the car is driven forward to the tracking station its suspension and steering settings are scrutinised and adjusted. Next the trim is examined and the car is passed (or rejected) before moving to the roller testing station.

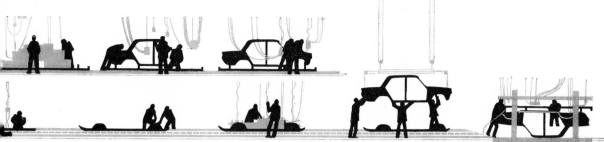

03.00 hrs: *fork lift trucks carry the steel pressings to pre-production line workshops. In separate processes the superstructure and the underbody are built. Smaller bits and pieces are put together by spot welding. Then these are fitted into jigs, and machines take over entirely. Automatic welders join the jig-held pieces together. The major superstructure and* underbody units emerge complete. Superstructure welding (roof, sides, scuttle) is going on at the upper level of the diagram, and underbody assembly at the lower. Finally, superstructure and underbody are joined, wings are fitted, and the whole lot is welded together. The unit is turned wrong way up at one stage to let the stitch-welders get at it.

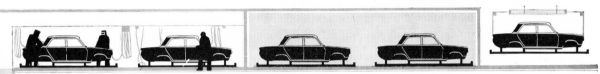

09.00 hrs: *painting is tricky. The car is washed first, and all joints covered with a sealer. Then it's dipped, waist-high, in a bath to give it an anti-corrosive finish. Men spray on priming coats by hand and the car is then cooked in an oven for 40 minutes before being wet-sanded* and dried again. Now three top colour coats are hand-sprayed on. Then the car's popped in an oven again to dry for an hour.

16.40 hrs: *there are still more details to be added to the car: horn, battery, brake fluid reservoirs, steering column, radiator and pipes —all the under-bonnet parts, in fact. On, too, goes the instrument panel, at this stage looking very gay. From it sprout lengths of brightly-* coloured wiring which will soon be connected with the engine. More externals are added finally: all the chrome fittings, including bumper, door handles, catches, strips. The car has a body: now it's got to have a heart.

19.20 hrs: *the loved one still can't move, of course. It has no wheels. But it's nearing completion. It goes on to a raised line so that men can poke about underneath it, to connect its arteries and veins. Joined up now are the oil,* petrol and brake pipes. Steering and pedals are connected, and a gear lever is added. On go the windscreen wipers. The beautification of the inside of the car is also in the final make-up stage. In go small details like the rear-view mirror as well as major elements like the carpets and the mats. All that remains is to make the car able to move around.

22.00 hrs: *in the roller station . . . the wheels roar round, but the car doesn't move. This test, however, will ensure that engine, transmission, steering, brakes and lights are O.K. If they are, the car is driven off for a brief road test. Another trial for it follows: 36 streams of water bombard the car at a pressure of 50 lbs. per square inch. Three hundred gallons drown it in* the space of 3 minutes, searching for leaks. If there aren't any it's dried down and has its final check. Then it's parked in the trade lines to await the delivery driver and the journey to (usually) a good home. If it's lucky, it will also get a room of its own. In Britain, around 1,000 models of a car like this will be turned out every 24 hours.

Heart of the loved one

No car ticks without a heart —the engine. Here David Frankland and Peter Sullivan show the process (cost £21 million) by which Ford build and test an engine.

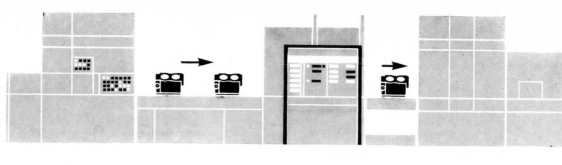

2 *The block continues to hang from carrier arm as it moves along assembly line. Specially-matched sets of pistons are now installed after careful grading (below and right). A 'tele-autograph' system continually signals the assembly area, indicating the grade of pistons needed. There are 'free loops' on assembly line so that part-made engines can be shunted off for inspection.*

3 *Sub-assembled cylinder heads are now added to the engine (right). To make assembly easier, the carrier arm can be turned so that the engine has timing and head face cover uppermost.*

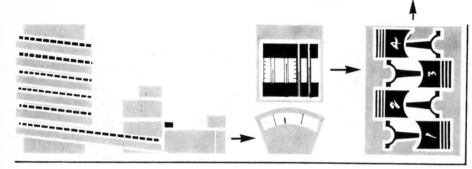

6 *The intake manifold bolts are tightened (first right) and the engine changes position again (second right) so that the operator can more easily assemble the distributor.*

9 *The front timing cover is assembled (left) and the block is turned (right) for water pump and hoses to be added.*

10 *Again the engine is turned to bring the oil pan face uppermost. The oil pan is positioned and the securing bolts are 'run down' (right).*

13 *The engine is next equipped with its flywheel and clutch assembly (left). Then, turned to its 'car' position, it receives lubricant (right). Fuel pump and carburettor are connected.*

14 *'Brain' of the whole assembly system is a mammoth control room (right), as intricate as the most modern rail signal box. From it, the operation of 3 miles of conveyor lines is observed and regulated.*

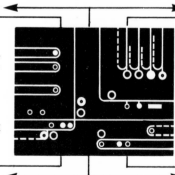

18 *In a 'hot test' area the engine is run under its own power (left). Here there is a further quality check on all sorts of items—correct tappet adjustment, secure gaskets, correctly-tightened cylinder head bolts, freedom from oil and water leaks, and so on. Then (right) the rocker cover is fitted.*

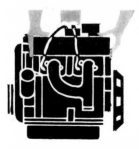

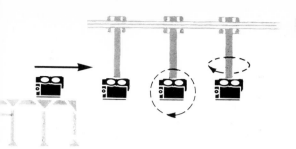

1 *The engine block and head components are machined. Then assembly takes place on special carrier arms to which each block is bolted (left). Crankshaft, camshaft, balance shaft are first items to be assembled (left and right).*

4 *In the next stage (left), with the engine block moving around on its arm as necessary, the oil filter is positioned and tightened. The cylinder head and exhaust manifold are then positioned on the cylinder block.*

5 *Critical bolts are checked for correct torque and cylinder head bolts are 'run down' with a multi-nut runner (left). The block changes position for the intake manifold to be added (right).*

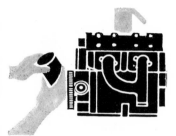

7 *The engine moves round yet again (right) to bring the oil pan face uppermost. Now the oil pump goes in.*

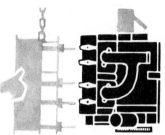

8 *The gear assembly is now completed. Two parts of the assembly—camshaft and balance shaft—had already been partially added to the engine at stage 1. Now the camshaft gear assembly is completed.*

11 *The cylinder head faces are now uppermost and the front crankshaft pulley is assembled (right) together with the rocker arms.*

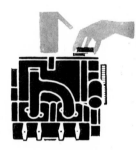

12 *Critical parts of the engine are masked or protected; it undergoes paint spraying and drying on a detour conveyor (right). Then an electric timing light effects the engine's final ignition setting.*

15 *Every conveyor line has its own drive and electrical field panel inside the control room (left). Should there be a failure on any of the 31 conveyors, a warning-light system locates breakdown point immediately. There are 150 warning lights to indicate every condition throughout engine assembly operations.*

16 *Now the fuel pump is mounted on the side of the crankcase (right). Mechanically operated, the pump is worked by means of an eccentric on the rotating camshaft.*

17 *Tappets are finally set (right). The engine is now completely ready for 'hot testing'. Quality-control staff check that all details are complete.*

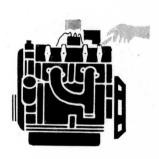

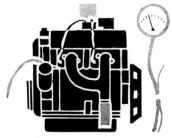

19 *The engine must now undergo a crankcase and gasket leak test (left) which calls for highly sensitive electro-pneumatic equipment to detect loose bolts and missing or damaged gaskets.*

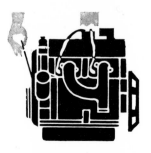

20 *The engine is finally dressed with dipstick tube and oil-filler cap (left). After a last quality check, it goes to the shipping area ready to move to the main car-assembly production lines.*

Detroit: the philosophy, psychology, sexology
by Pete Brock, talking to John Bentley

"What's good for General Motors is good for America." The sentiments of Charles Wilson, tycoon conscripted by Eisenhower as defence aide when he was President of the United States, have become part of American folk-lore. If the motor car has a spiritual, as well as a material home, it is certainly Detroit. What is in the minds of the men who rule the most important car-making city in the world? Pete Brock, who gives his idea of the answers, is young (b.1936) yet he is already a brilliantly successful sports car designer. At General Motors he helped develop the Corvette Sting Ray; working for Shelby American Inc. in California, he designed the Daytona Cobra coupé which in 1965 enabled Carroll Shelby's racing team to take the World Manufacturers' Championship for Grand Touring cars, the first time any American manufacturer had taken a world title. He has now, very successfully, gone independent as a consultant designer and stylist of international stature, working for, among others, Tomaso in Italy and Hino Motors in Tokio. John Bentley, besides being a successful racing driver (Sebring, Le Mans, etc.), has written hundreds of articles for British and American motoring publications; among his books are 'All the World's Cars', 'Great American Automobiles', 'The Faster They Go', and 'The Cobra Story'.

There *is* a philosophy (and a psychology too) behind American automobile design. But it is not what the automotive 'purists', both in the U.S.A. and in Europe, usually say it is. Detroit has, to this extent, been unfairly judged. To Britons who usually can't afford the enormous import duties on American cars anyway, the super-chromed Detroit automobiles they see parked bumper to gleaming bumper around Grosvenor Square in London may seem unreasonably huge and plush, though still desirable. But in American terms the cars make straightforward good sense, except perhaps for the chrome. There is little mystique, and little that's sinister (in the sense of a deep-laid plot!), about the psychology and so-called motivational research of our automobile industry.

Building automobiles in the United States means, essentially, building 'transportation'—reliable, generally inexpensive personal transportation that, at a glance, shouts the word 'luxury'; that will withstand abuse and neglect, year after year, while giving its owner a minimum of trouble. In this, the American car-makers can, as a whole, claim justly to have succeeded.

The reason why they have succeeded is not hard to find. The automobile industry—which after oil and steel is the largest in the United States—is a tough, hard-nosed, highly competitive business, prepared to spend millions to make a successful play for the public's dollars. There are therefore no longer good cars and bad cars; or at least hardly ever—whatever the American lawyer, Ralph Nader, may have alleged in his storm-raising book *Unsafe At Any Speed*. There are, instead, good cars and better cars, and the determining factor that separates the comparative from the superlative is simply how much the buyer wants to spend and the purposes for which he needs his car.

In general, of course, the great American public remains indifferent to the finer implications behind the ownership and the driving of cars—this despite its remarkable instinct for a good car. It simply does not care so long as an automobile meets two requirements: first, that it is a means of transportation, and second that it is a status symbol calculated to give an impression of prosperity and wealth. This also is true, however, of the bigger icebox, colour television, the inevitable washer and dryer and a dozen other household appliances, including the electric can-opener. These things save work, and at the same time represent well-being.

But, to return to the purists, individualists and die-hards, who delight in heaping scorn and ridicule on the Detroit product. The favourite weapons with which they choose to belabour Detroit have necessarily become somewhat blunted by time, and by the kind of performance American cars have shown themselves capable of putting up against the best European competition. But the trouble is that their arguments (like that old Goebbels propaganda) have just enough leavening of truth, especially when quoted out of context, to seem plausible.

The principal attack on American car manufacturers is five-pronged. Detroit is allegedly guilty of persuading the public that these basic tenets are true:

First, that in order to be comfortable, a car must be huge.

Second, that in order to be safe, an automobile must be heavy and should weigh something like two tons.

Third, that in order to deliver performance, a car must of necessity have gobs of horsepower.

Fourth, that the industry gives the average American exactly what he wants by way of a car (when in fact, say the purists, he merely gets what Detroit thinks he ought to have).

The fifth line of attack by the diehards is rather more subtle, and also contains rather more truth. It is that the terms 'styling' and 'engineering', which are two very different things, have been given an interchangeable meaning by advertising agency copywriters, handsomely paid to attract the buying public.

Are the attackers right? In my view these five arguments are, by and large, Five Myths about Detroit hammered home to the point of absurdity by socalled purists. Let's examine each of them.

First, Americans have scarcely had to be *persuaded* that they need large cars for comfort. A family of five, plus baggage for a two-week vacation, plus the golf clubs and baby carriage, cannot very well shoehorn themselves into a '2+2' coupé or roadster. Hence, the station wagon, which is the product of the vast shift of population out of many overcrowded American cities, from urban to suburban areas. Moreover, we have the best roads in the world, and the straightest. And we use them more. In England, if you drive 500 miles you have travelled from one end of the country to the other; in Texas, 500 miles

may not be too far to drive to a movie and back, or to go on a shopping trip. Comfort therefore becomes crucial.

It's true that many small European cars have suspensions offering as much comfort as may be found in any Detroit automobile—if not more—and perhaps the Porsche is a prime example of this. But it seats two people; not six. It's also true that some of our larger American cars become completely unstable if violent corrective measures become necessary.

But the large American car is designed for an American motoring environment—super-smooth highways and comparatively well-engineered streets and roads which theoretically eliminate the need for sudden and brusque manoeuvres.

It is certainly no myth to assume that for overall practicality (the basis on which the American car is designed) comfort and size go hand in hand.

If we accept this, then the second attack on Detroit also fails. It may, I agree, be true that the prime factor in roadability and safety is *not* simply weight, but *weight distribution*. But to build a big car of low weight with absolutely correct distribution of poundage would raise production costs prohibitively. The necessary use of exotic metals and highly sophisticated design is almost impossibly difficult to cope with financially even with a vast production programme.

Above: *Pete Brock and embryo design. During the four years he was with Shelby American he designed virtually everything— from the company's notepaper to the Cobra T-shirt, which became wildly popular in America.*

87

Point three, I would say, is just as much a myth as the other two. How else can you *get* performance, despite the handicap of weight, unless you match that weight with adequate horsepower? And what cheaper way is there of getting more power than by increasing cubic inches?

Someone once described the art of selling as an ability to make people buy something they don't need, don't really want, and can't afford anyway. This, perhaps, is relevant to the charge that Detroit gives people what *it* thinks they ought to have; a charge which still seems to me nonsensical. Not that I disagree with the description of selling —it's a pretty good one. But the automobile is scarcely susceptible to this particular technique since, even if the owner happens to regard his car as nothing more than a status symbol, he nevertheless *wants* it, regardless of whether he can afford it or needs it.

Some critics also love to point out that "so-called Detroit automotive surveys or public opinion polls" are often taken immediately following an intensive multi-million advertising campaign that conditions the buyer to the proper response. If this were generally true, then how do you explain the success of relatively expensive machines like the Cobra, Sting Ray, or the special Mustang GT350? No one told the young American, or even the middle-aged one, that he should buy such cars. Yet these became the most successful real American sports cars. The products simply spoke for themselves.

Only on the fifth point (the way in which copywriters have long since persuaded the buyer to accept styling and engineering as meaning the same thing) do I concede that there is some element of truth. And the entire automobile industry must accept responsibility for complicity in this deception.

When a car manufacturer proudly announces that an 'all-new' model has been 'engineered' for 1966, and then proceeds to list 57 new features in support of his claim, the copywriters are scraping pretty hard around the bottom of the barrel. Ford, for example, can justly claim a significant engineering development in their new 427 cu. in. single-overhead-camshaft engine; and Chrysler with their highly successful 'hemi-head' pushrod unit. But if a manufacturer simply relocates door handles or adds chrome or comes out with a different grille, such things can't honestly be called *engineering* improvements. They belong purely in the realm of *styling*.

I doubt, though, whether any great harm has been done by this deception. Those who don't know the difference between engineering and styling certainly don't care; and those who do know don't care either. They are immune from such blandishments. The whole thing is simply a bid for a bigger share of an immensely competitive market, and whether a change is one of styling or engineering the buyer as a rule still gets a better automobile than he did last year.

It would, in fact, be useful to define the three classifications of auto-men which are too often used interchangeably to everyone's confusion. The terms 'stylist', 'designer' and 'engineer' describe three distinct worlds.

The engineer is just that—an engineer; an extremely competent, educated man familiar with mathematical formulae for solving problems. His job is to calculate the stresses and strains necessary to create a strong, safe, yet relatively inexpensive product. The designer is something else—a man of new ideas and new solutions to existing problems not solvable by the usual engineering methods. A perfect example of a designer might be Alec Issigonis of the British Motor Corporation. Mr. Issigonis is without a doubt a superior engineer, but in my book he is first and foremost a designer. The Mini is the perfect designer's automobile, and as such probably one of the best solutions to a problem the world will ever see. Certainly it wasn't the work of a stylist! A stylist is a decorator. He adorns the product, supposedly to increase its sales appeal. He is an American concept, and probably one the world would be better off without; but he came into being because the engineer knew nothing of sales appeal. It thus became his job to *create* sales appeal, and the results are well known: the typical American car—a gaudy, chromed road-barge.

Yet though there are millions of these four-wheeled albatrosses around the necks of Americans, the public has gradually, across two generations, learned to resist intrinsically worthless blandishments. The revolution was

probably sparked by tasteful European cars, and as a result the Sixties have seen cars created by teams of men (led by designers) who have a broad-view understanding of all the problems: engineering, sales, costs, materials, and, most important, good design. The American automobile is evolving, design-wise, into a very desirable package. The car looks as handsome and *right* in London or Paris as it does in California, something that certainly could not be said ten years ago.

You cannot, however, completely round up the factors affecting the philosophy and psychology of Detroit without mentioning one more. America, like it or not, is a matriarchal society. Women not only exercise a direct influence on about 70 per cent of all automobile sales; they also own, directly or indirectly, about the same percentage of the country's wealth, in annuities, in stocks and bonds, in real estate and in hard cash. And women are not interested in overhead camshafts versus pushrods, disc brakes against drums. They *are*, however, very much interested in ease of driving, comfort and gadgets: in colour-keyed interiors and paint jobs. That's why the industry has often gone out on a limb to give them such things: power brakes and steering; power-operated seats and windows; automatic transmissions ('slush pumps' to that minority which still regards driving as an art).

We have today, in fact, 'slush pumps' that can shift faster and more accurately on a long-term basis than can the most skilled race driver, who necessarily gets tired. The racing success of the Texas-built Chaparral, with

its G.M. Chevrolet V8 engine, is proof positive of this; and both Ford and General Motors have an equally effective, dependable (and raceworthy) automatic transmission that will probably change much nostalgic thinking.

The overwhelming influence exercised by American womanhood on car purchase covers for me most of that area which some people call the 'sexology' of car design. Whether or not the ornamentation of some models has any significance or symbolism is open to question. Not that I think it of much importance anyway. Where women are concerned the point is a simple one. As a rule, they like their plumage bright, whether in automobiles, personal apparel or household decoration. They like it, and they demand it. Detroit thinks about that far more than about creating phallic symbols.

Even so, the picture of Detroit's automotive philosophy is scarcely complete. I am often asked whether that extremely tenacious, loyal and loud-spoken minority of 'purists', who claim to drive for pleasure alone, has exercised any real influence on the trend of American car design. The answer, I believe, is yes.

In immediate post-war years, it's true, the industry considered the purist attitude a passing fad. But there has long since been a change of mind in Detroit. We have, in fact, travelled full circle back to the four-speed floor shift, wood-rimmed steering wheel, and functional instrumentation of the past, and we have gone quite a bit further. Many models now have available what is generically called a 'performance package'. This means, among other things,

Above: *the car that really established Brock at the top —the Daytona Cobra coupé, which won Carroll Shelby the World Manufacturers' Championship for G.T. cars in 1965. Here it is undergoing aerodynamic tests, in which the tufts of wool attached to the front of the car help as guidemarkers.*

stiffer suspension, faster steering, wide-based rims, better brakes. And it can mean a great deal more in terms of the engine.

I am, of course, a sports car enthusiast myself. So the evolution of the Corvette into the Sting Ray, with which I was closely associated, was not at all hard for me to take, to say the least! I can well understand the idealistic side of automobile design and I do not always find it easy to reconcile this understanding with the rock-hard and purely objective demands that belong to the realm of automobile sales. Yet that is what manufacturers are primarily in business for—to out-sell the competition with an equally good product that costs less and has more appeal, or a better product that costs as much and has even more appeal. How this is done does not matter, so long as Detroit keeps faith with the public in terms of value and performance per dollar.

Yet orthodox automotive engineers are sometimes a strange tribe whose slide-rules seem tailored to provide mathematical answers exactly coinciding with their pre-conceived ideas. When, for example, I designed the body of the prototype which became known as the Daytona Cobra coupé, an aerodynamicist and engineer shook his head and sighed: "I'm afraid it'll never work."

Pressed by my then boss, Carroll Shelby, for further explanation, he said: "To propel this shape at anything like 160 m.p.h., you'll need at least 450 h.p. So you might as well forget the whole thing!" This engineer was simply that—an engineer. His figures and preconceived ideas told him that this new concept was unpractical, and because no one had ever done anything like this before he had no information upon which to base his thinking; so mathematically he rejected it. Luckily, Shelby wasn't an engineer either and he gave me the go-ahead. The Daytona coupé, until it caught fire during a pit stop in the 1964 12-hour Continental at Daytona International Speedway, led the entire field, lap after lap, and almost ran away and hid. Not even the Ferraris could stay with it. What's more, the Daytona coupé did so with 18 per cent better gas mileage and 15 m.p.h. more top speed than the hottest of the open-bodied Cobras, and with much less than 400 h.p.

This model won the G.T. class at Sebring and Le Mans that same year. And in 1965, the Daytona Cobras won the World Championship for G.T. cars, the first time an American car had ever done so.

As a side comment, I should point out that the Cobra is essentially 50 per cent British, since chassis and body were built in England by A.C. Cars under contract to Shelby American.

There's yet another question I'm often asked: do I believe that racing improves the breed? Of course it does. Private test tracks and artificial 'torture' roads are just great, but it's extremely difficult, probably impossible, to simulate scientifically and *consistently* the tremendous interplay of continually varying stresses and shock loads imposed by actual racing. You can't do it artificially for the simple reason that there are about as many different stress areas and combinations as there are drivers, to say nothing of race courses. And since racing is as old as the second car ever built, and is still going strong, we can assume that it has taught many vitally important lessons of direct value to the production line, and to the buyer: lessons that have produced better engines or safer brakes or more perfect tyres or whatever.

Of the Detroit Big Three, one firm only—Ford—has openly opted for racing, and achieved, of course, their great 1966 Le Mans 24-Hour Race victory. A second, General Motors, is sitting on the fence, and the third, Chrysler, is taking a 'benevolent' view of the sport. The pertinent question is: which of these three is collecting the marbles? Ford's intensive racing programme does not appear to be suffering any pains sales-wise. Quite the opposite.

Still, when you are in business to build and sell cars, racing is never more than the most expedient means to an end. It is not an end in itself, even though racing *success* is probably still the most potent sales medium a manufacturer can command. The buyer *identifies* with the race-winning marque. The pitfall is that racing does have a point of no-return, and it is crucial for the manufacturer to know when he has reached it. The object lesson here was provided, post-war, by Mercedes-Benz. No one was ever more successful in translating the enormous cost of a sustained and intensive racing programme into world-wide sales and prestige. No one was ever smarter in knowing when to stop.

Yet when all the theorising about Detroit's philosophy is done, there is still an element of chance about the approach of our manufacturers. Trying to forecast the wishes, wants, and sudden caprices of Americans is to some extent like walking blind through a minefield. The same, of course, applies to any country where free enterprise exists—but not, perhaps, to the same extent. Europeans are slower to accept change, to adopt or demand new ideas, unless such changes or new ideas have a definite intrinsic merit. The buyer in Europe (because he also has a higher degree of technical orientation in the automobile field) is more predictable. The abysmal flop of the Edsel, followed by the staggering success of the Mustang, for example, could probably never have occurred on the European side of the Atlantic. Again, how can we explain that while Americans cared not one jot about aluminium engines, they took to their heart almost immediately a radically new concept like the air-cooled, rear-engined Corvair? How do you explain the success of the front-wheel drive Oldsmobile Toronado?

It seems to me that Detroit, far from 'conditioning' the prospective buyer, faces perhaps its most demanding job in getting its marketing analyses and opinion surveys to come up with the right answers! Trying to find out what the average American is likely to want a year from now remains pretty much like trying to pick the winning number at roulette.

Basically, from what I have observed over in Europe—and especially in Italy, where I have done extensive styling and designing work for de Tomaso and other independents who have a genuine appreciation and knowledge of what Americans would call 'exotic machinery'—I would say that the psychological approach of car manufacturers does not generally differ a great deal from that of Detroit. A fine car in Britain (like the Aston Martin DB5 or 6, the Jaguar XKE, or the Jensen) is very much a status symbol, quite aside from its performance. The principal difference lies in the size of the market and the specific needs of prospective buyers.

Petrol consumption, for instance, still looms as a highly important consideration with the British motorist. Not so in the United States, where petrol costs only half what it does in Britain. Many owners haven't any idea of their car's m.p.g. and could hardly care less.

The average British car owner seems better informed, technically, than his American counterpart, to whom a tool-kit is an obsolete, useless and tiresome thing. This is related to the fact that in Europe the art of good driving has always remained much more of a pleasure than in America. We in the United States are only just coming back to this idea.

But what, finally, about the furore caused by Ralph Nader's book? How relevant is he? Nader (who is anything but an engineer) has accused Detroit of neglecting the problems of car safety in an immense way, and he has been a factor in governmental activity over automobile standards.

The pity of it is that he is crusading for the right thing in the wrong way. 'Safety' is a great word. It could perhaps save 40,000 highway deaths yearly —but not by padding car interiors with two feet of foam rubber, strapping the occupants as though they were in the electric chair and hoping that enough 'give' can be built into an automobile to cushion the shock of a 50 m.p.h. collision by having exactly two feet of chassis and body collapse in a smooth, evenly distributed way. Given *all* these factors, the occupants *might* survive 42 G's of deceleration without fatal effects. They *might*—but you'd never get them to buy that kind of car.

There's a more logical, more appealing and less costly solution. Let Detroit borrow another leaf from European designers and build into its *production* autos a much higher evasive capability. By this I mean improved steering, suspension and brakes, or the inherent ability to *avoid* a smash-up rather then try to survive it. At 60 m.p.h. you are travelling 88 ft. per sec. So 1/20th of a second can mean the difference between life and death. What chance have we now with power steering, poor brakes, awkwardly shifting weight distribution and marshmallow suspension? Equally culpable is the law itself, which allows suicidally inept drivers to fool with barely controllable 30 h.p. mastodons.

This is the area in which legislation would be useful. And as a philosophy—positive rather then purely negative—it appeals to me more.

91

Kandy for the kustomers
by Tom Wolfe

There is one aspect of the American car complex which Pete Brock did not discuss. Beyond the world of Detroit mass-production, there is another. The makers in this world turn out "customised" cars, usually adaptations of existing models, which are part of today's Pop Culture — cars which go with Beatlemania, new hair styles, flamboyant clothes, the affluent young. Of this culture (he calls it "the teenage netherworld") the American journalist Tom Wolfe has become the interpreter, writing a pyrotechnic sort of "new style" which is adored or abhorred. Here are extracts from the essay which threatens to become the classic of the style: 'The Kandy-Kolored Tangerine Flake Streamline Baby'. In its way, this particular automobile cult is the culmination of this century's loving of the motor-car.

I don't have to dwell on the point that cars mean more to these kids than architecture did in Europe's great formal century, say, 1750 to 1850. They are freedom, style, sex, power, motion, colour—everything is right there.

Things have been going on in the development of the kids' formal attitude toward cars since 1945, things of great sophistication that adults have not been even remotely aware of, mainly because the kids are so inarticulate about it, especially the ones most hipped on the subject. They are not from the levels of society that produce children who write sensitive analytical prose at age seventeen, or if they do, they soon fall into the hands of English instructors who put them on to Hemingway or a lot of goddam-and-hungry-breast writers. If they ever write about a highway again, it's a rain-slicked highway and the sound of the automobiles passing over it is like the sound of tearing silk, not that one household in ten thousand has heard the sound of tearing silk since 1945.

Anyway, we are back at the Teen Fair and I am talking to Tex Smith and to Don Beebe, a portly young guy with a white sport shirt and Cuban sunglasses. As they tell me about the Ford Custom Car Caravan, I can see that Ford has begun to comprehend this teenage style of life and its potential. The way Ford appears to figure it is this: Thousands of kids are getting hold of cars and either hopping them up for speed or customising them to some extent, usually a little of both. Before they get married they pour *all* their money into this. If Ford can get them hooked on Fords now, after the kids are married they'll buy new Fords. Even the kids who aren't full-time nuts themselves will be influenced by which car is considered 'boss'. They use that word a lot, 'boss'. The kids used to consider Ford the hot car, but then, from 1955 to 1962, Chevrolet became the favourite. They had big engines and were easy to hop up, the styling was simple, and the kids could customise them easily. In 1959, and more so in 1960, Plymouth became a hot car, too. In 1961 and 1962, it was all Chevrolet and Plymouth. Now Ford is making a big push.

I met George Barris, one of the celebrities of the custom-car world, at the Teen Fair. Barris is the biggest name in customising. He is a good example of a kid who grew up completely absorbed in this teenage world of cars, who pursued the pure flame and its forms with such devotion that he emerged an artist. It was like Tiepolo emerging from the studios of Venice, where the rounded Grecian haunches of the murals on the Palladian domes hung in the atmosphere like clouds. Except that Barris emerged from the auto-body shops of Los Angeles.

Barris invited me out to his studio—only he would never think of calling it that, he calls it Kustom City—at 10811 Riverside Drive in North Hollywood.... Barris grew up at the time when it was considered sharp to change all the C's to K's. He also sells Kandy Lac to paint cars Kandy Kolors with, and I know that sibilant C in City must have bothered the hell out of him at some point. It's interesting, I think, that he still calls the place Kustom City, and still sells Kandy Kolors, because he is an intelli-

HELP PROMOTE
STREET
RACING

GENUINE
STOLEN
PARTS

VOLKSWAGENS
FOREVER

CHEVY LOVERS
OF AMERICA

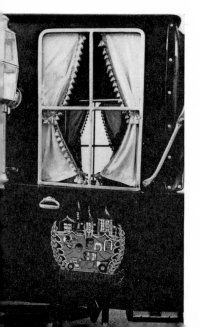

gent person. What it means is, he is absolutely untouched by the big amoeba god of Anglo-European sophistication that gets you in the East. . . .

Barris, whose family is Greek, is a solid little guy, five feet seven, thirty-seven years old, and he looks just like Picasso. When he's working, which is most of the time, he wears a heavy white T-style shirt, faded off-white pants cut full with pleats in the manner of Picasso walking along in the wind on a bluff at Rapallo, and crepe-sole slipper-style shoes, also off-white. Picasso, I should add, means nothing to Barris, although he knows who he is. It's just that to Barris and the customisers there is no one great universe of form and design called Art. Yet that's the universe he's in. He's not building cars, he's creating forms.

Barris starts taking me through Kustom City, and the place looks like any other body shop at first, but pretty soon you realize you're in a *gallery*. This place is full of cars such as you have never seen before. Half of them will never touch the road. They're put on trucks and trailers and carted all over the country to be exhibited at hot-rod and custom-car shows. They'll run, if it comes to that—they're full of big, powerful, hopped-up chrome-plated motors, because all that speed and power, and all that lovely apparatus, has tremendous emotional meaning to everybody in customising. But it's like one of these Picasso or Miro rugs. You don't walk on the damn things. You hang them on the wall. It's the same thing with Barris cars. In effect, they're sculpture.

For example, there is an incredible object he built called the XPAK-400 air car. The customisers love all that X jazz. It runs on a cushion of air, which is beside the point, because it's a pure piece of curvilinear abstract sculpture. If Brancusi is any good, then this thing belongs on a pedestal, too. There is not a straight line in it, and only one true circle, and those countless planes, and tremendous baroque fins, and yet all in all it's a rigid little piece of solid geometrical harmony. As a matter of fact, Brancusi and Barris both developed out of a design concept that we can call Streamlined Modern or Thirties Curvilinear—via utterly different roads, of course—and Barris and most other custom artists are carrying this idea of the abstract curve, which is very tough to handle, on and on and on and on at a time when your conventional designers—from architects to the guys who lay out magazines—are all Mondrian. Even the young Detroit car stylists are all Mondrian. Only the aircraft designers have done anything more with the Streamline, and they have only because they're forced to by physics, and so on. . . .

If Barris and the customisers hadn't been buried in the alien and suspect underworld of California youth, I don't think they would seem at all unusual by now. But they've had access to almost nothing but the hot-rod press. They're like Easter Islanders. Suddenly you come upon the astonishing objects, and then you have to figure out how they got there and why they're there.

If you study the work of Barris or Cushenberry, or Ed Roth or Darryl Starbird, can you beat that name?, I think you come up with a fragment of art history. Somewhere back in the Thirties, designers, automobile designers among them, came up with the idea of the streamline. It sounded 'functional', and on an airplane it is functional, but on a car it's not, unless you're making a Bonneville speed run. Actually, it's baroque. The streamline is baroque abstract or baroque modern or whatever you want to call it. Well, about the time the streamline got going—in the Thirties, you may recall, we had curved buildings, like the show-pieces later, at the World's Fair—in came the Bauhaus movement, which was blown-up Mondrian, really. Before you knew it, everything was Mondrian—the Kleenex box: Mondrian; the format of the cover of *Life* Magazine: Mondrian; those bled-to-the-edge photograph layouts in *Paris-Match*: Mondrian. Even automobiles: Mondrian. They call Detroit automobiles streamlined, but they're not. If you don't believe it, look down from an airplane at all the cars parked on a shopping-centre apron, and except that all the colours are pastel instead of primary, what have you got? A Mondrian painting. The Mondrian principle, those straight edges, is very tight, very Apollonian. The streamline principle, which really has no function, which curves around and swoops and flows just for the thrill of it, is very free Dionysian. For reasons I don't have to labour over, the kids preferred the Dionysian. And since Detroit blew the

94

thing, the Dionysian principle in cars was left to people in the teenage netherworld, like George Barris.

From the very moment he was on his own in Los Angeles, when he was about eighteen, Barris never did anything but customise cars. He never took any other kind of job. At first he worked in a body shop that took him on because so many kids were coming by wanting this and that done to their cars, and the boss really didn't know how to do it, because it was all esoteric teenage stuff. Barris was making next to nothing at first, but he never remembers feeling hard up, nor does any kid out there today I talked to. They have a magic economy or something. Anyway, in 1945 Barris opened his own shop on Compton Avenue, in Los Angeles. . . .

Most of the work he was doing then was modifying Detroit cars—chopping and channeling. Chopping is lowering the top of the car, bringing it nearer to the hood line. Channeling is lowering the body itself down between the wheels. Also, they'd usually strip off all the chrome and the door handles and cover up the wheel openings in the back. At that time, the look the kids liked was to have the body lowered in the back and slightly jacked up in the front, although today it's just the opposite. The front windshield in those days was divided by a post, and so chopping the top gave the car a very sinister appearance. The front windshield always looked like a couple of narrow, slitty little eyes. And I think this, more than anything else, diverted everybody from what Barris and the others were really doing. Hot-rodders had a terrible reputation at that time, and no line was ever drawn between hot-rodders and custom-car owners, because, in truth, they were speed maniacs, too.

This was Barris' chopped-and-channeled Mercury period. Mercuries were his favourite. All the kids knew the Barris styling and he was getting a lot of business. What he was really doing, in a formal sense, was trying to achieve the kind of streamlining that Detroit, for all intents and purposes, had abandoned. When modified, some of the old Mercuries were more streamlined than any standard model that Detroit has put out to this day.

At this point Barris and the other customisers didn't really have enough capital to do many completely original cars, but they were getting more and more radical in modifying Detroit cars. They were doing things Detroit didn't do until years later—tailfins, bubble-tops, twin headlights, concealed headlights, 'Frenched' headlights, the low-slung body. They made use of some twenty designs from him alone. One, for example, is the way cars now have the exhaust pipes exit through the rear bumper or fender. Another is the bullet-shaped, or breast-shaped if you'd rather, front bumpers on the Cadillac.

Along about 1957, Barris started hearing from the Detroit auto manufacturers. . . . Since then he has made a lot of trips to Detroit. The auto companies, mainly G.M. and Ford, pump him for ideas about what the kids are going for. He tells them what's wrong with their cars, mainly that they aren't stream-lined and sexy enough.

"But, as they told me, they have to design a car they can sell to the farmer in Kansas as well as the hot dog in Hollywood."

For that reason—the inevitable compromise—the customisers do not dream of working as stylists for the Detroit companies, although they deal with them more and more. . . . This is an old story in art, of course, genius vs. the organisation. But the customisers don't think of corporate bureaucracy quite the way your conventional artist does, whether he be William Gropper or Larry Rivers, namely, as a lot of small-minded Babbitts, venal enemies of culture, etc. They just think of the big companies as part of that vast mass of *adult* America, sclerotic from years of just being too old, whose rules and ideas weigh down upon Youth like a vast, bloated sac. Both Barris and Roth have met Detroit's Young Stylists, and seem to look upon them as monks from another country. The Young Stylists are designers Detroit recruits from the art schools and sets up in a room with clay and styluses and tells to go to it—start carving models, dream cars, new ideas. Roth especially cannot conceive of anyone having any valid concepts about cars who hasn't come out of the teen-age netherworld. And maybe he's right. While the Young Stylists sit in a north-lit studio smoothing out little Mondrian solids, Barris and Roth carry on in the Dionysian loop-the-loop of streamlined baroque modern.

3 The mystique and the mania

This is the heart of the matter. And there is a word for it – "Automania" – first coined and defined formally by a British publication, 'The Sunday Times Magazine'. The definition given below makes redundant any further description of what the third part of this book is about. The point is made another way by the Mini (right) which artist Alan Aldridge worked over. It took him five days – plus, among other things, 100 tubes of designer's gouache – to effect the transformation. This is the dream car, the fantasy world the twentieth century love affair evokes. For the male, the dream is all speed and power, Bond and Superman. For the female, the ideas of home, security and decoration predominate.

Automania ọ̄·to mē̆ı·niă (Gr. αὐτο 'self, one's own, by oneself, independently'. Used in names of self-acting mechanisms; short for AUTO-MOBILE 1895. Gr. μανια - madness. 1. Mental derangement characterised by excitement, hallucinations, and in acute stage by great violence. 2. A vehement passion or desire; a craze, a rage.) **1.** The state or condition of being crazed about cars. **2.** Immoderate passion for Motor Shows, new cars, and bits of cars. **3.** Predilection for decorating cars with slogans, devices, symbols, mascots *passim* **4.** Passionate tendency to build and design cars. **5.** Unbridled debate or discourse about cars. **6.** (of writers) Penchant for introducing cars into works of fiction, especially in glamorised varieties *passim* **7.** Ferocious inclination to drive cars in races or rallies *passim* **8.** Frenetic attendance at motor-race meetings *passim* **9.** Inordinate tendency to buy and sell new and secondhand vehicles. **10.** (esp. of women) Unnatural jealousy of, desire to be taken out in (home in) cars; urge to dress for cars; temptation to drive cars from back seat or (more recently) driver's seat. **11.** Fascination with power units of cars. **12.** State of wishing to be with others suffering from automania. **13.** Subconscious folk-wish to be maimed or killed by car. **14.** Universal proclivity to holiday or honeymoon by car. **15.** Temptation to eat or play games in cars. Hence AUTOMANIAC – anyone who is nutty about cars. First coined 1965 by The Sunday Times Magazine (q.v. *passim*)

The car as character

Novelists have written about cars with feeling, and often with great understanding, since the twentieth century began. Their characters may be fictitious; usually the car is real, perhaps the one the author himself drives, or fancies himself driving. The words writers choose to describe steel and rubber and wood show something of the fascination the automobile has for us. Sometimes the cars sound more human than the people. Bill Boddy comments on the extracts from novels and stories in the pages that follow. Bryan Wharton took the colour photographs below; other colour pictures are by Graham Finlayson.

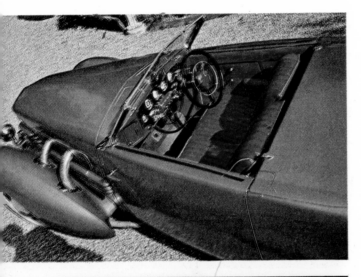

Ian Fleming

To Bond, American cars were just beetle-shaped dodgems in which you motored along with one hand on the wheel, the radio full on, and the power-operated windows closed to keep out the draughts. But Leiter had got hold of an old Cord, one of the few American cars with a personality, and it cheered Bond to climb into the low-hung saloon, to hear the solid bite of the gears and the masculine tone of the wide exhaust. Fifteen years old, he reflected, yet still one of the most modern looking cars in the world. (From *Live and Let Die*.)

James Leasor

He raised the heavy blue alligator mouth. Love saw the familiar glitter of the aluminium supercharger, flat as an inverted frying-pan; the polished alloy cylinder heads; the neat harness of multi-coloured wires to the gear-box solenoids; the long-throated horns. . . .

He ran one hand under the black four-branch exhaust manifold, where dust collected; his fingers came away clean. He looked beneath the tear-drop front wings on their smoothly contoured pontoons and under the clutch housing, but he could not find a drop of surplus oil, or a speck of dust anywhere. . . .

Love lowered the bonnet and stood back admiringly. . . . It was impossible for him to look at the horizontal radiator louvres, the four chrome-steel outside exhausts, the raked V-windscreen fitted with faintly tinted glass against the tropical sun, without feeling the same absurd, irrational thrill of pleasure that the sight of his own Cord always aroused in him. (From *Passport to Peril*.)

Comment on these passages is superfluous, for James Leasor writes at length about the Cord roadster on page 144.

Left: *Bryan Wharton took the pictures of the Cord which James Leasor owns. In the passage quoted, Dr. Jason Love, hero-figure of 'Passport to Peril', is examining a Cord he has found in the palace of a local ruler in the Himalayas. According to the book, it had been dismantled and carried over the moutains by coolies in 1937, then reassembled, and never used for thirty years. Leasor saw a car to which this happened in real life—at Srinagar, capital of Kashmir; but in this case it was a Bentley.*

99

Dorothy L. Sayers

Mr. Mervyn Bunter, patiently seated in the Daimler on the far side of Regent's Park, reflected that time was getting on. Packed in an eiderdown in the back seat of the car was a case containing two-and-a-half dozen of vintage port, and he was anxious about it. Great speed would render the wine undrinkable for a fortnight; excessive speed would render it undrinkable for six months. (From *Busman's Honeymoon*.)

Cars were as essential in thrillers when Miss Sayers started writing as they are today. But nothing sporting was envisaged by her for her famous character, Lord Peter Death Bredon Wimsey. His fans say he possessed fourteen Daimlers in his time. This one is about the most sporting his butler, Hunter, would have permitted—a rare low-chassis Double Six now captive in South-East London.

Nevil Shute

I produced a jet from my waistcoat pocket. "It's about the carburettor on your car, Miss," I said. "The makers sent a letter round to us agents to say as some cars was issued from the factory wiv jets as gives trouble in the morning, starting from cold, like. They was to be replaced without charge. So as I was passing along this evening the manager told me to look in."

"It's very good of him," said the girl, "but she's always been very easy to start. Beautiful." (From *Marazan*.)

Shute turned to novel-writing as relaxation while at Crayford working on stressing the R.100 airship. Aviator and motorist, he liked cars in his stories; this girl's Morris, for instance. He is accurate over details, though whether this make was ever afflicted with starting trouble I do not know. Usually you got a quiet start with the dynamotor.

Michael Arlen

Open as a yacht, it wore a great shining bonnet; and flying over the crest of this great bonnet, as though in proud flight over the heads of scores of phantom horses, was that silver stork by which the gentle may be pleased to know that they have just escaped death beneath the wheels of a Hispano-Suiza car, as supplied to His Most Catholic Majesty. (From *The Green Hat*.)

Arlen's juicy novel—regarded as naughtily daring at the time—portrays the mad Twenties much as John Braine's 'Room at The Top' and Rona Jaffé's 'The Best of Everything' reflect the present generation. He uses that great French luxury car, the 37·2 h.p. Hispano-Suiza, as his motor-hero. But history suggests that with the royalties Arlen invested in a Rolls.

Aldous Huxley

The wind in their faces increased from a capful to half a gale, from half a gale to a full gale, very nearly a hurricane. Lord Hovenden's spirits rose with the mounting speed. His lips curved into a smile of fixed and permanent rapture. Behind the glass of his goggles his eyes were very bright.

"Pretty good going," he said.

"Pretty good," echoed Irene. Under her mask, she too was smiling. Between her ears and the flaps of her leather cap the wind made a glorious roaring. She was happy. (From *Those Barren Leaves*.)

Huxley could look into the future, as his controversial novel 'Brave New World', in which Ford had replaced God, emphasised. But for his shy character, Lord Hovenden, in this romantic story, the author let cynicism drop and described delightfully the sense of achievement, the buoying up of confidence, that a fast run in a 30/98 sporting Vauxhall imparted.

The cars about which the novelists on this page are writing are shown on the left. Their names are . . .
Top left: Daimler Double Six (Dorothy L. Sayers)
Top right: Hispano-Suiza (Michael Arlen)
Lower left: Bull-nose Morris (Nevil Shute)
Lower right: 30/98 Vauxhall Velox (Aldous Huxley)

Rudyard Kipling

He beat his right or throttle hand madly on the side of the car till he found the bent rod that more or less controls the pump, and, neglecting all else, twisted it furiously.

My engineer grabbed the steering bar just in time to save us lurching into a ditch.

"If I was a burnin' peacock, with two hundred bloodshot eyes in my shinin' tail, I'd need 'em all on this job!" said Hinch.

"Don't talk! Steer! This ain't the North Atlantic," Pyecroft replied.

"Blast my stokers! Why, the steam's dropped fifty pounds!" Hinchcliffe cried.

"Fire's blown out," said the engineer. "Stop her!"

"Does she do that often?" said Hinch, descending.

"Sometimes."

"Any time?"

"Any time a cross-wind catches her."

The engineer produced a match and stooped.

That car (now, thank Heaven, no more than an evil memory) never lit twice in the same fashion. This time she back-fired superbly, and Pyecroft went out over the right rear wheel in a column of rich yellow flame.

"I've seen a mine explode at Bantry—once—prematoor," he volunteered.

"That's all right," said Hinchcliffe, brushing down his singed beard with a singed forefinger. (He had been watching too closely.) "Has she any more little surprises up her dainty sleeve?"

"She hasn't begun yet," said my engineer, with a scornful laugh. (From *Steam Tactics* in *Traffics and Discoveries*.)

Kipling's knowledge of radio, motor-cars, ships, guns and other things mechanical enabled our greatest advocate of Empire in poem or prose to get his technical references precisely right. These light-hearted accounts of pioneer motoring in a dubious 1900–1901 Locomobile steamer (above) and an air-cooled 24 h.p. Lanchester (above right)—Kipling disguising the latter, very advanced, extremely well-sprung car as the 'Octopod'—were certainly based on his own automobilism. Kipling, indeed, became an enthusiastic Lanchester owner; a 1901 10 h.p. air-cooled model was delivered to him in 1902. He was lent a later experimental water-cooled Lanchester, which he

102

christened 'Jane Cakebread', by the Lanchester brothers. It came to grief on Ditchling Green. The episode from which our second extract is taken involved Fred Lanchester and a kidnapped village bobby who had pestered the motorists into taking drastic action.

The long, low car slid forward and then dropped like a bullet down the descent our steam toy had so painfully climbed. Our guest's face blanched, and he clutched the back of the tonneau.... Our impetus carried us halfway up the next slope, where we steadied to a resonant fifteen an hour against the collar.

"What do you think?" I called to Hinchcliffe.

"'Taint as sweet as steam, o' course; but for power it's twice the *Furious* against half the *Jaseur* in a head-on sea."

Volumes could not have touched it more exactly. His bright eyes were glued on Kysh's hands juggling with levers behind the discreet backward-sloping dash.

"An' what sort of brake might you use?" he said politely.

"This," Kysh replied, as the last of the hill shot up to one in eight. He let the car run back a few feet and caught her deftly on the brake, repeating the performance cup and ball fashion. It was liked being daped above the Pit at

the end of an uncoiled solar plexus. Even Pyecroft held his breath.

"It ain't fair! It ain't fair!" our guest moaned. "You're makin' me sick."

"What an ungrateful blighter he is!" said Pyecroft. "Money couldn't buy you a run like this.... Do it well overboard!"

"We'll just trundle up the Forest and drop into Park Row, I think," said Kysh. "There's a bit of good going hereabouts."

He flung a careless knee over the low raking tiller that the ordinary expert puts under his armpit, and down four miles of yellow road, cut through barren waste, the Octopod sang like a six-inch shell....

I had seen Kysh drive before, and I thought I knew the Octopod, but that afternoon he and she were exalted beyond my knowledge. He improvised on the keys—the snapping levers and quivering accelerators—marvellous variations, so that our progress was sometimes a fugue and sometimes a barn-dance, varied on open greens by the weaving of fairy rings. When I protested, all that he would say was: 'I'll hypnotise the fowl! I'll dazzle the rooster!' or other words equally futile. And she—oh! that I could do her justice! —she turned her broad black bows to the westering light, and lifted us high upon hills that we might see and rejoice with her. She whooped into veiled hollows of elm and Sussex oak; she devoured infinite perspectives of park palings; she surged through forgotten hamlets . . . and, tireless, she repeated the motions. Over naked uplands she droned like a homing bee, her shadow lengthening in the sun that she chased to his lair. She nosed up unparochial byways and accommodation-roads of the least accommodation, and put old scarred turf or new-raised molehills under her most marvellous springs with never a jar. And since the King's highway is used for every purpose save traffic, in mid-career she stepped aside for, or flung amazing loops about, the brainless driver, the driverless horse, the drunken carrier, the engaged couple, the female student of the bicycle and her stagger-ing instructor, the pig, the perambula-tor, and the infant school (where it disembogued yelping on cross-roads), with the grace of Nellie Farren (upon whom be the Peace) and the lithe aban-don of all the Vokes family. (From *Steam Tactics* in *Traffics and Discoveries*.)

C. N. and A. M. Williamson

Certificate
Automobile
Club,
50 miles
trial.

£200

Greatly Improved Benz System. The Famous ORIENT EXPRESS, No. 1. (SOLE AGENTS).
Single-cylinder **6 h.p.** water-cooled motor, 3 speeds and one reverse, belt transmission, with jockey pulley, thus overcoming belt slipping, magnetic (Simms-Bosch) ignition, therefore practically perpetual ignition without the trouble of charging accumulators, automatic self-mixing carburettor, very solidly and strongly built and a very reliable car, is probably the prettiest car in the market, and the coachbuilding is of the very finest, speeds vary from 1 to 22 miles per hour, splendid hill climber.
Price £200. Extras: pneumatic tyres, £15 15; leather hood, £10 10; third lamp, £1 10; complete set tools fixed to car, £3 3.

I was proud of the car when I went out in it yesterday (November 14, 1901). Aunt Mary wouldn't go, because she doesn't wish to be the "victim of an experiment". Rattray drove for a long way, but when we got beyond the traffic, towards Richmond, I took his place, and my lesson began. It's harder than I thought it would be, because you have to do so many things at once. You really ought to have three or four hands with this car, Rattray says. When I asked him if it was different with other cars, he didn't seem to hear. Already I've noticed that he's subject to a sort of spasmodic deafness, but I suppose I must put up with that, as he is such a fine mechanic. One can't have everything.

With your left hand you have to steer the car by means of a kind of tiller, and to this is attached the horn to warn creatures of all sorts that you're coming. I blow this with my right hand, but Rattray says I ought to learn to do it while steering with my left, as there are quantities of other things to be done with the right hand. First there is a funny little handle with which you change speeds whenever you come to a

hill; then there is the 'jockey-pulley-lever', which gives the right tension to the belts (this is *very* important); the 'throttle-valve-lever', on which you must always keep your hand to control the speed of the car; and the brake which you jam on when you want to stop. So there are two things to do with the left hand, and four things with the right, and often most of these things must be done at the same time. No wonder I was confused and got my hands a little mixed, so that I forgot which was which, and went wrong for a second! Just then a cart was rude enough to come round a corner, I tried to steer to the right, but went to the left—and you can *think* how many things can happen with a motor-car in one second.

Now don't be worried! I wasn't hurt a bit; only we charged on to the sidewalk and butted into a shop. (From *The Lightning Conductor*.)

The Williamsons, husband and wife, turned early automobilism to good account by weaving romantic novels around their own travels and motoring experiences. 'C.N.' apparently did the driving and his wife

104

Alice the writing. Her first book, 'The Lightning Conductor', became a best-seller at a time when most people in horse-bound England looked askance at horse-less carriages. The book featured a titled hero, disguised as a humble chauffeur (the 'Lightning Conductor' of the title), driving his beloved—an American girl, Molly, touring Europe with her aunt—in his own efficient Napier after her Orient Express, the car shown left and described in our first extract, had broken down. Finally the Lightning Conductor returned to tour England in his big Sunbeam saloon (below) of about 1932 vintage.

You ask in your note whether I've bought a new car. I have, but it's the same make—a Sunbeam. I've been loyal to Sunbeam since the jolly old war, when they earned the best record of all, as you may remember. My latest would knock you in the eye. Black and gold, saloon, 24 h.p. and can do more than most other cars of higher power. A peach she is, as Molly says. Runs like satin on velvet. Nothing ever seems to happen to her except what one wants to happen. A very different story from the 'Lightning Conductor' in our hectic past! (From *The Lightning Conductor Comes Back*.)

G. R. N. Minchin

At the top of the hill, Pat changed into top. Seventy miles an hour was his speed over the undulating road, nor did he slow down through the tiny hamlets as they flashed past. Pont de Briques and Samer left behind, it was but a few more moments before they came to the outskirts of Montreuil. They wound up the hill, under the walls of the old chateau, British Headquarters in 1918, and went on through the town and on to the straight road, through the orchards, to Abbeville. . . . Pat swept on, through the suburbs and up the hill towards Brignais. On to the concrete stretch of road, laid down for the 1914 Grand Prix. Past the famous hairpin of Les Sept Chemins, round which the racing cars of eight nations had skidded. Just beyond lay the site of the *tribunes*, whence, on the eve of war, the spectators had watched, spellbound, the great duel between the French national hero, Boillot, in his blue Peugeot, and the stolid German, Lautenschlager, in the white Mercedes.

The memory of those stirring days and past heroes gone to his head, Pat drove like a madman down the road to Givors. (From *N.7: A Novel*.)

Minchin, a businessman having associations with Rolls-Royce through an accumulator company, wrote this thriller—about Pat's Bentley (forerunner of that shown below) and other cars—to win a wager with Sir Henry Royce. He used the intimate details of a Rolls-Royce Phantom's controls as clues to the unravelling of a mystery. He loved Continental travel in good cars. In 1966 he wrote to the editor of this book from South Africa.

F. Scott Fitzgerald

After half an hour, when the twilight had coagulated into dark, the silent Negro who was driving the buggy hailed an opaque body somewhere ahead of them in the gloom. In response to his cry, it turned upon them a luminous disk which regarded them like a malignant eye out of the unfathomable night. As they came closer, John saw that it was the tail-light of an immense automobile, larger and more magnificent than any he had ever seen. Its body was of gleaming metal richer than nickel and lighter than silver, and the hubs of the wheels were studded with iridescent geometric figures of green and yellow—John did not dare to guess whether they were glass or jewel. . . .

"Gosh! What a car!" This ejaculation was provoked by its interior. John saw that the upholstery consisted of a thousand minute and exquisite tapestries of silk, woven with jewels and embroideries, and set upon a background of cloth of gold. The two armchair seats in which the boys luxuriated were covered with stuff that resembled duvetyn, but seemed woven in numberless colours of

the ends of ostrich feathers.

'What a car!'' cried John again.

"This thing?'' Percy laughed. ''Why, it's just an old junk we use for a station wagon.'' . . .

He spoke a few words into the mouth-piece and immediately the footman turned on a searchlight and swept the hillsides with an immense beam.

''Rocky, you see. An ordinary car would be knocked to pieces in half an hour. In fact it'd take a tank to navigate it unless you knew the way.'' (From *The Diamond As Big As The Ritz*.)

Cars abound in the writings of Scott Fitzgerald: as instruments of pleasure, of envy and, in 'The Great Gatsby', of death. But this brilliant and tragic celebrant of the post-1918 Jazz Age—"with a whoop", he said in one essay, "the orgy began"— was somewhat unspecific about makes. And the car he described in 'The Diamond As Big As The Ritz' was pure fantasy. The model of it shown was made by Deirdre Amsden. She first constructed it from paper, then produced a second version using cardboard, silver paper, paste jewels and cloth.

107

Henry Miller

I feel like doing a little passacaglia now about things automotive. Ever since I decided to sell the car she's been running beautifully. The damned thing behaves like a flirtatious woman.

Back in Albuquerque, where I met that automotive expert Hugh Dutter, everything was going wrong with her. Sometimes I think it was all the fault of the tail wind that swept me along through Oklahoma and the Texas panhandle. Did I mention the episode with the drunk who tried to run me into a ditch? He almost had me convinced that I had lost my generator. I was a bit ashamed, of course, to ask people if my generator were gone, as he said, but every time I had a chance to open up a conversation with a garage man I would work him round to the subject of generators, hoping first of all that he would show me where the damned thing was hidden, and second that he would tell me whether or not a car could function without one. I had just a vague idea that the generator had something to do with the battery. Perhaps it hasn't, but that's my notion of it still.

The thing I enjoy about visiting garage men is that one contradicts the other. It's very much as in medicine, or the field of criticism in literature. Just when you believe you have the answer you find that you're mistaken. A little man will tinker with your machinery for an hour and blushingly ask you for a dime, and whether he's done the correct thing or not the car runs, whereas the big service stations will lay her up in dry dock for a few days, break her down into molecules and atoms, and then like as not she'll run a few miles and collapse. . . .

When I got back to the garage I found Dutter bending over the engine, he had his ear to the motor, like a doctor examining a weak lung. From the vital parts there dangled an electric bulb attached to a long wire. The electric bulb always reassures me. It means business. Anyway, he was down in the guts of the thing and getting somewhere—so it looked.

"Found out what's wrong yet?" I ventured to inquire timidly.

"No," he said, burying his wrist in a mess of intricate whirring thingama-jigs which looked like the authentic automotive part of the automobile. It was the first time I had ever seen what makes a car go. It was rather beautiful, in a mechanical way. Reminded me of a steam calliope playing Chopin in a tub of grease.

"She wasn't timing right," said Dutter, twisting his neck around to look at me but, like the skilful surgeon, still operating with his deft right hand, "I knew that much before I even looked at her. That'll heat a car up quicker'n anything." And he began explaining to me from deep down in the bowels of the car how the timing worked. As I remember it now an eight cylinder car fires 1, 3, 5, 7 with one cam and 2, 4, 6, 8 with the other. I may be wrong on the figures but the word cam is what interested me. It's a beautiful word and when he tried to point it out to me I liked it still better—the cam. It has a down-to-earth quality about it, like piston and gear. Even an ignoramus like myself knows that piston, just from the sound of the word, means something that has to do with the driving force, that it's intimately connected with the locomotion of the vehicle. I still have to see a piston *per se*, but I believe in pistons even though I should never have the chance to see one cold and isolate.

The timing occupied him for quite a while. He explained what a difference a quarter of a degree could make. He was working on the carburettor, if I am not mistaken. I accepted this explanation, as I had the others, unquestionably. Meanwhile I was getting acquainted with the fly-wheel and some other more or less essential organs of the mysterious mechanism. Most everything about a car, I should say in passing, is more or less essential. All but the nuts underneath the chassis; they can get loose and fall out, like old teeth, without serious damage. I'm not speaking now of the universal—that's another matter. But all those rusty nuts which you see dropping off when the car's jacked up on the hoist—actually they mean very little. At worst the running board may drop off, but once you know your running board is off there's no great harm done. (From *Automotive Passacaglia*, in *The Air-Conditioned Nightmare*.)

J. P. Donleavy

"George."

"I'm listening Shirl."

"I sound so loud in the dark."

"Beep beep."

"Don't do that George. Please."

"Beep beep."

"I know I deserve it George."

"Deserve what."

"Beep beep."

"Beep beep!"

"George are we cars."

"You said it."

"I wanted you to see my gold slippers George."

"Too dark."

"Yeah. But do you want to feel my gold slippers."

"Stand back."

"I know I deserve it George. Do whatever you want to me."

"Pretty risky talk. What are you doing Shirl."

"I'm undoing."

"Beep beep. I'm a car."

"This is the way we used to be, George."

"I've just stopped for traffic lights."

"Are you sitting up George."

"I'm waiting for the lights to change."

"And we should have been like this more often. Don't you think, George."

"Beep beep, I'm going again."

"Should we have a crash."

"Are you suggesting I'm not a careful driver."

"No George."

"Well watch it, beep beep."

"I can see you George. I can."

"He he. I can you too, Shirl."

"We've wasted so much time, George, haven't we."

"Don't drive your car too close."

"I want you to crash into me."

"Safety first."

"George."

"What are these Shirl."

"Feel them."

"Wow."

"Feel this."

"What is this Shirl."

"This is what I want you to feel."

"I'd be a fool to feel it."

"Be a fool and feel it."

"What a foolish feeling."

"Just because you're feeling foolish."

(From *A Singular Man*.)

Two of the stranger passages about cars: the first because it is by an author ('Tropic of Cancer' etc.) whose reputation, to say the least, does not rest on his association with the automobile; the second because of the way in which automotive symbols are employed. Henry Miller is seen by some (like Lawrence Durrell) as a brave adventurer; others use different words. Whatever one's view, few people would have expected to find in the work of so controversial a figure his 'Automotive Passacaglia', a piece (not exactly fictional!) about a car written with great care and affection. The car is unspecified, but it is plainly mass-produced and heavily-used: ripe for going wrong in New Mexico, where Albuquerque lies. Miller captures something of the hopes and fears, love and hate of all owners of ailing cars. The air of innocence is also neat. J. P. Donleavy arrived with a bang a decade ago when his first novel, 'The Ginger Man', was published. In this short extract from his second book, 'A Singular Man'—as bawdy, jaunty and oddly written as his first—he is using, very idiosyncratically, images of the motor age in a bedroom parley. His mysterious hero, George Smith, very rich and very lonely, even visits the vast mausoleum he is erecting in a bullet-proof and dreadnought-like limousine.

Eric Linklater

But age comes quickest and most irremediable to mechanical things. The life of a sparking-plug is a fierce tropical existence of days only. No healing leucocytes rush to the aid of a cracked cylinder, nor anastomosing tributaries expand to carry the life-blood of a choked feed-pipe. Old motor-cars grow asthmatic, systolic murmurs betray their weakened power, and carbon comes to poison them outright. And so the aged Morris staggered in its gait like an old lady in the rain, wheezing a little, anxious about her umbrella which the wind was bullying. It grew somewhat hysterical feeling itself so far from home, and began to run in an agitated manner, short bursts of speed striving to make up for more frequent laggarding. . . . Light showed ahead. The weary Morris sighed with relief and edged to the pavement in front of a red-curtained house with a swinging sign. "You can't expect her to run on two cylinders!" said Holly, and got out. (From *Poet's Pub*.)

She took off the frilled apron and threw it into the back of the car. Her apple-green dress was plain and non-committal, but she could not persuade herself that it was the kind of dress the owner of an Isotta-Fraschini would normally choose. (From *Poet's Pub*.)

Linklater's novels are full of gusty action and unpredictable people. Cars are well suited to these themes and he seldom shrinks from naming them, even if he is careful not to enter into too intimate a technical contact with them. Thus the solid old Morris (top picture) and the stately Isotta-Fraschini (above), both in 'Poet's Pub'. The latter was a sort of Italian Rolls-Royce with eight cylinders to its enormous engine, and an impressive, heavy body to match. No wonder the girl felt her simple dress to be inappropriate to such a car.

110

Gilbert Frankau

The car shot on, purring—Peter, nearly recumbent, notched wheel gripped easily in gloved hands—Patricia bolt upright, eyes on the speeding hedge-rows. They made the six miles to Henley in a fraction over twelve minutes; swirled right-handed at the railway station; took the water-front at a bound; skidded the bridge corner on two wheels. Church, bridge and river vanished like mad movies. "Going well," muttered Peter through set teeth. White Hill rose up like a roof ahead. "Open that cut-out for me." Exhaust roaring, cylinders throbbing, the Crossley hurtled up between the trees, slowed to twenty; felt herself flung back into second; topped the rise; raced engine for the fraction of an instant; took top gear again; shot on.

Houses, trees, a crawling dray, flashed astern. Grey tarmac zipped under. Ahead, the road rose; dropped; rose again. Now they were in open country. Peter took one deep breath; fidgeted the throttle-lever to full open; jammed foot on accelerator. Couple behind felt the car gather herself as if for a great leap; saw passing hedge-rows fade out to a continuous blur. Speedometer-needle clicked to sixty; held there for three-and-a-half ecstatic minutes. (From *Peter Jackson, Cigar Merchant*.)

The Etonian novelist who wrote non-stop, doped with aspirin, to meet financial crises, found that his motoring experiences helped to fill the pages of his books. Here one of his heroes, a successful cigar merchant, races to London to celebrate the Armistice of a war in which he had fought and suffered, and gets along so swiftly that I suspect his Crossley (above) was a Shelsey model! This book, which established Frankau's reputation in 1919, captures the spirit of an age, and Frankau, who loved good cars in real life, particularly his air-cooled six-cylinder Franklin, later wrote a motor-racing novel.

John Galsworthy

"This car," Val said suddenly, "wants rousing; she doesn't get her hind legs under her uphill. I shall have to give her her head on the slope if I'm to catch that train." There was that about horses which had prevented him from ever really sympathising with a car, and the running of the Ford under his guidance compared with its running under that of Holly was always noticeable. He caught the train. "Take care going home; she'll throw you down if she can. Goodbye, darling." (From the third part, *To Let*, of *The Forsyte Saga*.)

Some authors are shy of real cars and invent fictitious makes, like the 'Rollhard' owned by Soames in Galsworthy's classic study of English middle-class society, 'The Forsyte Saga'. But in this part of the 'Saga' he felt safe with the Ford T. Everyone in post-1918 England knew it.

111

The racer as movie star by Derek Jewell

In the hands of movie-makers, cars can become characters even more striking than in novels. No director has lavished so much love, or money, on an obsession with automobiles as John Frankenheimer, who in 1966 made the £2½ million Cinerama spectacular, *Grand Prix*. He went to endless trouble to ensure authenticity. He spent £100,000 on a fleet of racing cars which had phoney Formula I superstructures built on Formula III chassis. Two of his stars, Françoise Hardy and James Garner (left), are sitting on a B.R.M. replica. His actors, like Garner and Yves Montand (bottom right), had to learn to race-drive, speeding round European circuits being filmed alongside real-life drivers like Graham Hill and Jack Brabham. Frankenheimer fearlessly mixed sequences of genuine Grand Prix with his own contrived races—matching up every detail of cars and drivers. He produced a compressed-gas cannon to fire cars at 100 m.p.h. in simulated crashes. Brian Bedford (bottom left) acts injured in one of them. He also had a £20,000 remote-control camera based on cameras used to film space-missile launches. Other cameras shot film from a Ford G.T. (below). "I can," said Frankenheimer, "show people a race like they've never seen." These photographs were taken on location at Monaco by Duffy.

A simple little three-car trick by Ken W. Purdy

One last example of the use of the car in fiction—this time, a complete short story. Strangely, most 'motoring' short stories have been unsuccessful, usually because they soon begin to sound like 'Boy's Own' pastiche (all screaming tyres and set teeth). Ken Purdy, an American, is one of the few writers to practise the form with flair, and he also wrote, with Stirling Moss, the best book yet on motor racing, 'All But My Life'. His characters, Peter and Elisabeth Harmon, appear in several of his stories. Peter and the Morgan Three-Wheelers of the story were drawn by Roger Law.

"Peter," Elisabeth Harmon said to her husband, "why do you keep flailing away at your coffee like that?"

Peter Harmon swallowed a lump of largely unmasticated toast. "Because I am trying to cool it, woman," he said.

"Ah," Elisabeth said. "I had the impression you were intent on beating it to death with the spoon." She smiled sweetly.

Peter looked at her, as he thought, covertly—but she was staring him direct in the eyeball. He felt a sinking sensation. The woman knew something. He made a swift inventory of recent sinnings—small, insignificant, inconsequential. Still he had been married to this fragile little thing for seven years, and there were unmistakable signs well known to him: an air of concentrated interest, detached amusement, serenity full of portent.

He looked at his watch. Three minutes to blast-off. He picked up hat, umbrella, briefcase. Elisabeth walked to the side-door with him, where she would stand to see him mount his charger, a 1952 Buick convertible.

"By the way," she said. "I see The Folly is no longer domiciled with us."

"Domiciled?" Peter said.

"Yes. There's a hole, as it were, in the garage, a yawning emptiness, where The Folly was, the last time I noticed, a couple of days ago."

"If," Peter said, "if by The Folly you mean my Morgan Three-Wheeler, a rare and valuable antique automobile, then I dig you. I have removed it, yes. Temporarily."

"To have the frattistat gears gold-plated?" Elisabeth said. "To have the top done in virgin ostrich-hide, perhaps? While your wife and children go without bread? Once more to the money-lender, dear friends? Is that it?"

"Now, Elisabeth," Peter said, "let's keep a little grip on ourselves. Let's. . . ."

"Tell me, hero," Elisabeth said. "Where IS the thing?"

Peter looked at his watch. The reading was 8:02. It was going to be a squeaker. He leapt into the Buick and waved to Elisabeth as the gravel flew. She spoke. He couldn't hear her, but he could read her ruby lips. "Coward!" she was saying.

The train was all but moving when he boarded it, but luck was beside him and he found his man: Herbert Jellison, who might, had he wished, have called himself Herbert Jellison IV, but was far too rich for such ostentation. He was not the most popular fellow on the train—a compulsive necessity to make money on his friends had something to do with it—and the seat next to him was empty. He was no reader, card-player, nor worker, Jellison! He was a talker. He got under way before the train did.

"I was terribly tempted this morning," he said. "I wanted to fetch my wife a good slap in the mouth."

"Really?" Peter Harmon said. "What had the poor thing done?"

"Nothing," Jellison said. "But last night I read this piece by Harry Golden, he'd been in Puerto Rico, and it seems that in Puerto Rico there's an ideal called *machismo*, translated pretty freely, *masculinity*. A young married

114

woman says to her husband, at a party, it's time they went home. So he walks over and slaps her in the mouth—not hard enough to knock her down, just hard enough to let her know that *he's* boss, and when it's time to go home, he'll say so. That's *machismo*. A great idea."

"Hmmmm," Peter said. "You interest me. When you do this thing, let me know. Let me know if you get away with less than six months in jail. Because I have a slight problem of my own...."

"Tell me more," Jellison said.

Peter folded his *Times*.

"I have this Morgan Three-Wheeler," he said. "It's an automobile. You know, I'm nutty about old cars, I've had a Frazer Nash, a Mercer, an old La France fire-engine, that sort of thing, and I've got this Morgan now...."

"*Three* wheels?" Jellison said. "Like a kid's tricycle?"

"Two in front, one in back," Peter said. "It was a gimmick in British law, anything with fewer than four wheels was a motor-cycle, and the tax was less ... so a fellow named H. F. S. Morgan made about 40,000 of these things. Mine's about '36. It's a lot of fun, weighs about 900 pounds, and goes like the hammers."

"*How* fast, for real?" Jellison said.

"An Englishwoman named Gwenda Hawkes made one do 116 miles an hour once. No one ever did it before her, and no one since."

"So what's the problem," Jellison said. "You want your wife to beat the record, and she says she won't? I don't think slapping her will help. Not a time for *machismo*, I'd say."

"No, no!" Peter said. "No such notion. I've got a little problem because every time I want to get the thing painted up a bit, or a bit of chrome done over, Elisabeth goes berserker, claims I'm taking bread from the mouths of our children."

"Or the mink off her back, that it?" Jellison said.

"The point *did* come up once," Peter said. "Anyway, the other day, I sneaked the thing out of the garage. And this morning she made a couple of cracks. Back on the rocky road to the poorhouse, you know, that kind of remark."

"I see," Jellison said. "Where'd you take the car?"

"It's in a paint-shop," Peter said.

"You see, I've had a tremendous strike of luck. There are only about six-seven Morgans in the United States, a new one almost never comes on the market. I've just found *two* in Chicago." He lowered his voice and looked around the back of his seat. "I have solid options on *both* of them. You hear me? I own these cars, practically."

"No kidding!" Jellison said. "My, my! I see it all now. You're going to have one for every day, and a matched pair besides? Both bright pink, say? You know what could be a great idea? You could have one marked HIS and one marked HERS."

"You are a very funny man, Jellison," Peter said. "You are wasting your time in Wall Street."

"I wish I could return the compliment," Jellison said, "but you have to admit, the idea of beating up your wife because she doesn't want you to have two 1936 three-wheel automobiles that were once driven 116 miles an hour by some English dame who must have been braver than Dick Tracy, and I'll drink to that—well, you have to admit it doesn't make you look like a hero."

"On the other hand," Peter said, "*you* wanted to slap your wife for nothing."

"That, friend, is *machismo*," Jellison said. "What you're talking about is madness. There is a difference."

"You want to hear the rest of the story?" Peter said.

"Frankly, no," Jellison said. "But I'm trapped, and we haven't even got to Darien yet. So carry on."

"All right, there're these two other Morgans in Chicago. I'll whip out there and bring them back—I can drive one and tow the other, and then...."

"That should be a great ride, and the best of British three-wheel luck to you," Jellison said.

"Thanks a lot," Peter said. "Now, then. You're probably too far out of the mainstream of life to know about such things, but General Grain Products is planning to do a new campaign—a really big one—and the theme is going to be 'Three Is Best!' You get the picture, corn, wheat, rye, all three in the same cereal, Three Is Best, clear? Right. Now, at the same time, they're redesigning the package in three colours: red, gold, white. So, *I* have *three* three-wheel automobiles, wildly interesting, antique, exciting, one red, one gold, one white, and we set up a whole campaign around them. Take 'em to auto races, county fairs, country clubs, fashion shows—no end to it. I hit General Grain Products a fat fee for the idea, I *lease* them the cars, it's a G.G.P. operation from start to finish, and I get indecently rich. Right? And you, too, make a splendid profit!"

"I do?" Herbert Hellison said. "How nice for me! Why?"

"Because," Peter said. "I am temporarily just a little light in loot, and to swing this deal, buying the two new cars, having the three of them painted and done up a bit, will take a small sum, not much, but a bit more than I happen to be holding at the moment. Say 3,500 dollars. Or even 3,000 dollars, for an economy-type operation. Naturally, the smaller figure would mean less profit to you in the end, because I would plan on a return for you of 100 per cent. Which is the best offer you'll be getting today, tycoon."

Herbert Jellison looked at Peter. He reached into his pocket and offered, open, a silver box, half-full of green-and-brown capsules. "These are but two-toned," he said, "but my friend, each of them contains 15 milligrams of the strongest tranquillisers known to medical science. I suggest you take two. Right away. And in a little while, all these funny ideas that are at the moment so troubling you, they will magically go away."

Peter Harmon rose and pulled his briefcase off the rack.

"You are the kind of clot who saw no future in the electric light, or the air-brake," he said. "You are doomed to a life of faceless obscurity, when fame could easily be yours. . . . And all for lack of a little imagination." He marched down the aisle.

When Peter Harmon strode into his home that night the odour of the juniper berry floated well ahead of him.

"Before you open your pretty mouth," he said to Elisabeth, "let me tell you that you were right this morning: I have been to the money-lenders. I have a project in mind for which I require financing to the amount of 3,000 dollars. Further than that, I do not care to discuss the matter. With you."

"No reason you should," Elisabeth Harmon said. "I have had a full set of bulletins from Janey Jellison. You are

the only man in all recorded history foolish enough to have owned three Morgan Three-Wheelers simultaneously. You are a flaming idiot, tripled!"

Peter Harmon cranked up and threw his best right-hand slap. "*Machismo!*" he cried. His wife looked at him distantly. He had missed her by a foot.

"Go soak your head, tiger," she said. "And I'll make some black-coffee gravy for your mashed potatoes."

They dined in comparative silence.

Morning brought surprises, breakfast in bed. And a good one, with scrambled eggs and things. Those Puerto Ricans have something, he told himself. I wonder what I'd have got if I'd HIT her?

Elisabeth sat on the bed beside him. She had the *Times* in her hand. "When your strength returns," she said, "you might read this. . . ." It was a headline, a two-column headline. "GENERAL GRAIN ACCOUNT TO R.Y. & J. AGENCY. 'THREE-BEST' CAMPAIGN ABANDONED." There was a longish story. Peter saw no point in reading it.

"I thank you for the breakfast," he said to Elisabeth. "Also, it is kind of you not to gloat. Meanwhile, must up and dress. Back to the old drawing-board, so to speak." He smiled. It came out one-sided.

"You are a brave, but excessively idiotic idiot, Harmon," Elisabeth said. "I shall probably have left your bed and board by noon today. I had your pledged word that you would never, never buy another smelly old automobile without telling me in advance. You now own three of the smelliest and oldest. It is too much."

Herbert Jellison was lurking on the platform. He laid a restraining hand on Peter as he passed.

"Unloose me, oaf," Peter said.

"You're wrong," Jellison said. "I am your friend, your true friend. You see in me the man with the life-preserver. Your plight has moved me. Now, look. . . ."

"My commutation book ran out," Peter said. "I have to pick up the new one."

"I'll wait," Jellison said. "I have a message. Honest."

Charlie Morelli, proprietor of Morelli's Station Garage, and nothing genial about him, was waiting at the newsstand.

"Did he park at your place this morning?" Peter said softly.

"Sure, like always. Two minutes after you called."

"You give it to him?"

"I give it to him *good*," Charlie said. "The Morgan Company's 75th Anniversary, buying up every three-wheeler in the U.S., five thousand bucks apiece, minimum, the whole business, I give him."

"He go for it?"

"Like free liquor."

"Thanks. If it works, you get yours tonight."

All the way to Grand Central, Peter Harmon told himself, "I never thought the man had it in him. Barrymore should have lived to see this." Herbert Jellison's performance was inspired. He opened easily, gently. He had been stunned by the brilliance of Peter's conception of the deal. The failure of it had in no way been his fault but he hated to see a friend hurt. And, to tell the strict truth, he had rather envied Peter. The Morgan Three-Wheeler sounded pretty sporting at that. Of course, he wanted to be strictly on the level: he intended to sell two of the three cars, and at an honest profit, if he could. He might have to wait a long time, but even so . . . it was great. Almost hand in hand, they walked to Jellison's bank. Not a chance of a cheque, of course. Cheques can be torn up if the seller changes his mind. Peter left bulging with 9,000 dollars in cash.

Elisabeth met him at the door that night. He hadn't doubted she would. When Elisabeth had said "until death do us part" she'd meant it, Peter knew that well enough.

"Well, dear heart," she said, "at least they're still running the bar-car, right?"

"I have here," he said, "a trifling gift for you, a little something." He watched her open the box. She was, he could see, surprised beyond belief.

"Peter!" she said. "This is *mink!*"

"Right," he said. "And also, wild. It represents a vast profit, you may be interested to know, originating in the Morgan Three-Wheeler."

"Darling," Elisabeth said. "Is there anything I can get you?"

"A dry martini," he said. "And at once."

When she had brought it she said, "I never saw *anything* so lovely. I can hardly wait to tell Janey Jellison."

"That should be fun," Peter said. "Why don't you call her right away?"

He left the room. His glass was empty. When he came back Elisabeth was still sitting beside the phone.

"You call her?" he said.

"Sure," she said. "Funny thing. SHE got a mink jacket today, too!"

"Big day for girls," he said.

"There was a reason," Elisabeth said. "And you're not going to like it. She says that Herbie went to school with the chairman of the board of R.Y. & J. The minute he left you this morning, he went to see the man and he sold him YOUR idea: they're going to use the Morgan Three-Wheelers for exploitation. Janey says he got 6500 dollars apiece for them."

Peter Harmon drank. He even ate his olive. "It is a sad story," he said. "To think that Herbert Jellison could sink so low . . . appalling."

"Ah, never mind, darling," Elisabeth Harmon said. "There's always tomorrow."

A warming smile rewarded her. "You're so right, doll," he said. "There's always tomorrow. There's always the 8:11. There is, even, always the empty seat beside Herbie Jellison." He handed her his glass. "Make me another, doll," he said. "I must think, I really must think."

118

Artist and automobile
by David Sylvester

In the 1960s, the motor-car became a familiar ingredient in art. Pop artists pictured it; sculptors in metal used actual junked cars as their raw material. Earlier in the century the car's appearances in art were more sporadic, but it did get into the work of several leading artists. David Sylvester, who has written the commentary in the following pages, is a writer, lecturer and broadcaster on art, organiser of some major exhibitions at the Tate Gallery, and art adviser to 'The Sunday Times Magazine'.

Henri de Toulouse-Lautrec: The Motorist, 1896. Lithograph.
Collection, The Museum of Modern Art, New York. Gift of Abby Aldrich Rockefeller.

Lautrec focuses on the driver, not the machine. His motorist is ferocious, indeed demonic—he rather than the car seems the source of the belching smoke. He is juxtaposed with the lady pedestrian as if they were Beauty and the Beast. But the satire is rather affectionate. In fact, the motorist was the artist's cousin and companion, Gabriel Tapié de Céleyran, then a medical student. Lautrec had several friends among the pioneer motorists.

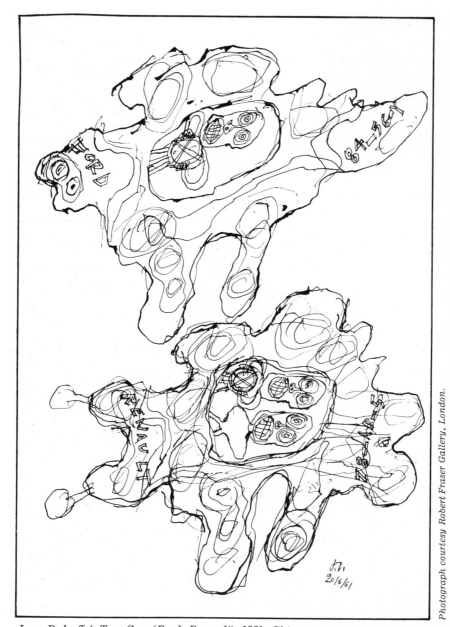

Photograph courtesy Robert Fraser Gallery, London.

Jean Dubuffet: Two Cars (Ford, Renault), 1961. Chinese ink.

Henri Matisse: The Windsc

Balla was one of the Italian Futurists; the first group of artists to fall in love with machines. Marinetti, their spokesman, published a poem in 1905 about a racing car: *To my Pegasus*. Severini enthused about "heavy powerful motorcars rushing through the streets of our cities". Speed was what most excited the Futurists, and they evolved a style in which several successive views of a body (or bodies) in motion are shown simultaneously. Balla's *Speed of an Automobile + Lights* is not about the automobile but about its speed. The

120

Giacomo Balla: Speed of an Automobile + Lights, 1913. Oil.

Collection, Mrs. Malcolm L. McBride, Cleveland; photograph courtesy Peter A. Juley, New York.

17. *Oil.*

spiral lines express the revolutions of
the wheels, the parallel diagonals con-
vey the forward motion: the car itself
disintegrates into these lines of force.

Matisse was inspired by no such
abstract and romantic ideas, but by his
pleasure in owning a car. One of this
master's recurrent themes is the interior of a room with a view: here the
room becomes the interior of a car, the
window a windscreen. The car is neither
a picturesque oddity, as it was for
Lautrec, nor a winged horse, a mythical
being, as it was for the Futurists. It is

something one uses and owns, like a
comfortable room. It's a machine for
living in.

Dubuffet's art, like Lautrec's, in-
volves satire and caricature, and he too
brings out the demonic side of driving.
The work illustrated is one of many
drawings and paintings of cars in his
series *Paris Circus.* One painting is
called *The Motor-car, Flower of Industry,*
and our drawing is another play on that
metaphor. And, maybe, a play on the apocalyptic image of Death on a pale horse
—in *Paris Circus* a pantomime horse.

121

Not surprisingly, American art is where the car and its adjuncts loom largest. **Edward Hopper** paints a silent filling-station as he paints deserted streets and empty rooms. The three Pop images here suggest that a juke box or transistor set is switched on. Pop artists paint life as processed by popular imagery. The **Lichtenstein** is a parody of an ad or a strip cartoon. **Rosenquist's** Dodge fender might be part of an ad or

Edward Hopper: Gas, 1940. Oil.

Roy Lichtenstein: In the Car, 1963. Magna on canvas.

part of a car as the ads see it. **Warhol** uses a blown-up news photograph: his picture consists of this same image repeated ten times. It is among several celebrations by Warhol of what has displaced TB as the most fashionable form of premature death. Larry Rivers is another notable American painter of cars. Willem de Kooning has painted landscapes inspired by driving along freeways out of New York City.

Andy Warhol: Green Disaster No. 2 (detail), 1933. Silkscreen on canvas.   James Rosenquist: Discs, 1964. Oil on canvas with metal.

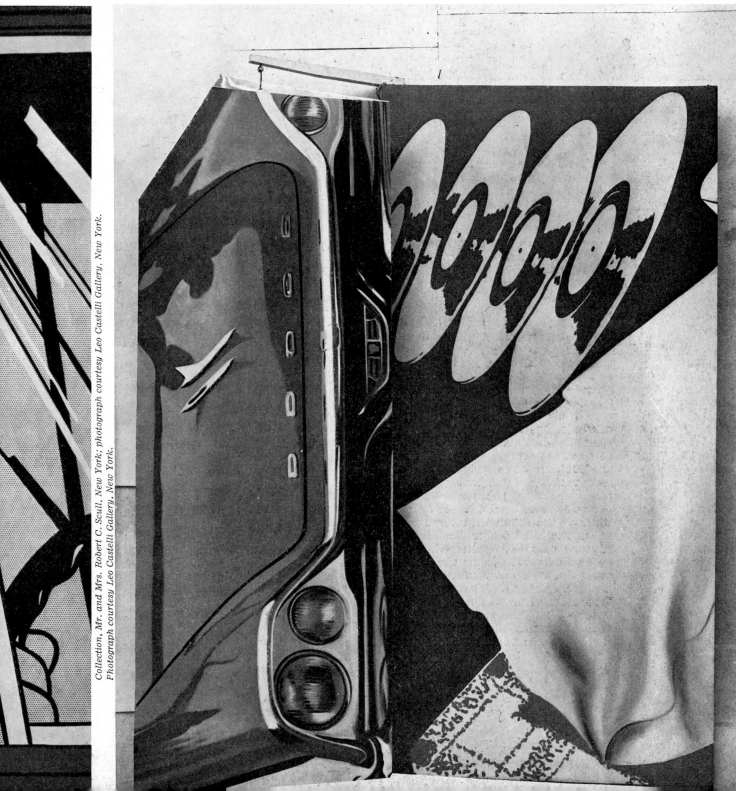

Pablo Picasso: Baboon with Young (detail), 1951. Bronze.

Several artists have employed parts of junked cars in making sculpture. The American Robert Rauschenberg has used tyres and doors. The Frenchman César has used cars compressed by the crusher. The American **John Chamberlain** treats car scrap as raw material for abstract sculpture, rarely seeks to remind us where the material came from.

The greatest exponent of junk sculpture has been **Picasso**—as in his sculpture of a bull's head made from nothing but the saddle and handlebars of an old bike. Picasso has never used car scrap, but he did use two toy motor-cars as the head of his *Baboon with Young*—the rest of the piece was modelled in clay.

The American Pop artist, **Claes Oldenburg,** works in the opposite direction—not using car scrap to represent something else but using neutral materials to represent cars in whole or in part, specifically the Chrysler Airflow. **Salvatore Scarpitta's** Pop sculptures of racing cars are, on the one hand, confessions of a boyish passion, on the other sophisticated games with our expectations as to what his artefacts are. We think we are looking at something assembled from real car parts: sometimes we are, but sometimes the parts have been carved in wood and painted. We wonder whether the cars will go: one of them does, the other doesn't. In making illusory cars and calling them sculptures, Scarpitta upends the art of the great Bugatti, who made real cars as if he were making sculptures.

From Pop image to popular image: **F. Gordon-Crosby's** magazine illustrations of motor racing have a magic that puts them laps ahead of all else of their kind.

124

Claes Oldenburg: Radiator, Hard Model, 1965. Paper, enamel.

John Chamberlain: Big E, 1963. Welded auto metal.

F. Gordon-Crosby: Szisz's Renault. Winning the French Grand Prix, 1906.

Salvatore Scarpitta: Exhibition Photo, 1965.

125

Cartoon and car

There is, obviously, a great deal of visual humour to be extracted from man's motor-car predicament. It has, for decades, been a staple theme of the daily newspaper cartoonist, like Giles or Osbert Lancaster. Sometimes, as with the work of the American, Saul Steinberg, it is difficult to know where to draw the line between cartooning and art. He chronicles the American scene in a very personal way. His drawings turn cars into fantastic baroque objects, often set against equally strange backgrounds. But the mood is more affectionate than savage. Tomi Ungerer, however, is depicting man infected by the mechanical world he has himself created and sanctioned. Ungerer is German-born, now lives in New York, and is a highly original talent. Jonathan Miller has called his work "a sulphuric moral experience".

Ronald Searle

Ungerer

Osbert Lancaster

"*Quite honestly, darling, I don't really know, but I think they must be fertility symbols.*"

Steinberg

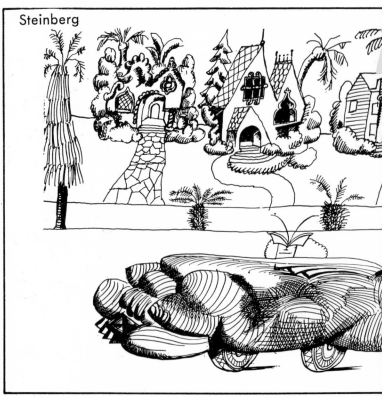

Giles

"Lady, don't ask me why they always have to have pictures of pretty girls to sell their cars—just go and eat your sausage roll somewhere else."

Thelwell

"I've got a three-litre Rover at the moment—about a mile outside Salford."

Companions of the road

Writers of fiction aren't the only ones in whose work the car plays an important role. Biographers, autobiographers, essayists, humorists are involved with it too. The pieces that follow, several of them written specially for this book, show in various ways how motors get mixed up in our lives. The opening words, from 'Great Morning', the third volume of Sir Osbert Sitwell's autobiography, evoke magnificently the feel of motoring in the early days: the exhilaration, the sense of freedom and power, which it has never lost. The turn-of-century advertisements opposite catch the feeling too.

Swimming in speed by Osbert Sitwell

Just as the swell had driven his tandem, so the nut essentially belonged, as much as a snail to its shell, to the fast, open motor of those days. This vehicle, so modern and of its time, induced in the young man a sense of being heir of all the ages, lord of all he passed by. For the sense of speed flatters the sense of power, raising the rich, and even the humbler lorry-driver, to a new and god-like level, as the houses rush past them, a peep-show, though filled with living people. In this matter, at least, the twentieth-century world had advanced upon the Roman (how greatly would the Romans have enjoyed rushing down their straight roads to the infinities of their Empire). Moreover, mine was the first generation in which the young men were allowed to take their sweethearts for drives—only fastest of fast actresses had ridden in tandems. . . . They would sit together, the two of them, the man at the wheel, the girl beside him, their hair blown back from their temples, their features sculptured by the wind, their bodies and limbs shaped and carved by it continually under their clothes, so that they enjoyed a new physical sensation, comparable to swimming; except that here the element was speed, not water. The winds— and their bodies—were warm that summer. During these drives, they acquired a whole range of physical consciousness, the knowledge of scents, passing one into another with an undreamt-of rapidity, the fragrance of the countless flowers of the lime trees, hung like bells on pagodas for the breeze to shake, changing into that of sweetbriar, the scent of the early mornings, and of their darkness, of hills and valleys outlined and tinged by memory; there was the awareness of speed itself, and the rapid thinking that must accompany it, a new alertness, and the typical effects, the sense, it might be, of the racing of every machine as dusk approaches, or the sudden access on a hot evening of cool waves of air under tall trees—all these physical impressions, so small in themselves, went to form a sum of feeling new in its kind and never before experienced. Even the wind of the winter, at this pace snatching tears from their eyes and piercing through layers of clothes, was something their fathers had not known. The open car belonged to that day. No other generation had been able to speed into the sunset.

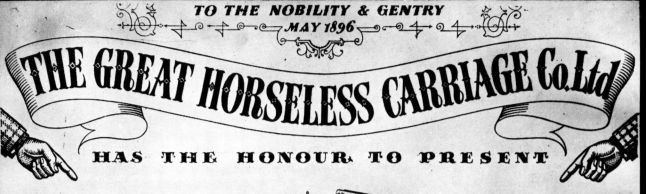

TO THE NOBILITY & GENTRY
MAY 1896

THE GREAT HORSELESS CARRIAGE Co. Ltd

HAS THE HONOUR TO PRESENT

This NOVEL vehicle is propelled by an **INTERNAL COMBUSTION ENGINE** OF 2 CYLINDERS AND 6 HORSE POWER *relying on petroleum for its motive force*

THE MECHANICAL carriage will attain the comfortable speed of **TWELVE MILES PER HOUR** on the level, while hills can be ascended and descended in safety

The Daimler Wagonette *is admirably suited to the needs of the* ⟨SPORTSMAN⟩ AND LOVER OF THE COUNTRYSIDE, *giving as it does* full facilities for the enjoyment of FRESH AIR AND AN **UNINTERRUPTED VIEW OF THE** *Scenery*

"A new mode of transport that has undoubtedly come to stay" — VIDE DAILY PRESS

THE TWIN-CYLINDER 6 H.P. WAGONETTE {See Engraving}

To mark the completion of their fortieth year of car manufacturing—"forty years of apprenticeship" they call it—the Daimler Company recently published a leaflet.

The place of honour on the front cover is given to the first Daimler—the wagonette of 1896. Our illustration is a reproduction of that front cover. It is typical of displayed advertising of forty years ago and, in a very marked degree, emphasizes the vast strides made by the motor industry in general, and the Daimler Company in particular. Especially do we like the phrases " the comfortable

---

❦❦ Warning. ❦❦

We beg to caution intending purchasers against certain unauthorised dealers and manufacturers **who are trying to palm off IMITATIONS of our Motors as genuine,** and we emphatically state that we have given **no license** to make our cars in England.

Messrs. HEWETSON Ltd., of Dean Street, Soho, London,

are our sole representatives for Great Britain, and only Benz Cars sold through this firm or their agents will come under our guarantee. We shall not supply any parts or replacements to persons obtaining here and there one of our cars indirectly.

The ORIGINAL BENZ Car is always the best.

It is the result of fifteen years' study and experience, and, since its invention in 1885, the first car in the world. Unscrupulous people copy our work, but

The ORIGINAL BENZ Car has never been surpassed.

We strongly recommend anyone, before buying a motor car, to carefully read the results of the Automobile Club trials last summer, and compare the performance of our cars with that of other makers. **WE WISH FOR NO BETTER ADVERTISEMENT.** This can be obtained from Messrs. HEWETSON'S at cost price, 1/3, post free.

We particularly caution purchasers of Benz Cars against parting with **ANY MONEY WHATEVER,** either as payment on account or deposit, **UNTIL THEIR CAR IS READY FOR THEM TO TAKE AWAY.**

BENZ & CO., Rheinische Gasmotorenfabrik A.G., MANNHEIM.

Established in 1883.

Reverie in a low gear by Patrick Campbell

"One of the last of the great herd of humorists that formerly roamed the paper plains of Fleet Street," said a blurb on Patrick Campbell. The critic who spoke of "this handsome, old-world property, so surprisingly developed" told us something more about him. Harder facts: born Dublin, 1913; educated Lancashire, Oxford, Paris, Germany; served with Irish Navy and 'Irish Times', a humorous columnist with 'Sunday Dispatch' and since 1961 with 'The Sunday Times'; also TV raconteur; became third Baron Glenavy, 1965. There is nothing, this editor believes, about which Paddy Campbell couldn't be funny — cars, of course, not excluded.

I was looking through the Automobile Association's new handbook, noting, I must confess with no great throb of interest, how many hotels in North Wales have hot and cold water in the bedrooms, when all at once, under the heading of 'Legal Summary', I came upon this astounding piece of information.

Under the Highways Act of 1835 any person who sees a motorist driving furiously to the danger of any person may arrest the motorist without warning.

I let the Automobile Association's new handbook fall to the floor. Any person who sees a motorist driving furiously to the danger of any person may arrest the motorist without a warrant. Can he, indeed? A picture begins to form in the fire. . . .

Say, now, I am making my way home along Western Avenue on a wet night, at the wheel of the 1938 drop-head coupé which I was privileged to buy for £230 in 1949. I am doing 43 m.p.h., with a slight smell of burning, and thinking what a satisfying thing it would be if I could pinch, under the Highways Act, one of that select band of brutes and brothers who flash about the country in illegally obtained new cars. I hold all new cars to be illegally obtained because I don't believe any dealer ever rings up anyone, in the straight course of business, and says, "Sir, your new car is ready."

Suddenly, there is the blast of a horn, and a small, *brand-new* saloon nips in between me and an oncoming lorry. The lorry driver and I swerve wildly, our hearts, enlarged, in our mouths. We just succeed in keeping on the road.

Down goes my foot on the floor-boards, and at 47 m.p.h., with an increased smell of burning, I am off in chase of the first prosecution, under the Highways Act of 1835, since 1835.

My quarry is going like the wind, well up to 50 m.p.h. It looks as though I'm in danger of losing him. I can get a little more out of my machine, but if I do the dynamo begins to discharge the maximum 25 amps and the lights start to go out, for no reason. Several garages have pitted themselves against this problem, and have had to give it best. It means that I have to be content with 45 m.p.h., and illumination equal to two strong paraffin lamps, or face the alarms of 50 m.p.h., preceded, apparently, by a glow-worm.

Several other cars flash by, without, however, infringing the regulations of 1835. I am still bent upon the small, brand-new saloon in front.

I catch him at the next lot of traffic lights. Catch him good and proper, too, because at the last moment he decides not to try to slip across against the amber, and slams on all his brand-new brakes.

I am only 50 yards behind him when he plays this desperate card and, from previous experience, I know what is going to happen next.

I put my foot on the brake pedal. Then I wedge my knee under the steering-wheel, shut my eyes, and push with everything I've got.

On a good day, with a fresh head wind, I can bring the drop-head coupé up, all-standing, within about 30 yards, but tonight I'm tired, and the same drive isn't there in the right leg.

I rap the small saloon sharply on its rear bumper, wait for a second to see if I'm going to go on fire, and then leap out to make my arrest.

The driver of the other car turns out to be a small, elderly man—might be a retired dry-cleaner's manager. He wears glasses, a black overcoat and a black, rather pot-shaped homburg hat. A full-bodied woman in red occupies the other front seat.

They seem to have been alarmed by the recent slight percussion behind, because both of them are peering out anxiously into the night.

I go to work without delay, modelling my manner on previous experience of my colleagues, the police.

"Pull in there to the side, and look sharp about it."

The small man cranes his head out of the window, to see what it's all about. I step back, just out of his range of vision. I don't want him to see my jumper, when he's expecting the terror of a navy-blue uniform. And, in any case, my colleagues the police always do this, particularly on a wet night, so that the motorist can't tell if he's been stopped by the constabulary, or held up by the boys from the Elephant and Castle. It softens the motorist up, and ensures that he will be unable to prepare an immediate defence.

"Well, Neville, do what you're told, can't you?" says the full-bodied woman in red.

The thing is going so well that I begin to wonder if I may not be able to stick him with the charge of fiddling a new car, on top of the furious driving lot.

"Put her down this side turning," I tell him, "and get your driving licence and insurance ready."

I go back to my own car, which is still in the middle of the road, jump in, and find a moment or two later that it's not going to start.

I know what's happened. Although the engine is nearly red-hot the carburettor, in its own hysterical way, has decided to flood itself with petrol, and then soak the plugs and everything else. The only

cure is to turn the engine rapidly, with the accelerator right down, until in some unaccountable fashion the machinery dries itself out. This means I've got to wind the handle, because the 50 m.p.h. chase, with the subsequent discharge from the dynamo, has probably reduced the battery to a state in which it is only just capable of illuminating the rear light.

I get the starting-handle out of the boot, with an old hat of my wife's wrapped round the end, and wind savagely, with the engine switched off, in the hope that this will clear the juice.

So intense is the physical effort that I do not notice for some time that the small man and the full-bodied woman are standing on the pavement. In fact, it isn't until Neville says, "Excuse me, sir, did you see a police officer anywhere?" that I become conscious of his presence, and, indeed, of the nature of his problem. And of the nature of mine.

A moment of intuition makes it clear that I can no longer persist, without a warrant, in making an arrest under the Highways Act of 1835. The initiative has passed to Neville, and if I don't exercise an almost finicky care *he's* going to arrest *me* not only for furious driving and crashing into him, but also for false pretences and any number of other things.

The first thing I must do is to make sure that Neville does not recognise my voice.

Without thought for how it is going to develop I turn to Neville with a politely bewildered look.

"Excuz, pliss?" is my plea. "My Eengleesh ees too vairy smoll. . . ."

Neville doesn't get it, but his wife is sharper.

"Come away from him, Neville," she says. "He's a foreigner. Leave him alone." Her name is probably Gwen.

The trouble is, if they do leave me alone, I'm never going to get my car started at all. Someone—obviously Neville—has to get inside and keep the throttle down while I wind the engine from the front.

"Vould youse, plizz," I say, "be helping me?" I address myself to Gwen, who has a quicker ear for dialect. "The leetle jaintleman," I tell her, indicating Neville with the starting handle, "moost seet at my steering-veel and poosh down trattle piddle."

Both of them look at my car. To their

astonishment the direction indicator slowly hoists itself out of the door pillar and glows, orange-red, in their faces. Gwen starts, and seizes Neville.

I cannot possibly begin to explain, in my present accent, why the direction indicator should suddenly erect itself without human agency or warning. Although I know the reason.

The direction indicator has a delayed action. It's said to have become 'lazy'. When I switch it on, forgetting its peculiarity, it doesn't work until twenty minutes later. I've often come out to the garage in the morning to find it erected, and burning brightly, as it has been doing since the previous evening, or, rather, as from five minutes after I put the rug on the bonnet and left the car, as I hoped, quiescent for the night. That's one of the mornings when I have to get a tow, because the battery is dead, having poured its life-blood into the direction indicator, signalling bravely, and without any purpose whatever, the intention of an empty car to turn left, in a garage, from dusk till dawn.

But there is no purpose in going into this elaborate matter for the benefit of Neville and Gwen. Neither of them seem mechanically minded, and only one of them understands what I am saying.

I don't, however, have time to go into the matter of the direction indicator at all, because Neville suddenly steps forward and says, ' Here—what's this?''

He picks up what appears to be an iron bar off the road. I am able to identify it immediately as one of the chromium plated strips which go along my running-boards, lending the drop-head coupé an air of speed and grace. It must have fallen off when I crashed into Neville's bumper.

The same idea occurs to Neville.

"Here," he says, "are you the chap what crashed into my bumper . . . ?"

With a shudder, I banish Neville, Gwen, and the whole miserable incident from my mind.

I take up the Automobile Association's new handbook again, and fall to studying their table of metric weights and measures.

I ignore the page which contains the information about the Highways Act of 1835.

A pursuit vehicle like mine, with a self-actuating indicator, is not the stuff *those* dreams are made on.

The Road
by T. E. Lawrence

Here this book, for once, breaks its rule: that it is about motor-cars. But rarely has the love of man for speed, for the open road, for the engine that transports him, been more sharply expressed than in this description by T. E. Lawrence — Lawrence of Arabia — of a race between a motor-cycle and an aeroplane. At this point the worlds of two wheels and four overlap. The extract comes from 'The Mint' which Lawrence published under the name of J. H. Ross while he was trying to hide himself in the R.A.F. with the rank of aircraftsman. Later he became T. E. Shaw. He was killed, of course, riding his motor-cycle, on May 19, 1935; he was still in the service.

Left: *Lawrence, alias Shaw, as an aircraftman in the R.A.F. astride the kind of motor-cycle which inspired his writing in 'The Mint'. This picture was taken in 1927.*

The extravagance in which my surplus emotion expressed itself lay on the road. So long as roads were tarred blue and straight; not hedged; and empty and dry, so long I was rich. Nightly I'd run up from the hangar, upon the last stroke of work, spurring my tired feet to be nimble. The very movement refreshed them, after the day-long restraint of service. In five minutes my bed would be down, ready for the night: in four more I was in breeches and puttees, pulling on my gauntlets as I walked over to my bike, which lived in a garage-hut, opposite. Its tyres never wanted air, its engine had a habit of starting at second kick: a good habit, for only by frantic plunges upon the starting pedal could my puny weight force the engine over the seven atmospheres of its compression.

Boanerges' first glad roar at being alive again nightly jarred the huts of Cadet College into life. "There he goes, the noisy ——," someone would say enviously in every flight. It is part of an airman's profession to be knowing with engines: and a thoroughbred engine is our undying satisfaction. The camp wore the virtue of my Brough like a flower in its cap. Tonight Tug and Dusty came to the step of our hut to see me off. "Running down to Smoke, perhaps?" jeered Dusty; hitting at my regular game of London and back for tea on fine Wednesday afternoons.

Boa is a top-gear machine, as sweet in that as most single-cylinders in middle. I chug lordly past the guard-room and through the speed limit at no more than sixteen. Round the bend, past the farm, and the way straightens. Now for it. The engine's final development is fifty-two horse-power. A miracle that all this docile strength waits behind one tiny lever for the pleasure of my hand.

Another bend: and I have the honour of one of England's straightest and fastest roads. The burble of my exhaust unwound like a long cord behind me. Soon my speed snapped it, and I heard only the cry of the wind which my battering head split and fended aside. The cry rose with my speed to a shriek: while the air's coldness streamed like two jets of iced water into my dissolving eyes. I screwed them to slits, and focused my sight 200 yards ahead of me on the empty mosaic of the tar's gravelled undulations.

Like arrows the tiny flies pricked my

cheeks: and sometimes a heavier body, some house-fly or beetle, would crash into face or lips like a spent bullet. A glance at the speedometer: seventy-eight. Boanerges is warming up. I pull the throttle right open, on the top of the slope, and we swoop flying across the dip, and up-down up-down the switch-back beyond: the weighty machine launching itself like a projectile with a whirr of wheels into the air at the take-off of each rise, to land lurchingly with such a snatch of the driving chain as jerks my spine like a rictus.

Once we so fled across the evening light, with the yellow sun on my left, when a huge shadow roared just over-head. A Bristol Fighter, from White-wash Villas, our neighbour aerodrome, was banking sharply round. I checked speed an instant to wave: and the slip-stream of my impetus snapped my arm and elbow astern, like a raised flail. The pilot pointed down the road towards Lincoln. I sat hard in the saddle, folded back my ears and went away after him, like a dog after a hare. Quickly we drew abreast, as the impulse of his dive to my level exhausted itself.

The next mile of road was rough. I braced my feet into the rests, thrust with my arms, and clenched my knees on the tank till its rubber grips goggled under my thighs. Over the first pot-hole Boanerges screamed in surprise, its mud-guard bottoming with a yawp upon the tyre. Through the plunges of the next ten seconds I clung on, wedging my gloved hand in the throttle lever so that no bump should close it and spoil our speed. Then the bicycle wrenched side-ways into three long ruts: it swayed dizzily, wagging its tail for thirty awful yards. Out came the clutch, the engine raced freely: Boa checked and straight-ened his head with a shake, as a Brough should.

The bad ground was passed and on the new road our flight became birdlike. My head was blown out with air so that my ears had failed and we seemed to whirl soundlessly between the sun-gilt stubble fields. I dared, on a rise, to slow imperceptibly and glance sideways into the sky. There the Bif was, 200 yards and more back. Play with the fellow? Why not? I slowed to ninety: signalled with my hand for him to overtake. Slowed ten more: sat up. Over he rattled. His passenger, a helmeted and goggled grin, hung out of the cockpit

reasonable living by writing about golf and sensible enough to remain a bachelor, so my thoughts turned naturally towards owning a 'proper' car. How I came to be acquainted with it I do not remember but my 'attention was drawn', as they say in the libel actions, to a superb machine, of which most people had never heard, namely the Hudson Terraplane 8. I have always had a weakness for what are now called 'convertibles' and this was an open four-seater. Furthermore, it was a beautiful opalescent light blue, which all my cars have been from that day to this. I am not sure, but I believe the Terraplane 8 represented almost the first example of the 'power-weight ratio' in a standard car, i.e. the marriage of a light shell-like body to an immensely powerful engine. At any rate it would accelerate from 0 to 60 m.p.h. in 13 seconds, a not unremarkable performance even today, more than 30 years later, and once it accelerated two golf balls out of a quite deep cubby hole into my lap. It would also do 3 m.p.h. in top gear and a popular trick was to get it going at about 80 m.p.h., then take one's foot off, let the speed die down, and eventually get out and have it follow along at walking pace, like a dog on a lead. This never failed to impress and entertain.

At last, however, the time came for my old friend and me to part company and I sold it for a song. It was with mixed feelings, therefore, that I saw it a year or two later, spick and span and apparently in splendid order, in the car park at a tournament at Wentworth. I naturally left a note in it, asking after its health and incidentally how much did its owner pay for it, but was disappointed to get no reply.

Thirteen years later in a night club in Honolulu I was introduced to a reddish-haired soldier of fortune called Hanson, who was flying transport planes into Tokio, so he told me, for Sabena. He apologised for not answering my note. "I was the chap who bought your Terraplane," he said.

I suppose the best car I ever owned was a ten-year-old 1937 Morris 8 open tourer, which I bought after the war. This maid-of-all-work plied between Chelsea and our cottage at Nettlebed, loaded like a three-tonner, and once carried up Watlington Hill four adults, two children, two suitcases, two bi-cycles, and the bull terrier. It was at the crossing between Grays Inn Road and Theobalds Road, at the busiest time of the morning, that smoke began to pour from the bonnet. I opened it up and for want of a better weapon started banging at the flames with one of the front seats. A great multitude at once assembled. Not less than a dozen people came up and said, "You're on fire!" "What the hell do you think I think I'm on?" I began to reply. At last one with rather more sense said: "Would you like me to send for the fire brigade?"

A few minutes later, with the police now having to control the crowds, there came the clanging of distant bells and round the corner dashed what I still think must have been the biggest appliance in the whole of the British Empire. A gigantic ladder, protruding far over the head of the driver, came to rest towering over my poor little car. A fireman got slowly down and, with a very small extinguisher and a single very small hiss, ruined the spectators' morning and what was left of the Morris 8.

It was in about 1950, with the roads beginning to fill up and motoring destined clearly to be reduced to a matter of getting from A to B, that I decided, deliberately and with my eyes open, to commit a final act of folly. I would own, before it was too late, one of the last of the Gentlemen's Motors. My eye fell on a 1937 drophead Lagonda and the fact that I was introduced to it by Patrick Campbell should alone have been sufficient warning. It was a "d-d-elicate shade of d-d-duck-egg blue," he said, and that settled it. No sooner had I paid the cheque than oil began emerging from everywhere and soon I discovered that one firm had a monopoly of the remaining spares. Never mind. The Duck-Egg Blue was indeed a Gentleman's Motor. Its patrician lines made it an object both of beauty and of envy and what it would have done, had it collided with one of the 'family saloons' of today, I shudder to think.

I have, however, a shrewd idea. The Surrey or Sussex reader may be familiar with the Alfold crossroads, near Loxwood, between Guildford and Horsham, in the centre of which an A.A. box stood on a triangle of grass. I was returning one night in a blinding snowstorm, peering through the half-moon cleared on the windscreen, when the acute left hand bend took me by surprise. I turned the wheel sharply but too late. At perhaps 25 m.p.h. the Duck-Egg Blue passed serenely forward on to the grass and a dozen yards later pulled up, its headlights shining and the engine continuing with its steady, deep-throated "P-rr-m, P-rr-m, P-rr-m", as though waiting for further orders. In the intervening period, however, though without any sense of physical impact, there had been a sound as though of someone crushing a large empty matchbox.

It had been easy enough to see where the people had sprung from in Theobalds Road. From what quarter a crowd of about twenty could spring instantly from nowhere at an obscure country crossing in pitch darkness and a blinding snowstorm I still have no idea, but there they were, uttering the usual fatuous comment, "Bin an accident?" Among them came the A.A. man himself, who, it turned out, lived in a cottage nearby. He flashed his torch on the bits and pieces which but a few minutes ago had been his box. "Perhaps, with luck," I said brightly, "the telephone is intact." It did not take us long to find out. Alas, the back wheel must have passed directly over it and there it was, like a pancake, flatter than any telephone can ever have been squashed before. The usual courtesies having been exchanged, I got one or two of the lads of the village to give us a shove up the snow-covered bank and we proceeded on our way. In the morning I examined the Duck-Egg Blue. Not a single scratch revealed that only a few hours ago it had passed nonchalantly through an A.A. Box and reduced it to firewood. Now there is a beautiful new Box at the Alfold Crossing, to which I never fail to lift my hat in passing. I notice, however, that it stands respectfully out of the way, hard again the distant hedge.

Finally, about eight years later, I found myself saying to Mr. Bob Scruton, of Lincoln Cars, "I come down to the Great West Road and take delivery of a car like this every 31 years." This time it is the Duck-Egg Blue Ford Mustang, indistinguishable almost in character from the Terraplane but with refinements which can make it, for all its fearsome performance, a real Old Man's Car. Its acceleration, it is true, is limited only by the grip of the tyres on the road and it does its 'ton' with the greatest of ease.

On the other hand you drive it with one foot; manipulate its power steering with one forefinger and thumb, the little finger delicately extended, as at the vicarage tea party; and, oh blessed virtue to us last lovers of open-air motoring, it opens and shuts its hood—sorry, 'top'—at the press of a button. In 10,000 miles I have only opened its bonnet—sorry, 'hood'—once, and that was to see what the engine was like. I can only say that there seemed to be an awful lot of it.

Incidentally, having made it go 100 m.p.h., I took my foot off and waited to see whether, like the Terraplane, it would do 3 m.p.h. in top gear and let me walk along beside it. Alas, I had forgotten about these modern gadgets and felt a trifle foolish when, being 'automatic', it came, of course, to a standstill and just sat there waiting for me to tell it what to do next.

Musical rides
or you too can learn to play the gear-box
by John Dankworth

There is, for some, a music in the sound of cars; sustained chords from Ferraris, characteristic screams from B.R.Ms. John Dankworth has his own approach to cars and music. He is among Europe's very finest musicians, led the best full-time jazz orchestra Britain has known, and still produces jazz records which win massive acclaim

from American magazines like 'Down Beat'. He extends his range constantly—playing with the London Philharmonic or Yehudi Menuhin, writing handfuls of excellent film scores (including those for 'Darling' and 'Modesty Blaise'). He is married to Cleo Laine, a wonderful jazz singer, and a performer of lieder too.

It all began in 1953 as my Jowett Javelin somersaulted through the French evening air (and I through the hole where its windscreen once was) and we landed upside down with a thud—it disconcertingly near a large tree trunk, I in a ditch some 40 feet further on.

Thus was born my interest in driving. At this rather shattering watershed of my driving experience, I decided that the weak link in my driving knowledge this incident had exposed—love of birds and beasts, and a consequent attempt to avoid a chicken in my path—could only be eliminated by a serious study of driving methods.

My ownership of cars had started some seven years earlier with the purchase of a 1931 Singer Junior Saloon, which I housed in a garage six doors away from me in the suburban avenue where I lived. One day I garaged it and the engine caught fire. Embarrassed, I knocked at the door of the neighbour who owned the garage and asked for a bucket of water. She obliged, but her curiosity grew as during the ensuing four or five minutes I asked for about ten more buckets. She asked what was wrong and I told her. Alarmed, she went to fetch Jake, a large American G.I.

Jake was undoubtedly the most relaxed person I had ever met. He gazed for fully two minutes at the conflagration before he leaned on the garage doorway, looked into my eyes. "Son, never put water on a gasoline fire," he drawled. He repeated this slowly, several times, then moved sluggishly to an old blanket and, in one great heave, placed it over the blazing engine, reducing it to a withering puff of smoke in seconds. A lesson well and memorably learned.

My Singer Junior and I parted company after a brief acquaintanceship with

a trolleybus in Seven Sisters Road in Tottenham. But it was a week's enforced stay in France, with my wounded family around me after my acrobatics in the Jowett, which made me decide that I really must drive properly. On my return to England I formed a large orchestra and thereafter 95 per cent of my touring was done at the wheel of my new car, a Ford Zephyr.

Thirty-five thousand miles a year was about the average. The ice-blackened roads of England were my skid pans. The closing stages of my rallies were the last hectic miles to an elusive dance hall or an obscure theatre.

Motor associations' warnings to avoid using the roads were of no use to me; I just packed a shovel in the boot next to my saxophone. And on nights when we were caught without shovels, the bowler-hat mutes of my trumpet-players were useful to shovel grit under the rear wheels—as well as to produce unusual sounds from the brass section.

Neither was the weather always the chief enemy. At Suez-time I remember fitting a special carburettor to my Renault Dauphine, increasing tyre pressures, and coasting half the way to Amesbury in Wiltshire in order to achieve 73 miles on a gallon of petrol to get to a job. But the hundreds and thousands of miles in all weathers gave me lots of opportunities to practise and improve my driving skill, and some years later George Eyles of the Institute of Advanced Motorists was able to pronounce me competent to join that worthy band of road-users.

Cars very often have special significance to a musician. When I defended a speeding summons in court myself, the police prosecutor asked me whether I was watching my speedometer at the

time of the offence. After I had replied in the negative, he asked me how I knew I was not exceeding the limit. I told him that my gear-box sounded A-flat in top at 30 miles an hour, and I knew by the note that my speed was not higher at the time in question. The court laughed disbelievingly and fined me £10, although the press coverage next day was worth a few thousand.

Gear-boxes are the most usual source of musical sound. I once knew a drummer who could play the National Anthem on the cogs of his vintage Bentley gear-box by using the lever without the clutch, and revving the engine according to requirements. Windscreen wipers are a source of melodic as well as rhythmic inspiration when the wipers have a slightly noisy electric motor. Bossa novas are usually suggested. But suction wipers, on which one can vary the speed by altering the throttle opening, are very amusing things to keep in time with the music on the car radio by accelerating and decelerating—on a deserted road, of course!

With such important appointments to keep, and with such valuable cargoes of people and instruments—my vehicles have delivered things as precious as Sarah Vaughan and Yehudi Menuhin (complete with Stradivarius)—cars just have to be reliable. Most of them are, especially French cars, which even when stricken by some minor ailment generally achieve a spontaneous recovery.

But not always. One sunny Saturday afternoon I was stranded at my own Bedfordshire home with a journey of 40 miles to a nearby American Air Force base to cover without a car. I eventually managed it by borrowing an Italian moped from my housekeeper. I tied my saxophone in a canvas bag on the carrier and wore a cloth cap and the white evening suit—complete with cycle clips —which I was to wear in front of my band that night.

I tried to sneak into the camp so they didn't see me, but it was not to be. A large banner over the archway of the N.C.O.s' Club proclaimed: "Welcome Johnny Dankworth". I don't think they expected a Cadillac, but the sight of me certainly was a surprise. I explained later; I'm sure they didn't believe me.

After a freezing midnight journey in the white suit on the return, I managed to recover enough next morning to take

t, *Wednesday, July 15, 1964* 15

DANKWORTH SPEEDS ON WRONG NOTE

£10 A-FLAT FINE

DAILY TELEGRAPH REPORTER

JOHNNY DANKWORTH the jazz musician, said in Bedford magistrates court yesterday that he can tell the speed of his M.G. sports car by the musical note of its engine.

He said he heard the note A-flat when he passed a radar check in M...

the moped down to the local garage and magnanimously fill the tank in return for the loan of the machine. The total came to 2s 4d.

When one changes cars as often as I do, one cannot help noticing that one becomes regarded as a different person in each successive car. In an MG one gets glances from female pedestrians and other car occupants usually reserved for wolfish bachelors-about-town; in a Mini one is regarded either as a madman or a senile idiot; while in an Aston Martin one is treated with politeness, good road manners and the sort of special attention that one could scarcely believe existed as the driver of a less expensive car.

Likewise, one's manners tend to adjust to the car; one tends to be cheeky driving a Mini in the morning, yet the driving seat of a DB5 that same afternoon can transform one into a courteous, benevolent and strictly-to-the-book driver.

But all cars have in common a strange illusion of privacy, in spite of the fact that one is surrounded by large windows in every direction. I was rather taken off-balance once when introduced to a man's wife at a cocktail party. "I've always wanted to meet you," she chirped, "ever since I saw you picking your nose at the traffic lights in Tottenham Court Road".

I am not a snob. All the same, I hope it wasn't in the Aston!

Opposite page: Dankworth with Aston Martin DB5 outside Nether Hall, his home in Bedfordshire—basically eighteenth century Georgian. The story of the musical-plea-that-failed is contained, in brief, in the newspaper tear-out (above).

James Leasor — seen on the previous page with his Cord roadster — is author, businessman, car-lover. After coming down from Oxford he was a 'Daily Express' reporter and feature-writer. He has written well over a dozen books, fiction and non-fiction, among which 'The One That Got Away' was made into a very successful movie. Another major project — a series of suspense novels involving Dr. Jason Love, who of course drives a Cord — may make even more impact in the cinema. The first film-of-the-book, 'Where The Spies Are', starring David Niven as Love and based on Leasor's 'Passport to Oblivion', was well received.

I remember, I remember, not only the house where I was born, but, more important to the old-car buff, the exact time and place when I first saw the car that has ever since appealed to me more than any other — the 812 supercharged Cord roadster.

As any psychiatrist knows (and at the drop of a fiver will tell you) the car with which the enthusiast embarks upon his most lasting love affair tends to be one that impressed him when he was at a most impressionable time of life: puberty, what else.

The moment I fell in love with that most expensive and intractable mistress, the 812, I was walking to Blackfriars Underground station from the City of London School on Victoria Embankment.

It was an autumn evening in 1937, young Leasor's work was done, and he was in no hurry whatever to catch an early train, for what lay ahead but homework and maybe *Monday Night at Eight*?

So, when a set of garage doors opened below street level in Unilever House, next to the school, I waited to see who or what was coming out.

One second, the drive up from this basement garage was empty; the next, it was completely filled by a bronze monster, bonnet blunt as a blue-nosed whale.

Four glittering chromium exhaust pipes plunged into teardrop wings. A young man, Icarus in a trilby hat and a camel-hair coat, sat nonchalantly at the cream steering wheel. Before him, the dashboard lights glittered briefly like a box of jade splinters, as green as my own envy. Then, with a woof from the exhaust, this vision swept along the Embankment in a glow of twin tail lights, red as lobsters' eyes.

Such was my first sight of a Cord; I have always remembered it, for the car represented all that seemed infinitely desirable, infinitely remote on that chilly evening. It stood for the open road, the open roadhouse, and away again over the hills into the everlasting sunset. How much more desirable than my Science IV homework with a batch of questions about Boyle's Law $(P_1V_1 = K)$ in my satchel!

More than a car, the Cord seemed a symbol of the good life, a key to freedom. Of course, at £995 in those days, it remained a fairly expensive and exclusive key. There were so few in circulation that I can list where I saw them. A roadster outside an undertaker's shop in Erith, Kent, a year later; a saloon in Bombay when my troopship docked there in 1943; another in Penang at the end of the war; a fourth in a showroom in Great Portland Street in 1946.

In the early 1950s I also inspected the late Amy Johnson's blue Cord roadster which was for sale on a bomb-site used car lot in South London. The dealer wanted £425 for it, but the car seemed so enormous, so horrifyingly unpractical in that grey, mercifully forgotten world of austerity and furnished rooms off the Cromwell Road, that I did no more than inspect it.

Age and the infinite, remorseless mechanical complexity of the beasts had thinned their numbers, but to the true believer this only made them more desirable. In 1959 or thereabouts, when I owned a house with a spare garage, I felt the virus infecting me again. I began to seek a lasting cure — a Cord for myself, not to use every day, but, as the Americans say, as a 'fun car'.

I advertised intermittently and unsuccessfully in various places, and then put a small advertisement in the London *Evening Standard*. Some weeks later, I received a reply from Australia. It was written by a ship's engineer who explained that he had seen my advertisement in Sydney; he owned a Cord roadster which was currently lying at Chandlers Ford in Hampshire. (All these huge old mastodonic vehicles are like ships in that they always *lie*; they are never simply *at* anywhere.)

I found an excuse to drive down to inspect the car. It bulged out of the garage, an enormous bloated pumpkin in maroon. As with most Cords, the

144

claim was that it had been owned by a celebrity; in this case, Walt Disney. The engine was partly dismantled; pistons as big as chimney pots sulked at the bottom of enormous bores. Valves the size of artichokes rested thankfully in their seats.

We agreed a price, and two friends who own a garage went down one Sunday intending to patch up the engine and drive the Cord to my home on trade plates.

In this intention they were over-optimistic, for, once reassembled, the engine declined to turn over on the starter, and they had to tow the car away. This proved an interesting 100-mile journey through the traffic of a summer Sunday afternoon. The tow rope broke six times.

Finally, it was stabled in my garage. Every time I opened the doors I smelled again the composite incense all old-car hunters know; the sad, nostalgic amalgam of ancient oil, tired leather, rust, damp and mildew. The task of restoring the Cord also produced some convincing reasons for the collapse of the Cord empire before the war. Every mechanical part was almost impossible to reach. Bolts had threads of unknown measurements; no part from any other car seemed to fit the Cord; and the more that was removed, the more there remained to remove.

Eventually Lord Montagu graciously accepted the car into his Midland Motor Museum at Measham to renovate it for me.

I took it back again before all the work was done, because, in an attempt to justify the expense of this mechanical anachronism, I had given a Cord roadster to Dr. Jason Love in *Passport to Oblivion*, and the car had to go through its paces in the film based on that book.

Writing about this one day, I mentioned that I thought I owned the only roadster left in this country. At once, a reader corrected me; he had seen another outside a garage in Staffordshire. I was glad to be proved wrong, for this second car was in such good condition that I bought it.

The garage reconditioned the car for me and the finishing touches were done by that expert restorer of antique automobiles, Alan Goodyear, of Rickmansworth. Now, at 70 m.p.h., with the tachometer registering 2,000 revs, the only sound is the swish of the tyres on the road—and the level of the petrol falling in the tank. The Cord, by the way, is a thirsty beast; 10 miles to the gallon with a following wind is the most one can expect.

With its original Motorola radio, no larger than a small suitcase, two amber-lensed Marchal spot-lamps, a Grebel signpost lamp and the long-throated horns of the era, the Cord is now everything I longed for as a boy before the war. In this lies the car's fascination; the realisation of a dream in which desire does not outstrip performance. For this we endure temperament that we could not stand at any price from any other car.

Many must agree with me, for of the 2,320 Cords produced in 1936 and 1937, when the original company went out of business, about 2,000 are still running, largely in the States, in the care of members of the Auburn-Cord-Duesenberg Club.

The Cord is a male car, blatant as a bull. It is impossible for a man not to be moved, either to admiration or disdain, by its blunt, aggressive coffin-nose, devoid of chromium, mascot or other frippery. You either dig the beast or you don't, and certainly, to an America on the dole, the car must have represented the absolute in motoring luxury; a vision of the Waldorf Towers from the methylated mists of Skid Row.

The Cord offered built-in one-upmanship and, with this, revolutionary design; advertisements played skilfully on this natural wish to be envied. "A champion never pushes people around," they declared. "Any driver that passes the supercharged Cord knows he does so only with the Cord driver's permission."

Front-wheel drive is now universally fashionable and acceptable, from the Mini, through the Citroen to the Toronado—the Sixties' equivalent of the Cord in its size and exclusiveness. But in the early Thirties, although it had been tried in the States by Ruxton and the Cord L.29, it was still too *avant-garde* for general acceptance.

Other Cord innovations were to use sound-proofed bodies of chassisless construction, also now virtually universal. They had no running-boards or outside door hinges, and the floors were flat. Overall height was low for its time— 4 ft. 10 in. on the convertible; power was

145

correspondingly high (170 b.h.p. with the Schwitzer-Cummins supercharger). The Cord also used a high-beam headlight indicator, three rear lights, rheostat-controlled dashlights, variable speed windscreen-wipers and the famous retractable headlamps, now reintroduced on the Lotus Elan and the Chevrolet Corvette Sting Ray. Maximum speed was 102·27 m.p.h. with acceleration, according to *The Autocar* of the day, "altogether exceptionable and remarkable . . . tremendous".

It *was* all tremendous, but although the car was made (but not designed) by one of the greatest salesmen of the age, Errett Lobban Cord, it offered too much, too soon and too expensively. Like the Phoenix, it had to die to live.

Possibly part of the car's attraction stems from Cord's own personality which symbolises, consciously or unconsciously, a 1930s determination to succeed in a world of dole queues, soup kitchens and slumps. His car was the crystallisation of all this; brash, flashy, but powerful, and with enormous drive.

As things like manners or accent can betray the self-made man, so the car betrayed its origins with irritating little faults—such as an electric gear switch that took seconds to select neutral, oil and water fillers concealed beneath a single flap to save opening the heavy bonnet, but confusing for service station attendants.

Cord the man and Cord the car were the apotheosis of the 1930s. He proved he could make a living while others starved; his car was visible proof of his success.

He began his career as a boy, when he bought up old Model T Fords, resprayed them in gayer colours than the universal black Henry had ordered, and sold them at a profit. After the First World War, as a salesman for Moon cars, he was making 30,000 dollars a year on commission.

Then someone introduced him to the ailing Auburn Car Company in Auburn, Indiana. This company suffered from commercial constipation; it couldn't shift 700 of its own dreary, uninspired products. Cord found a freelance artist to sketch some more exciting models, took the drawings to a board-meeting and talked the directors into giving him a free hand. He cut prices, and, using advertising as his enema, was rid of the ugly old Auburns at miniscule profit in

quick time. In their place he had new models—long, big, bright; like all Cord's cars, a salesman's car—on view at the next New York motor show.

This move coincided with the roaring prosperity of the Twenties. Cord's star soared. He helped it by selling off blocks of Auburn stock when the price was high, then buying back when such huge selling had depressed the market. Soon, largely by stock deals, he swallowed Duesenberg, then America's finest car; Lycoming engines; various body building companies; Stinson Aircraft; the Checker Cab Company; New York Shipbuilding and American Airways.

By 1929 he was a millionaire many times over—and marked the year by producing a car to bear his name—the front-wheel-drive Cord L.29. He sold 5,600—and lost on every one. The car was novel, but the depression killed it. More setbacks followed, but in the early Thirties Cord hired Gordon Buehrig, a professional body-designer of rare talent, to salvage what he could, as soon as he could.

Within a narrow budget, Buehrig did some revamping on the Auburns, but buyers were still rare. Then he came up with a car that had headlamps winding out of the wings and a square bonnet, with horizontal louvres, like a Venetian blind. The result looked like something out of *Things to Come* and Cord was delighted. He had intended that this would be a 'baby' Duesenberg, but he changed his mind and said he'd put his own name on it instead.

As an afterthought, since the first Cord had front-wheel drive, he wanted this to be the same. By the end of 1934 die models were ready, and then Cord lost interest; as with many men of financial genius, his enthusiasms were changeable as the sirocco. The project hibernated and the Cord car empire sank ever more deeply into the red.

The next year, and quite as unexpectedly, Cord changed his mind again. He wanted production, but the late decision meant a race against time and creditors. To collect essential publicity, the new Cord would have to be on view at the New York motor show, opening on November 1. But to be eligible to exhibit a new model, a manufacturer had to have at least 100 units; prototypes were not allowed. There was only one solution—to build 100 cars by hand.

This was also the costliest way, and so every other sort of economy was called for. They used only two dies for the doors, right front and left rear. They formed the window flanges with a cheap pinch weld. They had to make a roof in several pieces and weld them together because they could not afford a big enough press to bang out each roof on its own.

Door and window handles were bought as a job lot from a bankrupt maker, and fitted with huge round plastic knobs to make them look new. Buehrig was given a jumble of unwanted bought-out instruments and designed an aircraft-type panel to hold them. The dials had figures engraved on their glass and fitted in an engine-turned dash, lit with indirect green lights. Out of improvisation, beauty was born; the dash is still unsurpassed by any American design for its functional appearance.

The show cars were ready on time, some with fancy trim and copper plate instead of chrome. Unfortunately, they wouldn't work—the complicated front-wheel-drive transmissions were not ready. So the show cars were pushed on to trucks to carry them to the show—with nothing working under their bonnets. They had engines and gearboxes, but with no gears inside!

In New York, the salesmen were overwhelmed by orders for these sleek, futuristic cars, and promised delivery by Christmas. On November 1 this seemed distant enough to be safe. The promise was kept in that each customer did receive a Cord on December 25—but only a one-thirty-second scale model on a tiny marble slab. Transmissions were still not ready, and it was early spring before the first full-size Cords were delivered.

This could be forgiven, but what proved unforgiveable was that even though they were late, the cars still had teething troubles; engines tended to boil, and dealers in rival makes lost no opportunity in putting in the boot. All the early bugs that can afflict any new model were caught and killed, but too late. The first fire of enthusiasm for the new models gave way to doubts.

In 1936, 1,174 Cords were sold; in the following year, only 1,146. By the end of 1937, Cord admitted defeat, his car empire disintegrated and he moved to Nevada to build another fortune in property and television.

Auburn body dies were shipped to Russia and never heard of again. The Cord dies were used by Hupmobile for their 'Skylark', and then by Graham for their Hollywood coupés. Neither car sold well, for no Cord could ever live by any other name.

Now Glenn Pray, a former schoolmaster from Oklahoma, (who also saw his first Cord when he was a boy), has resurrected the name and the car. Working to a scale of eight-tenths of the original Cord, using a Chevrolet Corvette engine and a Royalite plastic body, he is manufacturing Cord cars again in the States.

But although Glenn Pray's car will be mechanically far superior and infinitely more reliable than its eponym of 30 years ago, it can surely be at best only an interesting mechanical anachronism, a manufactured antique.

To many of us, the Cord belongs to the Thirties, and half our love for it stems from its failings, its shortcomings, for in them we can see our own. The Cord is as much a part of its age as Pratts' High Test, as Ginger Rogers and Fred Astaire, as Croydon airport and beach pyjamas.

It is impossible to transplant this aura and era to the electronic, computerised Mini-world of today. For like any other old champion, the Cord belongs to the time when it was young and on top of the heap, somewhere long ago, halfway between the thunder and the sun.

A likely story
or how I learned to start worrying
after loving the R.R.M.P.W. 2D.S.
by Peter Sellers

'Dr Strangelove', 'What's new Pussycat?', 'The Pink Panther' and so on. Cadillac, Lotus, Mercedes, Lincoln, Aston Martin etc. . . . It would be as exhausting to name all Peter Sellers' films as to list every car he has owned. Let's leave it that he is probably the world's finest character actor and its leading automaniac. "Perfection in one vehicle is impossible to attain," he said once. "The only thing is to have a selection of cars and enjoy the best of each." Pursuing that philosophy, he has had around a hundred cars in the last 15 years or so.

Some he has kept for only half a day. He has said he is "car-crazy". He has been known to wipe mud from a gleaming bonnet with his handkerchief. His passion has cost something approaching a quarter of a million pounds. He is now the sponsor of a racing team using Lotus Formula III cars. Of one of his past loves, a Bristol Viotti, he said: "I fell in love with her at first sight. I was seduced by her good looks and was unable to fight back my desire." Over to Mr Sellers, vintage 1966 . . .

Left: *the unending game of car-loving . . . and this was the stage it had reached for Peter Sellers in December, 1963. He is seen with Mini-Cooper; coachwork by Hooper, interior finish by Rolls-Royce.*

At present I've got:
1 maroon Rolls-Royce Mulliner Park Ward two-door sports.
1 Ferrari Superfast 500.
1 Radford Mini-Cooper S (1275).

Very nice, of course, but I mean, once you've seen 1 maroon Rolls-Royce Mulliner Park Ward two-door sports, you've seen 'em all. What can you do with one, after all? You can drive it, true; but you can drive most things with wheels and an engine. You can paint it some other colour. But it's amazing how quickly an R.R.M.P.W. palls. Before you've had it for long, you're wondering what you ever saw in it.

You almost come to envy the fellers who don't have one. It was good, not having a maroon Mulliner.

But of course, when you haven't got one, what you think to yourself is, it would be nice to have a maroon Rolls-Royce Mulliner Park Ward two-door sports, wouldn't it. And before you know what's happening, along you go to the showroom, and say, "This Dong Feng," you say, "made in the People's Republic of China, and acquired by me from the proprietor of the Shanghai Restaurant, East Finchley, as the price of silence when I threatened to report his Fried Lobster Rolls to the Public Health Inspector, is all very well; but I rather fancy myself in a maroon Rolls-Royce Mulliner Park Ward two-door sports. I don't suppose you've got any in stock?"

The car man then says either yes, or no, or phones for the police. If he says no, that's it. If he phones for the police this story, already involved, will get right out of control. Let's say the man says yes.

"Yes," says the car man, as agreed. "As a matter of fact we have somewhat over-ordered. This was due to a clerical error: the man responsible has since been severely defrocked. But I wonder, sir, if you wouldn't prefer a Ferrari Superfast 500, sir?"

"And what," you query, surprised, "makes you wonder that?"

"We have something of a surfeit of those too, sir, as a matter of fact. Ferrari Superfasts are ten a penny in this place."

"I'll take ten!"

"Not er—not literally, sir, of course. But seriously, don't you think the Ferrari might be your cup of tea?"

"Well," you confess, "it might at that." After all, why not? Life is short, and Ferrari Superfasts are faster.

"It's no invalid carriage, is the Ferrari Superfast, sir," says the man, turning on the sales talk.

"No," you muse. You decide to take it, anyway. "I'll take it," you announce. "But what I really had in mind, as I intimated at the beginning, was a Rolls-Royce Mulliner Park Ward two-door sports."

"Certainly," says the man. "I'm just getting round to that. You'd look very well in one too, sir, if I may say so. But you'll want something a little more relaxed for the shopping. I would suggest for you, sir, this Radford Mini-Cooper S (1275)."

"Yes, yes, yes," you say, "I'll take it. But I insist on one of those Rolls-Royce Mulliners. A maroon one. My wardrobe won't be complete without it."

"You mean a maroon Rolls-Royce Mulliner Park Ward two-door sports?" says the feller.

"You took the words out of my mouth."

"How about that one, then, sir?" The feller stands aside. You stare at the vehicle indicated. In disbelief.

"You mean you call *that* a maroon Rolls-Royce Mulliner?" you gasp. Readers will recognise this as the first shot in a heroic attempt to cast nasturtiums and get the old R.R.M.P.W. cheap.

"Why—yes."

"Well," you snort, "I suppose there's one born every minute."

"You mean a maroon Rolls-Royce—?"

"No, I mean a gullible fool, sir. You've been had, haven't you, my good fellow. That's no more a maroon Rolls-Royce Mulliner two-door sports than I am. And you can see I'm not."

"No, sir?"

"No, sir." This is going well. "It's sky blue. What's the matter with you? Colour blind? And another thing. I can see only one door from where I'm standing."

By this time the wretched man is too confused to suggest that you come round and have a look the other side.

"Come round and have a look the other side," the feller says, contrary to expectation.

"All right," you concede. "All right, cleversticks, you win. I'll buy it." The attempt at casting nasturtiums has failed. "You'll take a cheque, of course?"

Fellers will always take cheques if it's over £10,000.

"No," says the feller.

"In that case, my good man, put it on the slate please."

The man eyes you askance—difficult for a feller as cross-eyed as he—and indicates a little notice saying "No tick". This, frankly, is the time to take the appropriate old school tie out of your pocket and tie it round your middle to stop your trousers falling down.

"Now look old chap," you tell the feller, lowering your voice to the ground, where you can both see it and it can't get away, "the fact is, I've had a spot of bad luck recently. An uncle of mine who went to Canada when I was a nipper seems to have died—"

"I'm sorry," the man says decently.

"My uncle," you continue, "happens to have left me, in his will, seventeen million pounds—so go and boil your head!"

The man is, naturally, impressed, and decides, on his own initiative, to waive all the usual formalities.

He aims for your midriff in a brave attempt to spit you on his fist.

"Whump!" he goes.

"You can't do that!" you gasp.

"No?" says the feller.

"No," you confirm.

"Thrunk," goes the chap, catching you a good one on the point of the stomach.

"I was brought up," you say, as soon as you can, "in the goods lift, where they taught me to believe the customer is always right."

"Ker-plow," goes the feller.

"My dear old—"

"Wham!" goes the feller. "Pow. Zunk. Biff."

"Good day to you, sir," you pant. "You will, I fancy, be hearing from my solicitors."

"Boff!"

It is about now that you lose your

150

temper. This was inevitable.

"I hope you get piles!" you explode suddenly. "You can keep your mouldy old maroon Rolls-Royce Mulliner! I wouldn't have one thrown at me."

You duck skilfully as the vehicle hurtles overhead.

"And as for your lousy Ferrari Super-fast," you rasp, bitingly, "I wouldn't can a sardine in it!"

The feller is eyeing you abashed.

"And I don't suppose your blown-up, supercharged Mini," you cry, warming to your theme, "could overtake a one-legged aubergine!"

By now a crowd has gathered and the management, fearing a scene, intervenes.

"Is there anything wrong, sir?" enquires the management.

"Is there anything wrong, sir?" you echo. "Yes, I'll jolly well say there's something wrong. I came in here, sir, to buy a car, sir. And the best this feller of yours can offer is that!" (pointing to the maroon thing). "And this!" (pointing to the Ferrari). "And that!" (you indicate the Mini). "Well, you can't fool all of the people all of the time, you know. You've been landed, haven't you? Who's going to buy that old load of scrap? I said, scrap?"

The management stares at you in astonishment.

"I for one," you continue, "wouldn't give a brass farthing for the lot! On second thoughts, that is my offer."

"Done!" cries the management delightedly, never having dared to think the matter would end so cheaply.

"I haven't got one on me."

"Later, later," says the management. "Any time."

And that is how I come to have, at the time of writing:

    1 maroon R.R.M.P.W. 2-D.S.
    1 Ferrari Superfast 500.
and 1 Radford Mini-Cooper S (1275).

Above: *more cars from the Sellers collection. The Ferrari (opposite page) and the Rolls (top right) are the ones he writes about in this article. But the Mercedes-Benz is one of his discards.*

151

A clutch of poets

The poets of our century haven't, as a body, been hooked by machines on two wheels or four—though even so austere a figure as T. S. Eliot did have one very evocative line in his Choruses from The Rock: "...And daughters ride away on casual pillions". But the motor-car still gets into verse, often surprisingly. Who would have thought that John Masefield would have devoted more than sixty resounding stanzas to a journey in a car? Less surprising is the way that pop-song versifiers have bent the automobile to their ends; the two examples given in this selection of verse that features cars could have been multiplied many times over, especially in the 1960s.

John Betjeman

The Hillman is waiting, the light's in the hall,
The pictures of Egypt are bright on the wall,
My sweet, I am standing beside the oak stair
And there on the landing's the light on your hair.

By roads 'not adopted', by woodlanded ways,
She drove to the club in the late summer haze,
Into nine-o'clock Camberley, heavy with bells
And mushroomy, pine-woody, evergreen smells.

Miss Joan Hunter Dunn, Miss Joan Hunter Dunn,
I can hear from the car-park the dance has begun.
Oh! full Surrey twilight! importunate band!
Oh! strongly adorable tennis-girl's hand!

Around us are Rovers and Austins afar,
Above us, the intimate roof of the car,
And here on my right is the girl of my choice,
With the tilt of her nose and the chime of her voice.

And the scent of her wrap, and the words never said,
And the ominous, ominous dancing ahead.
We sat in the car park till twenty to one
And now I'm engaged to Miss Joan Hunter Dunn.
                    From *A Subaltern's Love Song.*

The slow drive home by motor-car
    A heavy Rover Landaulette,
Through Welwyn, Hatfield, Potters Bar,
    Tweed and cigar smoke, gloom and wet.
                    From *Hertfordshire.*

Morris Bishop

I got pocketed behind 7X-3824;
He was making 65, but I can do a little more.
I crowded him on the curves, but I couldn't get past,
And on the straightaways there was always some truck coming fast.
Then we got to the top of a mile-long incline
And I edged her out to the left, a little over the white line,
And ahead was a long grade with construction at the bottom,
And I said to the wife, "Now by golly I got'm!"
I bet I did 85 going down the long grade,
And I braked her down hard in front of the barricade,
And I swung in ahead of him and landed fine
Behind 9W-7679.   *Ambition.*

Right: *few people realised that the heroin of Betjeman's most celebrated poem, Miss Joan Hunter Dunn, really existed until in 1965 sh was rediscovered and interviewed by an English journalist, Pete Crookston. She was photographed taking tea in the garde of her house in the Home Counties—pine trees in the driv and croquet hoops on the lawn. With her are her sons, (left to right) Andrew, Edwar and Charles. The Hillman of the poem is the car on the left, and the Rover of 'Hertford-shire' is on the right.*

Betjeman is, of course, the recorder of English bourgeois life: of suburbia, the stockbroker belt and all that. Naturally, the cars he mentions are those which have an aura of bourgeois respectability about them (see Maurice Wiggin's essay on page 168) and to which the middle classes extend a genteel warmth, if not love. Austin, Hillman, Rover—sound, solemn cars. Mr. Bishop's poem is 1950-'New Yorker' vintage, but the predicament it laughs at is now pretty universal.

Harry Graham

63

I COLLIDED with some 'trippers'
    In my swift De Dion Bouton;
Squashed them out as flat as kippers,
    Left them *aussi mort que mouton.*
What a nuisance 'trippers' are!
I must now repaint the car.

Inconvenience

Ogden Nash

They who make automobiles,
They hate wheels.
They look on wheels as limbs were looked on by Victorian
    aunts,
They conceal them in skirts and pants.
Wheels are as hard to descry as bluebirds in Lower
    Slobovia,
The only way you can see a wheel complete nowadays is
    to look up at it while it is running ovia.
They who make automobiles,
They are ashamed of wheels,
Their minds are on higher things,
Their minds are on wings.
The concept of earthly vision is one that their designers
    stray from;
Currently, a successful parking operation is one that you
    can walk away from.
Unremittingly the manufacturers strive
To provide turnip-heads with cars that will do a hundred
    and twenty miles an hour where the speed limit is
    fifty-five.
The station wagon that shuttles the children between
    home and school is hopelessly kaput
Unless two hundred and thirty horses are tugging at the
    accelerator under Mummy's foot.
I don't like wings, I like wheels;
I like automobiles.

154

I don't want to ride to the station or the office in j[e]
    propelled planes,
All I want is a windshield wiper that really wipes t[he]
    windshield, and some simple method of putting [on]
    chains.

Detroit, Spare That Whe[el]

e. e. cummings

she being Brand

-new; and you
know consequently a
little stiff i was
careful of her and (having

thoroughly oiled the universal
joint tested my gas felt of
her radiator made sure her springs were O.

K.) i went right to it flooded-the-carburetor cranked he[r]

up,slipped the
clutch (and then somehow got into reverse she
kicked what
the hell) next
minute i was back in neutral tried and

again slo-wly;bare,ly nudg. ing (my

lev-er Right-
oh and her gears being in
A 1 shape passed
from low through
second-in-to-high like
greasedlightning) just as we turned the corner of Divini[ty]

avenue i touched the accelerator and give

her the juice,good

                        (it
was the first ride and believe i we was
happy to see how nice she acted right up to
the last minute coming back down by the Public
Gardens i slammed on
the

internalexpanding
&
externalcontracting
brakes Bothatonce and

brought allof her tremB
-ling
to a:dead.

stand-
;Still)

she being Brand

John Masefield

We halted near Newport: the drive had gone slowly
From press on the road, and the way little known,
Now here nothing passed, but a grocer's van solely
That ran by for Shifnal and left us alone.

Most sweet was the hot summer drowse as we rested,
But Shifnal to Oxford meant many miles still.
I went through her spark-plugs and cleaned them and
    tested,
And climbed back aboard and went on with a will.

Two miles beyond Shifnal, the road gangs were tarring,
The width of the roadway was wet with hot tar,
A driver sped by us and sent it all starring
In black flicks and splashes all over the car.

Mist clung here and there as the summer day ended,
We drew near to Severn, but now on the road
With barking of sheep dogs the milking-cows wended
From meadow to byre and often we slowed.

By the red sandstone rocks under Bridgnorth the olden,
By Bowman, we went, through the fast dying day,
As we neared Kidderminster the sunset was golden,
When the car ceased to run there, the twilight was grey.

After halting and working, the engine re-started;
We drove across Bromsgrove, through Redditch and on.
The day (and the joy of the drive) had departed,
And all save the effort to end it was gone.

At Alcester, we passed gipsy caravans going
To camp by some copse on their way to a fair,
A glimpse of lit windows and foreign eyes showing,
And ponies with ears back and yellow teeth bare.

At Stratford we halted to dine at the Arden,
The full night had deepened with stars in the sky.
The oars of the boatmen who rowed past the garden
Made ruffles of glitter go loitering by.

Then on, for the last lap, though aching and dizzy,
The last fifty miles, through the moonless dark hours;
A crowd seemed about me, all talking and busy,
And the road seemed a tunnel deep-burrowed through
    flowers.

And at times all the flowers arched up, tall and splendid,
Like a Gothic church roof in a vault overhead,
And I longed as I drove for the drive to be ended,
And the swift beating engine at peace in its shed.

Long Compton was passed, and the bend in the hollow,
Near Enstone, and still all the way seemed alive
With people loud-talking, all running to follow,
Till the car had more voices than bees in a hive.

Then we drooped towards Woodstock and slowed to go
    through it,
Past the old English house where the Black Prince was
    born,
I thought of the maxim—seek peace and ensue it;
I longed for my peace as a starved horse for corn.

But mixed with the longing was rapture of knowing
The four hundred miles that the wheels had whirled by,
The things swiftly seen in the scene swiftly flowing,
The fields and the homes where men struggle and die. . . .
From *The Long Drive*

W. H. Charnock

I knew a man who loved Mercedes
More than liquor, lucre, ladies,
Wore the proud three-pointed star
On tie as well as motorcar,
On handkerchief and undervest
And, in tattoo, upon his chest . . .
From *Combustio Ad Infernum*

Oh damsel fair, beware the car
Where seating space is wider far
Than any man of reason needs
Except to further his misdeeds;
The steering-column change eschew,
No good can come of it for you,
And likewise any motor shun
From which you can't bale out and run.

Let maiden modesty decide
To take a summer evening ride
In something of the vintage breed,
For virtue's friend was ever speed.
No vulpine sibilance can come
From guileless lips of vintage chum,
With passion he is never dizzy,
(His motor keeps him far too busy)
And vintage bucket seats preclude
The acrobatic interlude. . . .   From *Counsel To Maidens*

The poems on the opposite page are all complete. Cummings's piece is typical of his liking for typographical oddities, his use of syncopated, jazzy rhythms and slangy style; he is one of the few successful verse experimenters. Harry Graham's (the drawing is also his) comes from his book 'Ruthless Rhymes', which was rather more of a rarity in the Twenties than it will seem in today's satire-impregnated atmosphere. Nash may be a humorous, sometimes even nonsensical, poet— but there is always an undercurrent of good sense and philosophy in his work, as 'Detroit, Spare That Wheel' illustrates. The Masefield verses above are taken from his poem 'The Long Drive' recounting a journey from Edinburgh to Boars Hill. Born in 1878, he became Poet Laureate in 1930. W. H. Charnock is one of the few men, if not the only man, to have published a complete book of verses about cars.

Grant Clarke and Edgar Leslie

Johnny O'Connor bought an automobile,
He took his sweetheart for a ride one Sunday,
Johnny was togged up in his best Sunday clothes,
She nestled close to his side.

Things went just dandy till he got down the road,
Then something happened to the old machin'ry,
That engine got his goat,
Off went his hat and coat,
Ev'rything needed repairs.

Chorus
He'd have to get under, get out and get under,
To fix his little machine.
He was just dying to cuddle his queen,
But every minute, when he'd begin it,
He'd have to get under, get out and get under,
Then he'd get back at the wheel.
A dozen times they'd start to hug and kiss,
And then the darned old engine it would miss,
And then he'd have to get under, get out and get under,
And fix up his automobile.

From *He'd Have to Get Under, Get Out and Get Under*

Brian Wilson and Roger Christian

It happened on the strip where the road is wide,
Two cool shorts standin' side by side,
My fuel-injected Sting Ray and a Four-Thirteen,
Revvin' up our engines and it sounds real mean,
Tak it up, tak it up, buddy gonna shut you down.

Declinin' numbers at an even rate,
At the count of one we both accelerate,
My Sting Ray is light, the slicks are startin' to spin,
But the Four-Thirteen's wheels are diggin' in,
Gotta be cool now, power-shift here we go.

The super-stock Dodge is windin' out in low,
But my fuel-injected Sting Ray's really startin' to go.
To get the traction I'm a-ridin' the clutch,
My pressure plate's burnin', that machine's too much.

Pedals to the floor, hear his dual-quads drink,
And now the Four-Thirteen's lead is startin' to shrink,
He's hot with ram injection, but it's understood,
I got a fuel-injected engine sittin' under my hood.
Shut it off, shut it off, buddy now I shut you down.   *Shut Down*

'Get Out and Get Under', for which Maurice Abrahams wrote the music, is of fairly venerable vintage so far as modern pop songs are concerned. 'Shut Down', featured by the Beach Boys, is very much of the Sixties and the modern hot-rod and surfing cult in America. The lyric describes a drag-race—a sport which has boomed in the United States, and to a lesser extent in Europe. To the dragster, to 'shut down' your opponent means to beat him; the rest of the cult language (e.g. 'slicks' equals smooth-surfaced tyres with virtually no tread) is fairly obvious in intention.

Right: *Horst Baumann took these pictures, which capture all the bizarre fury and Pop-Art feel of dragster racing. It is quick, spectacular, brutish. Two cars race from a standing start over a 440-yard strip and the most powerful machines— stripped-down monsters of up to 1,600 h.p.— may be hitting well over 200 m.p.h. when they slurp over the finishing-line. The smoke and flame and noise which accompany all this make the need for protective clothing for drivers obvious. In the less fearsome races, teenagers use ordinary saloon cars with beefed-up engines, spawned in the world about which Tom Wolfe writes on page 92.*

The lily gilders
by Lord Montagu of Beaulieu

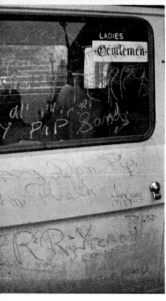

Today we're used to it. People try to beautify their cars in all sorts of ways. Curtains and flowers for homely types; tiger tails and joke slogans for rococo merchants; wire wheels and spotlights for the sporting brigade. Could love go further, or be more bizarre? But the game of gilding our cars began a long time ago. If it wasn't things to hang on cars, it was clothes to wear in them, as the 1902 poster below suggests. If the mania has ended up in the modern examples on the left, which you can see down any street, then perhaps it was inevitable. Overleaf, Lord Montagu of Beaulieu, who runs one of the finest motor museums in the world at his Hampshire home, traces the changing fashions in car beautification from the beginning.

We motorists are saddled with the 'bolt-on goody' industry for keeps. We can cover our bodywork in detachable plastic cane panelling, to give it the stately town-carriage look; we can smear the waistline in chequer-tape, and add a theoretical 10 m.p.h. to the top speed; and we can festoon the long-suffering vehicle with a plethora of lamps calculated to dazzle our neighbours. As the number of basic types of car on the market dwindles, so the disease of 'personalisation' spreads—as a counterbalance to the ever-growing risk of helping oneself to somebody else's Mini after a hard morning's shopping.

As might be expected, the infection in its most virulent form is a post-war phenomenon, though its roots dig deep into the past. Most Edwardian motorists were, however, not so concerned with beautifying their cars as they were with equipping it adequately, a thing manufacturers seldom bothered to do. "Equipment other than standard extra" is a terse phrase beloved of the modern American public relations man, and in fact the 'stripped' price of a transatlantic behemoth may well not include a spare wheel. But in 1906, the catalogue price of a cheap two-seater anywhere did not always include the tyres, and the odds were that hood, lamps and tools would also be extras. Argyll, then one of the largest firms in Europe, offered some thirty-three different items, from magnetos for cars normally issued with coil ignition (£25 fitted), through windscreens (£8), to "crests on side doors" (one guinea), while a comprehensive outfit of lamps and tools could be ordered for £11 10s.

The accessory catalogues proper as yet concentrated on expensive apparel for driver and passenger, calculated to transform a wasp-waisted beauty into a creditable imitation of a bear, but there were some gems on the market, such as the "Neptune portable and collapsible bath". Its presence could not be said to beautify anything, but it certainly helped to restore the occupants' appearance after a tussle with a recalcitrant inner tube. The luggage boot was still a thing of the future, so enormous trunks for mounting at the rear of a car were matched by wickerwork holders to take umbrellas, sandwiches, or a change of clothes, while for 2s 9d the Civil Service Stores could supply a hanging basket

for the dashboard.

The beautifiers played little part in these operations. Baskets could be shaped to fit the sides of any style of *tonneau* body. As cars grew quieter, more and more ornate warning devices were introduced, culminating in 1913 with a "cavalry horn with several different cardboard records, and several plain records which can be perforated to any tune". Mascots were, of course, a

160

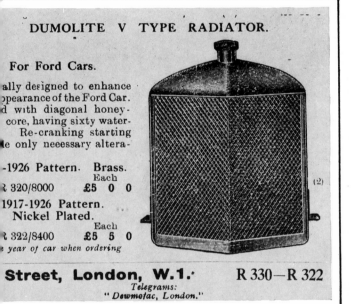

DUMOLITE V TYPE RADIATOR.

For Ford Cars.

...ally designed to enhance
...ppearance of the Ford Car.
...d with diagonal honey-
...core, having sixty water-
... Re-cranking starting
...e only necessary altera-

...-1926 Pattern. Brass.
　　　　　　　Each
R 320/8000　　£5 0 0

1917-1926 Pattern.
　Nickel Plated.
　　　　　　　Each
R 322/8400　　£5 5 0

...e year of car when ordering

Street, London, W.1.　　R 330—R 322

Telegrams:
" Dewmotac, London."

h.p. runabout into a miniature Napier or Mercedes, and later to camouflage the ubiquitous Model T Ford as almost anything.

The disease had little scope, however, as long as making the vehicle reliable engaged 90 per cent of the owner's time. The spare wheel was not destined to make its appearance until quick-detachable wheels were accepted, and this standby of the 'customiser' was thus absent from the accessory catalogues. By 1914, leather tyre and wheel covers were listed, and thereafter the beautifiers were to amuse themselves by putting the spare wheel in stylish rather than useful locations. The early 1930s saw the craze for "dual side-mounts"—an installation where the extra wheels lived in wells in the front wings, furnishing excellent water and corrosion traps, and, incidentally, enhancing the vehicle's snob-value in old age. Chromium-plated covers made them even more U, and also lengthened the process of a wheel change. Twenty years later the spare wheel had finally been banished to the boot, and thus inevitably there was a short vogue for "Continental spare wheel kits" incorporating an unsightly vertical mounting at the rear of the car.

Wheels themselves have kept the beautifiers happy for half a century. We may pass by the spring wheels of the 1905–1910 era, since they were as ugly as sin, and were intended solely as a substitute for the pneumatic tyre, but the 1920s were the era of the disc, which tidied up unsightly artillery and hard-to-clean wire wheels, at the cost of often-inaccessible tyre valves. The craze for streamlining brought in its wake the rear wheel spat, which failed to improve appearance, and sometimes fell off. By 1949, the disc wheel was universal save on sports cars, and recourse was had to the meretricious chromium-plated 'rim trim', a real brute to keep clean. As if this were not enough, the following decade saw a fashion in clip-on mock-wire wheels, sometimes even with 'spinners' designed to resemble the knock-on hub-caps of a more functional age.

Closely allied with the fake-wheel industry is the cult of the whitewall tyre. Cab drivers of the Teens and Twenties used to achieve the desired effect with French chalk, but the white-wall proper arrived in the Thirties and has been with us ever since, though

Left: the portable bath (1906) really did have a function in motoring. After struggling on dusty roads with a difficult automobile, the owner might well be in need of beautifying. But where did he bath? Behind a hedge? The radiators which came later, were more spurious; entirely spurious, indeed. They were meant to disguise the fact that you were only driving a plain Ford.

regular item, the themes being topical, such as comic policemen (in protest against the constabulary motorphobia then at its zenith), imperialistic eagles, aircraft and aero-engines, and even swastikas, publicised as 'lucky' for motorists. Perhaps the most blatant manifestation of pre-1914 Jonesmanship was a brisk trade in spurious radiators, enabling the Man in the Street to transform his third-hand 6

nowadays it is seldom seen outside European motor shows and the U.S.A. generally.

The lightweight wood-rimmed steering wheel which makes one's Mini go faster is no novelty—similar affairs were around in 1906. If the customised instrument panel was not, it was only because what few instruments there were on early cars were tucked away in a sort of Cave of Ali Baba under the scuttle where they were of little use for reference purposes, let alone anything else. The 1930s, the heyday of the gimmick, saw little advance in this direction, if only because outside America enormous soup-plate dials were the order of the day, and it was not until just before World War II, when these gave way to a single large and indecipherable white-faced instrument, that the subsidiary panel for ammeters, clocks, and suchlike came into its own. This was an admirable if untidy antidote to the manufacturers' new credo of 'warning lights for everything'. From these beginnings stems the cult of leather-covered and wood-framed facias for Minis, to distinguish the Jonesmobile from the same object as conducted by Robinson, who doesn't care anyway. Useless instruments like altimeters and brake pressure gauges were fitted by the luxury-car manufacturers, and therefore imitated by the gadget industry.

Fancy electrical equipment has always been handicapped by the attitude of the Law. It took the British authorities (as well as the average driver) a long time to reconcile themselves to the now ubiquitous winker. Weird and wonderful early traffic indicators also had only a short vogue. Man-sized and anatomical hands were tried (and are still used by Australian lorry drivers), but Morris's ingenious traffic-light-in-miniature was stifled at birth in 1932. Swivelling spotlights are, and always have been, illegal. Around 1931 some cars wore curious little red-and-green illuminated masts on their front wings, but I have never been able to ascertain their actual function. Most of the more attractive warning devices, however, such as the wolf whistle, lived on the exhaust system and were thus concealed from view, but the early 1930s saw a vogue for twin trumpet horns, flanking the radiator or grille, and capable of some peculiar dissonances. Though they are now one of the hallmarks of what the Americans term 'classicism', they were an affront to the devotees of streamline, and soon disappeared. In any case, their peculiar music has now become the preserve of the emergency services and the purveyors of ice-cream; in New South Wales, these latter cry their wares to the melody of *Greensleeves*!

Some external trimmings have a practical value, such as the bug-deflectors which burst upon us around 1952. Visors painted to match the body colours are regular wear in hot countries. Others, however, are quite valueless unless one is anxious to make one's car look like some other, costlier make, or like nothing at all. When Buick

162

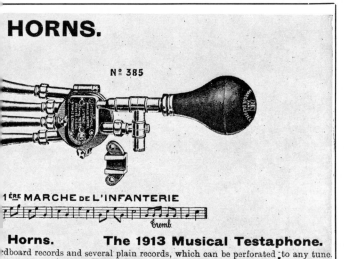

HORNS.

Nº 385

1ᴱᴿᴱ MARCHE DE L'INFANTERIE

Horns.   **The 1913 Musical Testaphone.**

rdboard records and several plain records, which can be perforated to any tune. own at once.   Each, Brass or Nickel-plated **£5 8s.**

introduced the porthole bonnet *motif* in 1949, so did a whole generation of customised Citroens, Peugeots and Simcas in Paris. The vee-grille used on early postwar Fiats stemmed from a *trasformazione* offered by accessory-makers in 1939. Superfluous chromium trim on the slab-sided bodies of the later 1940s served to break up large masses, and was applied, not only by the amateur lily-gilder, but later by the manufacturers themselves in an endeavour to cut down tooling costs and still make their 1952 model look different from its 1951 counterpart.

Trunk bars at the back of the car, telescopic luggage grids, and step plates in lieu of running-boards were fashionable in the 1920s, while dummy "landau irons" affixed to the rear quarters of the body suggested ownership of the more expensive convertible rather than the basic saloon. This whole trend was to be reversed a quarter of a century later, when the hardtop replaced the true convertible as the automobile of fashion. This style started as something that looked convertible, but wasn't: it ended up as the exemplar of all things, encouraging the with-it brigade to paint the tops of their cars in a lighter colour. I would not, incidentally, include the wrap-around rear window (common on old-type *traction avant* Citroens in their native land) under this head, since these really did help reversing on cars with blind rear quarters, and seldom, if ever, improved the appearance.

Mascots prospered until safety be-

came the world's watchword in the later 1950s. The comic horrors of 1910 inspired some things of beauty such as Charles Sykes's *Spirit of Ecstasy*, commissioned by my father for Rolls-Royce, and Hispano-Suiza's *cigogne volante*. On a less expensive car, Humber's snipe pleased the eye, until it acquired a rubber beak. But the factory-produced guided missiles of a later era were ugly and messy, while the less said of the Lalique insects of the late 1920s and early 1930s the better, for all their cost and superb craftsmanship. Their effect was (dare I say it?) comparable to the bobbing birds and dangling dollies that obscure vision and usually indicate the kind of driver who hugs the crown of the road at 35 m.p.h., come hell and high water.

The last decade has seen a mounting interest in foreign travel, and thus the 'we've-been-somewhere' motif on cars was inevitable. Before the war, 'GB' plates were offered by some makers as an optional extra, and 'plaqueitis' has never been confined to the Veteran and Vintage motorist, though he is all too often the worst offender. Mail-order firms dispense badges of foreign automobile clubs much as stamp-dealers offer 'assortments', and horribly-shaped badge bars can be purchased to reconcile the collection of such emblems with modern styling. Where the motorist of yore confined himself to an occasional notice in his rear window, advising following drivers that "If you can read this, you are too d . . . . d close", his descendants are determined to broad-

Above: *the number-plate, mascot and horn shown all belong to 1913. In those pre-Hitler days the swastika still had a reputation as a lucky emblem. As for the policemen, they may look jolly, but they were intended as figures of fun; coppers (of any nationality) were the motorist's natural-born enemy. The 'cavalry horn' could play any tune you wanted, via a cardboard record. The woman (with her own line in horns) was the ideal of the well-dressed female driver in 1905.*

163

cast all their movements. Nasty little stickers proclaim their progress from Blair Atholl to Bognor, from Ilfracombe to Inverness. Some Scotsmen like to carry little 'Ecosse' plates on their rear bumpers, and I have even seen an Isle of Wight-registered vehicle with a spurious 'GBW'. In 1963 there developed a rash of little county plaques with armorial devices, and these have spread far beyond the bounds of the dolly-dangler. There is an organisation that purveys bogus VIP passes, and tigers with eyes linked up to the stop-lights were around long before a certain oil company put them in the motorist's tank. To my mind, however, the cream of this Chamber of Horrors is the sign displayed in the rear window of a certain f.w.d. car, which tells the newly overtaken driver: "You Have Been Mini'ed".

Within the vehicle, no holds are barred. Bogus radio aerials are permissible when they are standard equipment, and the set itself an optional extra, while (dare I whisper it?) air intakes that take in no air were originated by factory stylists in Detroit. The ship-type scuttle ventilators popular during the 'nautical' period of sports-car styling in the 1920s did, however, purvey draughts in the region of the knees. The normal selector for an automatic gearbox is an unlovesome thing, so first the customers, and now the manufacturers, have transferred it to a console on the floor, where it looks like a proper central shift, and suggests that the owner not only knows how to change gear, but prefers the manual process. Seat belts and windscreen-washers are essential: not so fancy 'sports car' seats, which are frequently lacking in comfort and support alike. The seat-cover industry has burgeoned. The original slip-ons were intended solely to protect the upholstery and thus increase the trade-in price; but now the plastics industry has learnt to simulate anything from tapestry to ocelot skin. A catalogue of approved accessories issued as long ago as 1953 by a prominent American factory offered four patterns in nylon, seven in 'plastic', and four in fibre, plugged as being "as colorful as Autumn". The star turn was a "multi-color plaid with bolta-quilt one-and-one-quarter-inch channel bolster trimmed with vinyl leatherette and rayon".

164

Left: *the 1960s cult of the personal number-plate* (bottom row) *and the mania for badges deserve a caption to themselves. Whatever one's view of the Numbers Game, it's certain that Sir Gerald Nabarro, M.P., is king. He has seven NABs, from NAB 1 to NAB 7 —the largest collection in Britain. Two of the plates are for his gardeners. Once you could buy your own number-plate for a fiver. You applied to the licensing authority in the district using the letters you wanted and hoped no one else had got in first. That was stopped in 1962. Now you must search and hope even more fervently, and as a result prices have rocketed. Numerological status-seekers sometimes buy cars, scrap them, and keep the plates. R 1 went for £1,250 in 1965. Some examples are too good to be true, if you like that sort of thing. BRA 1 is owned by a brassiere maker; a doctor has SAY 99; and the grocer who has 00 7 doesn't aim to part with it.*

Flower vases, now mercifully defunct, were still available in the early 1930s, and Sears Roebuck, the famous mail-order house even listed the "Donna Lee Automobile Disseminator" (what a name!) in Model T Ford days. This was "a porous vase guaranteed to fill the car with a faint, clean odor of lavender". And if you want to introduce a home atmosphere into your vehicle, what price an "AM Radio Stereophonic Tape System" (one's own Muzak), "highway pilot controls" (to help you maintain a set cruising speed) and an "overhead safety panel", with lots and lots of warning lights for everything, including loose seat belts and doors left ajar? A sequence from a goody-merchant's nightmare? No, an excerpt from a 1966 American automobile catalogue.

There are other ways of dispensing fake performance apart from adhesive chequer-tape. 'Deep-note' exhaust systems with huge chromium-plated fishtails have always had their adherents, though a similar effect could be obtained on the old Morris Eight by sawing off the tailpipe abaft of the front seats. 'Speed

spray' on the bonnet sides was common in America in the 1930s, and so were the costly chromed stub exhaust pipes sprouting through them, which looked just right on a supercharged Mercedes-Benz or Auburn, but resembled the amateurish plumbing it was when applied to a Ford V8!

Even more fantastic are the Californian 'customs', elderly and mundane American sedans that are given face-lifts from stem to stern. Recognised tricks are to lower the roof line several inches, to remove superfluous chromium plate, and to simplify the radiator grille. The end-product is often painted in an exotic candy-stripe colour scheme, and can be very expensive. It can also be diverting to drive, due to reduced vision in all directions.

War cannot stop the beautifiers, as the 1939–45 period showed us. All sorts of alternatives to the unsightly Government Issue headlamp mask were propounded, some of them with proper lacquer finish. Even the regulation which required vehicles to be daubed in white paint produced quite a few bright

ideas, though the majority of users were content with smearing their bumpers and the edges of their wings. White flashes down the body sides were tried. The one wartime adjunct that defeated the artists was, however, the gas producer, though the attempts to hide this unsightly object probably sparked off the bulbous boots later offered on popular cars such as the original Issigonis-designed Morris Minor.

Yes, we've come a long way from merely rendering the motor car habitable. The bolt-on goody industry—I quote from the display advertisements of one of our best-selling monthly motoring magazines—can offer, *for Minis alone*, customised instrument boards, 'Grand Prix' steering wheels, rally-type seats, remote switch panels to allow for the mounting of overflow instruments on the doors, magnetic drain plugs, tachometer cowls (an extra for an extra!), steering column adjusters, 'Victory plaques', rear spare wheel covers (why?), wheel spacers to widen the track, and 'de luxe' radiator grilles, as well as a host of purely practical accessories that don't show.

And the motivational research boys hover in the background, as witness a fascinating salesman's catalogue, again from America, in my possession. Most of the old familiar gimmicks are listed—spats, wheel trims, several varieties of radio, a bug deflector, fancy steering wheels, and even our old friend the trunk bar. Salesmen were advised to appeal to the buyer's desire for "comfort, real comfort" when peddling 'foot hassocks'. "Convenience and safety" were considered to be the correct motives for purchasing a cigar lighter—these, incidentally, were available from accessory houses in London in 1912, price 12s. 6d. each, and I would hazard a guess that they were as temperamental as they have always been. Motive had to be studied carefully if a radio was to be sold, and matched correctly with one of the four types of antenna on the market. Says the author of this guide darkly of the under-car type, "strictly an alternative, use only to save a radio sale". And this booklet was published in 1942!

Above: racing cars may be functional, but they still make very striking examples of the gilding art—from their multi-coloured bodies, through the subtly individualistic helmets of the drivers, to the serpentine coils of their engines, which have an aura of modern sculpture. This was Jack Brabham winning the British G.P. of 1966 in the Repco-Brabham which quickly asserted its superiority in the first 3-litre season.

167

The gospel according to St Marque
by Maurice Wiggin

Maurice Wiggin has three passions: ang-
ling and the open-air life in general; poetry;
and cars, preferably rather old, beautiful
and noble cars. A journalist and critic all his
life, he has written hundreds of articles, and
some books, about all three. He has also
been, apart from one break of a few
months, television critic of 'The Sunday
Times' since 1951. No man knows more
about the social subleties of automania.

The one with the blue rinse said to the
one with the Marjorie Proops glasses,
"I wouldn't have bought my MG 1100
if I'd known they were going to bring
out a Riley 1100. Rileys *always* have
better engines."

Useless, I fear, to break it to the dear
sanguine soul that so far as the engine
goes, or indeed the entire mechanical
specification, there isn't one discover-
able difference between the MG and the
Riley 1100s. And the Wolseley, for that
matter. And the little Princess, too, if
you insist. It would be a waste of time.
Fanciers who have always fancied
Rileys will go on fancying them, long
after they have ceased to be Rileys in
anything but name. So will Wolseley
addicts. They will opt for their favourite
name even though the more knowledge-
able among them know "for a fact" that
the last *real* Riley was the RMF—or,
stretching a point, the Pathfinder—and
the last *real* Wolseley Superintendent
Lockhart's old 6/90. Indeed and indeed,
there are devotees who believe that
there hasn't really *been* a Wolseley, or a
Riley, since the war. Yet the names,
and the loyalties, persist.

Now some find all this a subject for
dreadfully biting satire, but I don't
know. Isn't it possible to argue that
there is involved here a certain delicate
and rather appealing sensibility, and a
touch of old-world loyalty, which give a
relish to the brute business of mere
transportation?

In a rather strange way, motoring in
Britain has never become mere transportation, as I think it has become in
some countries. It arouses feelings,
absurd or not, it is part of people's

emotional lives. Loyalty to a particular
marque has been a feature of the motoring scene ever since there were motors.
It is no more bizarre than most loyalties, and considerably more harmless
than some. The fact that the British
Motor Corporation find it entirely
worthwhile to produce what is fundamentally the same car under five different brand names (Austin, Morris, MG,
Riley, Wolseley) is of course an affront
to diehards who remember (so they say)
how different they really used to be; yet
it really means no more than that the
'conformist' British are loyal, which is
nice even when the loyalty is what some
might call misplaced, and refreshingly
keen to see at least a touch of individuality preserved in an age of stan-
dardisation.

It is not only the more exotic marques
which inspire this fervour. You expect a
man who has once been hooked by a
Straker-Squire, a Hispano-Suiza or an
Iso Grifo to stay hooked—he can hardly
get *more* distinctive—but the mystique
of the marque operates just as strongly
in the world of bread-and-butter machines. The Englishman by and large has
never regarded his car simply as utilitarian transport, but as an extension of
his personality, a means of self-expression.

To fanatics of my generation, the
incredible happened when Austin and
Morris merged. In fact we still, sub-
consciously, refuse to accept it as a
fait accompli, just as some Frenchmen
still mistrust Germans (and some
Englishmen, even longer in the memory,
still mistrust Frenchmen). When I was
young the Ford Model T, or Tin Lizzie,
was the rock-bottom basic heap, a car
used for want of anything better by
the most impecunious stratum of
society. (We owned about five, at one
time and another). You hit bourgeois
respectability only when you got on to
the Austin-Morris level. Anything else
was ever so slightly demonstrative and
eccentric. Clyno, Swift, Star and Jowett
spoke of a rather too obvious desire to
be different: Austins and Morrises were
'real'. But people rarely owned both.
The rivalry between those who sold
them was matched by the rivalry between those who bought them.
As a Black Countryman I was naturally brought up in the sure and certain
conviction that anything made by the
sturdy craftsmen of Longbridge was

168

inherently sounder than anything thrown together by the effete and irresponsible foreigners of Cowley (not to mention *Oxford*) in the decadent south. Austins stood for utter dependability: for years and years they advertised in that sublime phrase, "You buy a car, but you invest in an Austin". This we believed as gospel: the fact that it was equally true of the Morris was never allowed to enter our tight little minds.

Wesleyans were quietly proud of not being Primitive Methodists. The almost imperceptible differences were much more important to us than the overwhelming similarities. We avoided heresy.

But, of course, there were deviationists (the Wiggins among them) spurred on by an inexhaustible curiosity and delight in mere diversity. Thus, though we would almost rather have walked

169

than bought a Morris, we fell for several Standards, probably, I fancy, because they were virtually Austins plus a touch of decorative gaiety. (Austins *were* dour: pre-eminently the car of the Calvinist). On the other hand, we did not deviate so far as the Bean, an excellent car which deserved to do better; and we avoided the Hillman on the grounds of frivolity.

The apocalyptic Morris-Austin divide, as intense as the theological war between Leica and Contax believers and infinitely more widespread, is curiously paralleled today by the Vauxhall-Ford division. Luton and Dagenham have taken over the roles of Cowley and Longbridge, and probably with no better justification.

In a higher income bracket you found people who were utterly devoted to Humbers, Rovers and Lanchesters; three cars whose very names were redolent of sobriety, discretion, decorum and balance (including bank balance). These three attracted, in their day, the most solid citizens of the land. The publicists at Rootes's have been trying hard to revive or perpetuate the Humber legend, even going so far as to call their plushiest product the Imperial limousine, which is pretty brave of them. The Lanchester is gone from us, more's the pity, and is hardly perpetuated by the new Daimlers, which have much more in common with Jaguars. But the Rover mystique survives in a remarkable way, virtually undiluted. I know families who have never owned anything else but Rovers, and others equally well-heeled to whom the idea of owning a Rover simply never occurs. Somehow that estimable car inspires strong emotions, one way and another. To some it is the junior (I won't say 'poor man's') Rolls-Royce; or at least the patriot's or indigenous Mercedes. To others, it seems to represent a withdrawal from the lively world of fun motoring. The new generation at Rovers, while sedulously perpetuating the older image with the three-litre, have been brilliantly engaged in making the best of both worlds by attracting the more dashing conservatives too, with the delightful Rover 2000. This is awfully clever of them and makes Rover shares, to my mind, the best bet in transport equities. The British being what they are.

Between Rover men and Jaguar men is fixed a gulf unbridgeable, as wide and deep as that which separates the hatless from the hatted. The Jaguar, to those who do not own one, is specifically the marque of the beast. Jaguar-hatred may just conceivably be rooted in envy, as Rover-worship is certainly founded on a perceptive appraisal of the eternal verities. In fact the Jaguar is fast, quite well-made (for the price), luxurious, sporting, and extremely pretty: it is also wonderful value for money. But, of course, it attracts extroverts who like gaiety more than decorum. I'm afraid you *can* recognise 'the Jag type'; and vulgarity is not unknown among them. Flashy is the word I am trying to avoid.

I would have said, quite a short while back, that there was no instance on record of a family turning from Rover to Jaguar, or vice versa. They are polar opposites. Yet it happened. I myself, after owning three new Mk II Jaguars (2·4, 3·4 and 3·8), tired suddenly of the burden of being hated and despised, associated with jewel thieves and cosh robbers, motorway madmen and property developers. The fact that my brakes failed may also have had something to do with it. However that may be, and whatever the multiple and complex and recondite and unrecognised reasons, I bade a fond farewell to the last of the Jags and bought a lovely little Rover 2000, chastely finished in the darkest of green. Instantly I felt a different man: a respectable citizen, modest and unassuming but quite perceptive, you know, quite on the ball and *au fait* with what's what. Somehow it seemed to symbolise the coming of sober middle age, the end of irresponsibility: I felt that I had put away childish things. Nice. But I don't know anyone else who has sloughed a skin in the same way. Nor how long it will last. . . .

We haven't yet begun to touch on the special enthusiasms associated with *foreign* cars. This is altogether a trickier and more complex subject, since it is held to involve the delicate and difficult question of patriotism. Such nonsense!

There are those who hold it as an article of faith that *all* foreign cars are inherently better than all British cars, and those who believe the exact opposite. Neither view, it need hardly be said, is strictly accurate. In matters of design, the foreigners are ahead of us in some ways, behind us in other ways. But

170

in matters of workmanship—ah well, now, y'see. . . . One does find it difficult not to believe that an export model is more carefully assembled and checked than a model meant for the home market. This (one feels) must be true even of British cars, and certainly foreign cars do *seem* to have been inspected more thoroughly. The standard of assembly, simple craftsmanship, and the intensity of inspection and control, seem hideously sloppy in Britain: so many brand-new cars one hears of (and buys) should never have left the factory. Yet I have owned a British car which happened to be an export model that never got exported, for some mysterious reason—it was quite superb, infinitely superior to its brothers (or sisters) which flooded into the British showrooms.

Whether or not the foreign cars available here are actually better *made* than our native models (and I think they tend to be, I am sorry to say I do) there is no doubt whatever about the cachet of owning one. Personally I wouldn't feel particularly taller just because I happened to own, say, a Fiat 600D, which is plainly inferior to a Mini on every count except assembly and reliability. But to own a Lancia, a Maserati or an Alfa Romeo is obviously something. I owned an Alfa once, a Giulietta Sprint, but mine, alas, was well on the way to being worn-out and failed to arouse any particular feelings in me, except possibly disdain. However, it impressed the outsider satisfactorily.

Considerations of patriotism do not disturb me over-much. I did my time in the war and thereby earned a perfect freedom to buy as I chose. If I could not bring myself to buy a German car—and I couldn't—this is not because I am so inordinately proud of the British, but partly because I hate the Germans and partly because German cars tend to be heavily Teutonic and rather hideous. Is there anything on the road so Gothic as the Merc? But Italians, of course, are impossible to hate. And they make such very nice cars. They always had style, and nowadays it comes out in their cars, the best of which are the most desirable in Europe.

The French are trying, of course; very; and people with no ear and only a minimal sensibility swear by the Citroen. People who don't particularly like the sound of a sewing machine are less enthusiastic. One hears that the Peugeot has all the French peasant virtues, just as Renault has the brittle ethos of a Paris suburb written all over it. They are hardly names to conjure with.

It is undeniable that cars do manage, somehow, to express national characteristics, in however attenuated a form, What could be more expressive of the drabness of Eastern Europe than the Skoda, of provincial Russia than the Moskvitch, of the suicidal Scandinavians who don't get enough sun than the Saab and Volvo, of the placid Dutch than the Daf? And what, one asks, could better express America's vast optimism and certitude than the American car? Of course they are flatulent, far too big, vainglorious, flashy and hideously wasteful—it is the Teuton coming out in Detroit—and yet, you know, they are most marvellously engineered, they are simply wonderful cars—for America. The names, the actual marques, don't possess the quality of *cachet*, any more than do the dreary European bread-and-butter jobs: but the know-how is there, and in a very few years, when Detroit turns its mind to making a different sort of car to suit a different sort of era, monopolising the best Italian thought and assimilating it to its own native engineering genius— then, brethren, we are going to see the finest production cars the world has seen rolling off the lines in Detroit. Until then, I think one can wait.

Enough. Let us summon up the last reserves of tolerance and say that it is the hunger for individuality which makes people who are otherwise eminently docile—people who will uncomplainingly eat mass-produced, devitalised bread and pay ridiculous taxes— believe that there is really a worthwhile difference between Hillman Super Imp and Singer Chamois, between Cresta and Zodiac, between Elf and Hornet. What's in a name, except its fame? But these are innocent preferences, and good for trade. Of what embattled ideologies can we say so much?

4 The future and the facts of loving

Left: this car is part of what's coming—new beauty combined with new safety. In this form it was a hand-built Alfa Romeo turned out in Turin as a one-off prototype, partly for prestige display at motor-shows, but also—like most Turin prototypes—to test ideas which may later percolate to the mass-production industry. The smoothness of line made the car glamorous and desirable, but also eliminated projections which can be so damaging in accidents. Headlights were recessed, outside door handles set flush. This car also pioneered rubberless windscreen and rear-window sealing, resulting in a thinner and neater steel frame. Six months after it was first shown, many of its characteristics had been built into the limited production Alfa shown overleaf. Turin has been the centre of the bespoke car tailoring business for many years and the biggest influence in exterior car styling. But the American automobile industry —with its wealth and talent for serviceability, safety and ergonomics—may ultimately take Turin's place.

Although our passion for the motor-car still runs hot as ever, there are signs that in some directions at least it is being tempered by hard fact. Society is looking more critically at the less palatable results of the affaire: especially the carnage on the roads and the spoliation of cities. So the last section of this book is sweet and sharp in flavour, loving and unloving. It looks into a future where cars will be still more beautiful and efficient, but where they will be safer too. And it sees the realities of our involvement with the car through the eyes of those — a woman, a researcher, and a second-hand dealer, among others — whose affection for it is strictly qualified.

173

Where we're headed
by Maxwell Boyd

Safer cars? Lovelier cars? New engines? New shapes? Maxwell Boyd gives his assessment of where the car business—and the love affair—is going. Motoring Correspondent of 'The Sunday Times' since 1960, he was assistant editor of 'Autosport' before that. He is also a photographer who trained with Baron in London.

I bought a new car just the other day. One of the very latest models.

New! Startling! Sensational! Revolutionary!

The advertisements screamed at me when it was launched, and carried on screaming. The critics in the newspapers and magazines carrying those advertisements raved. Never before had there been a car like this one. It was the last word, and the first. The alpha and omega of cars rolled into one.

By the end they were all growing a little breathless over adjectives. But they had achieved the desired effect. They bludgeoned me into mental acceptance of the car. I had to have one. Life wouldn't have been complete without it. My family would have ignored me and my wife would almost certainly have left me. So I bought one. After all, it was new, *new*, NEW!

Or was it? Frankly, no. Not very. Certainly the shape was slightly different. The engine, the gearbox and so on, were rather more sophisticated. The trim was made out of modern materials. There was more glass around which would shatter into pretty patterns, and some very clever tyres on the wheels which worked best when they looked flat. And I could buy the car in just about every imaginatively-named rainbow colour except black.

But when you got down to basics, this veritable miracle of modern industry was surprisingly like all my previous cars, my father's cars before me, and even my grandfather's cars before him. It had four road wheels and a steering wheel, brakes that worked by pressing a pedal in the floor, a gearbox operated by a stick and an engine, fed on petrol, in which pistons went up and down in cylinders. Even the rear suspension dated itself by being described as cart springs. Nothing essentially different,

in fact, from the cars of twenty, forty, even sixty years ago.

If the basic car design has changed so little in the last sixty years, will it remain equally unchanged in the future? I doubt it. It seems that, at last, technology is overtaking the traditional conservatism of the motor industry, while mass-production methods of manufacture are making innovation commercially viable.

In the end, you see, it all boils down to the vicious circle of cost versus production. The manufacturer believes the customer will not pay much extra for novelty. Therefore he tends not to go in for it much. Consequently the novelty remains expensive because it is made in limited quantities.

An example of this in recent years has been the a.c. generator, which is now quickly replacing the d.c. dynamo in a car's electrical system. All cars are going soon to have an a.c. system, which keeps the battery fully charged even at tick-over speeds and provides extra current for all the electrical gear the modern car carries. The a.c. generator has been around for years, but it was only by the mid-1960s that sufficient were ordered by the industry to bring the price down to an economic level.

Cars have been powered by conventional piston engines since the dawn of motoring, and this form of power unit is now so reliable and cheap to build— though it is very wasteful of power and petrol—that the industry has been understandably loth to reject it. But three possible alternative power sources have existed for some time: gas turbines, electric drive and the rotary piston engine. I have had personal experience of cars driven by all three methods.

Opinion on the gas-turbine engine as a practical proposition for motor cars has been divided more or less equally in the industry. Not unnaturally, the weight in favour has been on the side of those who have been closest to its development. In Britain this means the Rover Company, who have been running prototype gas-turbine cars for more than a decade, and whose efforts culminated in the highly successful Rover-BRM racing car exercise at Le Mans in 1965.

Right: *haute couture produc. of Turin. Detai. shown come from experimen- tal prototypes— except for the re. Alfa (top of page) which wa. developed from the prototype or page 173. Some c. these prototype. are interesting simply for their beauty of line. Others have built-in safety factors. The palish blue car (top right and lower left) is a Pininfarina design; it has direction-winke. at the end of wrap-round fror bumper, covered double head- lights, intriguin. rear-window styling. A Vigna. design based on the rear-engined Fiat 1000 (red c. just below the Alfa) has fared in headlights an. (right of page) near-flush, pres. button door catch. A Ghia design based on an American Shelby Cobra (darker blue car with tan seats, centre page) also has flush door catch. Other pictures illustrate strikin. tail assemblies and (bottom left) swing-asid. steering wheel.*

The Vauxhall XVR, a British prototype, has aerodynamic curves, retractable headlights, flushing door handles, collapsible steering column.

The Ford J, first unveiled in 1966 as a sports racer. Featured automatic transmission and speeds up to 250 m.p.h. Cut-off back led to nickname—the 'bread van'.

In America, General Motors, Ford and Chrysler have also been engaged on gas-turbine development. Chrysler gave out fifty turbine cars to private owners and these cars covered over a million miles. Reaction was enthusiastic for their smooth operation, and in 1966 Chrysler reaffirmed their ultimate objective of a production turbine car.

Despite these passenger car experiments, most authorities believe that the real future of the gas-turbine engine lies in the long-distance commercial vehicle field. They envisage a truck, or even a train of trucks, cruising along transcontinental motorways at a steady, unwavering speed, using the characteristics of the engine to their best advantage. Car use, they maintain, would be impracticable because of the gas turbine's lack of acceleration, lack of engine braking, heavy fumes and high fuel consumption. The physical size of the engine would also dictate cars of at least American proportions.

Driving Rover's T4 prototype, I found that the first thing you had to get used to was the rev-counter needle pointing to 40,000 r.p.m. at tick-over! But the car proved to be exceptionally docile in city traffic, sufficiently smart off the mark to keep up with and overtake other traffic and, once you had mastered the different technique, surprisingly easy to drive. Unlike using the petrol engine, you have to build up the revs with the gas turbine. This means you must anticipate the need for acceleration, holding the car on the handbrake and throttling it up to about 80,000 r.p.m. before the traffic lights go green. You must also put your foot down well in advance before driving through a corner on power. The Rover turbine

engineers are convinced there is still a future for gas turbines in cars.

Whereas the future of the gas-turbine car lies principally on the open road, that of the electric 'bubble'-size commuter car lies in those heavily populated urban areas which conventional vehicles are now reducing to a state of traffic paralysis. But at their present stage of development, it would be difficult for them to share the roads with petrol- or oil-powered vehicles. The battery-driven electric car has a good deal of initial acceleration, but it runs out of breath at about 20 m.p.h. and is, for all practical purposes, flat out at 30 m.p.h. Since town traffic ebbs and flows in bursts of rapid and momentary acceleration, the electric car in crowded streets at present might be more of an obstacle to other traffic than a fumeless pint-sized blessing.

Their miniature dimensions may also be a handicap. Certainly the battery cars demonstrated in 1966 were too cramped for comfort for anyone over average size. Moreover, one remembers how the German two-stroke 'bubble' cars used to get under the wheels of buses and lorries at the height of their post-Suez popularity a few years ago. For safety's sake electric cars should share the road with none but their own size.

This presupposes the ideal conditions for running electric cars—town centres free of all other traffic. One can visualise fleets of them owned, perhaps, by the local authority and kept on the perimeter of the centre. People would park their conventional cars and hire an electric vehicle by the hour for shopping or business.

Many people, including the British

'Fill-up' of the future? This is one of the British 1966 two-seater electric cars being recharged. Bulky batteries have in the past proved a major handicap to electric cars.

Padded bucket seats and head-rests in Pininfarina-designed Sigma—a prototype in-tended as the ultimate in safety.

motor industry, hold that the electric car is quite unpractical as a commercial proposition while its power source remains the cheap but heavy and bulky lead-acid battery. But the problems of noise, air pollution and overcrowding in urban areas are becoming so acute that it would be foolish to pigeon-hole the electric car project until equally cheap forms of more sophisticated batteries have been evolved.

Since electric traction will provide the only form of transport to overcome our objections to liquid fuel propulsion in towns, its further development should be encouraged both by the motor industry and by the town planners who will have the responsibility of accommodating it. The car itself must be quite ready to take new power sources, including eventually the fuel cell, as soon as they are developed, which will happen sooner rather than later if the need is pressing enough. The whole outlook for electric cars was, indeed, enhanced by the announcement in September, 1966, that the Ford Motor Company would test a prototype electric car in Britain in 1967.

With the development that remains to be done, however, both the gas turbine and the electric car are not immediate alternatives to the conventional piston engine. A more short-term option is the rotary piston engine, of which the German Wankel design is the furthest advanced, though the Japanese have also been pushing ahead with similar rotaries. One principal advantage of this power unit is that it will produce at least 50 per cent more power than a conventional engine of a similar size.

The secret of the Wankel is its single, triangular rotor. This is pushed round by three petrol-air mixture explosions, one against each face of the rotor, to each complete revolution. The rotor takes the place of the pistons in a conventional engine and is virtually the only moving part. There is no camshaft or valve gear, while the 'crankshaft', transmitting the power to the clutch and gearbox, runs through the centre of the rotor. And since the drive is rotary in the first place, it doesn't have to be converted from an essentially jerky up and down movement, as in an ordinary engine, with a resultant loss of efficiency. Nothing could be simpler, or smoother.

The Wankel engine got off to a slower start in Britain than in continental Europe. N.S.U., the German firm who originally took up Dr. Felix Wankel's brain-child, have already produced a Wankel-powered car. Citroen in France have been making one, while Mercedes-Benz have backed the idea to the hilt. Indeed, their chief development engineer, Rudolf Uhlenhaut, told me in 1966 that although a good deal of development remained to be done, he couldn't see a practical alternative to the Wankel for passenger cars.

At present the main problems are excessive fuel consumption, wear on the points of the rotor, and inefficient combustion which results in excessive exhaust fumes. Engineers like Uhlenhaut quite frankly maintain that, to justify its introduction, the Wankel must be better than the best piston engine in some ways and equal to it in all other ways. In time, it will be. And when it is, it will be cheaper to produce en masse than piston engines.

At first, Britain's motor industry appeared supremely indifferent to the

178

Wankel rotary engine, showing
its single, triangular rotor which
takes the place of pistons.

possibilities of the Wankel engine. But things are different now. Rolls-Royce have been investigating the engine; so has the Government; and engineers in the popular-car industry have begun to see its potential. It is my bet that, if the Continental motor industry produces a Wankel-engined car by 1968, Britain will do the same by 1970 or so.

I cannot see any radical change in the shape of the motor car in the years to come, though the usual current three-box format—engine, passengers, luggage boot—may well evolve into a layout of two boxes, one for the engine and the other for the passengers-cum-luggage. Instead of having a huge container overhanging the back axle, remaining empty for probably eleven months of the year, it would be far more logical to use the spare space for passengers when there is no luggage or goods to be carried. Consequently I see an extension of the principle pioneered on France's Renault 16, a car which is nearly halfway between a saloon and an estate car.

I certainly can't see the front or rear engine compartment disappearing. The engine is far better where it is, outside. If proper precautions are taken, the engine and its box also provide a welcome safety buffer between the passengers and the accident. The precaution, of course, is a bulkhead to deflect the engine beneath the car, rather than into the driver's lap, on impact. Provided this happens, then the biscuit-tin metalwork of the bonnet will absorb much of the shock. Mercedes-Benz already claim that, in a head-on collision, the front of their car will crumple so that only one-tenth of the impact on the bumper will reach the driver.

Resistance to change in the overall shape of the car does not mean that styling will remain unaltered, that technical advances will not be made long before we have alternative forms of engine. In fact we can expect quite soon many improved ways of doing simple but important things beneath the bonnet. Fuel injection as a substitute for carburettors is a practical possibility since Lucas in 1966 introduced equipment specially designed for the medium-price passenger car. By means of the more accurate metering of fuel, and the *injection* of the fuel/air mixture into the cylinders—rather than its being drawn in somewhat haphazardly by suction as at present—petrol will be both saved and used to greater advantage. This will also result in fewer toxic by-products being left over to be expelled from the exhaust.

Among the 'electrics', contact breaker points, which forever need cleaning and resetting, will be replaced by transistors to perform the essential 'make and break'. Electronics will switch the side-lights on automatically at dusk, while flexible printed circuitry will not long hence replace the matted tangle of multi-coloured cable that makes up a car's wiring system. Automatic transmission is bound to make further inroads in the small car field, especially since the introduction of the Lockheed automatic for the BMC Mini.

Manufacturers both here and abroad have bubbled over with enthusiasm for this incredibly ingenious two-pedal transmission, while Lockheeds themselves have already developed several improved versions of the original. I don't think it is even now realised just how fundamentally this invention is

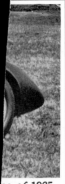

...ce of 1965.
...e future of

going to affect the history of the motor industry. Lockheed may not even realise it themselves, for it will only become apparent as millions of the world's small car motorists reject the nuisance and effort of continually having to change gear in ever denser packs of traffic.

Although Britain has often led the way in motor engineering, she seldom has in styling, particularly in the 1960s. Clothing the car has long been the prerogative of Italians, led by the 'fashion house' of Pininfarina, an establishment which cleverly and profitably combines the exclusivity of *haute couture* in metal with the semi-mass-production of the restricted assembly line. They build imaginative one-off prototypes, and they produce perhaps three or four dozen a day each of various French and Italian production models for which they have designed the body. In addition, as consultants, they have styled bodywork for mass manufacturers in many countries—BMC in Britain, Peugeot in France, Fiat in Italy, Opel in Germany.

But Pininfarina, though the largest and most successful, is only one of about 40 firms dotted around the ancient city of Turin who are engaged in influencing and changing the fashionable shape of the motor car throughout the world. Some—like Pininfarina, Ghia and Bertone—work from big, glossy premises. Others make do with a drawing board in a side-street office, with perhaps a tiny workship next door. But their ideas, new lines and fresh approaches, first embodied in hand-built prototypes, eventually percolate through to the mass-production industry.

Occasionally the new lines may have a major influence. A whole car may go into production almost as it leaves the Turin workshop. But more often than not the influences are marginal, though certainly not insignificant. In the mid-1960s Turin started fitting flush exterior door catches, often of a push-button type, on its prototypes. Since their safety advantages are obvious, they are plainly due to be incorporated in to mass-production cars before long.

But Turin's supremacy in the influence of styling may be in peril. For the Italian stylist and his metal worker, the man with the hammer, are essentially 'skin men' who fashion the outer casing of the car. They only smarten the detail of the interior rather than change it. The Americans, on the other hand, have the almost unfathomable resources to change and develop everything from the instrument dials to the gear lever and seat adjustment controls. Prototype cars from Detroit have increasingly shown how details such as these can be improved in function and in visual attractiveness by imaginative styling. The Americans, too, have a talent for serviceability, safety and ergonomics which is not always shared by the Italians. Consequently, some think, Detroit could take Turin's place within a decade as the hub of the bespoke car tailoring business.

The word safety in connection with Detroit is important, though. A growing body of opinion in America began to be heard—and heard loud—in the mid-1960s. It said that in terms of safety Detroit had lagged behind for many years.

The claim, vigorously disputed by Detroit, gained strength from various revelations: that General Motors, for

180

instance, were endeavouring to call 1,500,000 1965 Chevelles and Chevrolets back from their owners to attend to a deficiency in their accelerator linkage. The throttle, apparently, could be jammed open by snow or ice. Chrysler and Ford also called in tens of thousands of vehicles for detail modification.

Pressure was put on the automobile manufacturers from a number of sources. In Congress, the Road Safety Committee was making alarming noises. Its chairman, Senator Ribicoff, declared: "The air of confidentiality adopted by auto manufacturers with respect to deficiencies in their products constitutes what might almost be called a betrayal of public trust." President Johnson initiated legislation designed to enforce higher safety standards on car-makers.

In a nation with 80,000,000 vehicles on the roads, it was certainly a novelty to find Detroit in the dock. Quite how it will react in the long-term—or how it will be forced to react—is still not absolutely predictable.

At the 1966 New York Motor Show there were (from the Americans) some half-hearted claims about safety—concentrating on things like padded visors and instrument panels, with some models offering safety belts as standard.

There were stories of Thunderbird owners smashing the red roof warning light installed as a reminder if seat belts weren't fastened—which perhaps tells us something about customer reaction to safety as a selling weapon.

But in serious and fundamental matters of safety there was, even in 1966, no convincing American sales pitch. Detroit still appeared to be selling what car manufacturers have always sold: performance, glamour, status, sex, what-have-you. The safety end was left to the Europeans, and certainly the European lead in *applied* safety in cars was in the mid-1960s lengthy.

Experimental safety cars like the Pininfarina Sigma symbolised this. Production cars which pitched part of their sales-drive on safety, like Mercedes-Benz and Rover, demonstrated the fact in action. There was nothing coming out of Detroit in 1966 like the Rover 2000, which could almost be called a production safety car, with its steel bulkhead deflecting the engine beneath the car in a head-on crash; the steel division between fuel tank and passenger compartment; the steering machin-

ery designed not to spear the driver in a collision—and so on. British Fords also took a long safety lead over their American counterparts with their new Zephyrs and Zodiacs of 1966, offering impact-absorbing bodywork, unburstable door-locks, steering wheels made to yield under impact, spare wheels under front bonnets as extra shock-absorbers, and many other features.

But safety must come to Detroit, mustn't it, as it must come all over the world? If one believes that America will ultimately take over the leadership in design and styling of cars, then the safety factor must be part of it. I believe that public opinion, both in America and elsewhere, is definitely moving round to demand greater safety in cars. And announcements like that of mid-1966 giving the news that, by the early 1970s, all Detroit Fords would have collapsible front-end structures to absorb the shock of a collision showed the way the wind was blowing.

Quite how safety will be inbuilt one can't comprehensively forecast in detail. I have not, you will notice, even mentioned cars that don't need steering, or cars powered by atomic energy, or whatever. They will come, I suppose, for world supplies of petroleum are *not* inexhaustible. But my crystal ball doesn't have an indefinite range. I'll leave such things to the next generation.

But I do suspect that we are standing in mid-century at a great watershed in our relationship with the motor-car. Slowly our love affair with it is being tempered by reality: rather in the way that after the honeymoon period of a marriage, any couple learns that it isn't all bedroom and storybook. As roads get more crowded, people will have to view the motor-car as something other than simply an escape-fantasy, a status symbol and the rest of it. Cars will become safer; they will become more efficient, along the lines of the detail I have laid out earlier; they will be made (in size, for instance, and also in curbs on their freedom to rove where they want) more to fit our cities and countryside, rather than having our landscapes made to fit them. I see no reason why they should not become more beautiful. The love affair, in other words, is going to become less of a fantasy, more like real life. That, fellow-lovers, is where we're headed.

181

Women, as you know, are different

by Elizabeth Benson

Women see cars in their own way. If they love them, which they often don't, their motives are not the same as men's. Elizabeth Benson is a rare bird: a woman whose test reports on cars have appeared in print nationally—in 'The Sunday Times Magazine'. This is usually an all-male corner. She isn't mad about cars, but she still enjoys them. She has, over 15 years, driven a wide variety of them.

The Kingston by-pass, any morning; or any other of the roads that plunge in and out of our towns and cities. Stand and observe. See the gentlemen ride by, usually alone in their cars, aerials whipping in the wind, snatches of *Housewives' Choice* (of all things) squirming through the roar from the occasional open window. See the women ride by. On the school-run. Three, four, five active passengers hide them. Afterwards, perhaps, it's away to Fine Fare or MacFisheries.

Our urban, monogamous society gives men and women different things to do with cars. Men are more often alone with them, communing with them, driving them. Life is not the same for passenger and driver, nor for shopper and non-shopper. It's not surprising that men and women seek different qualities in the cars they drive.

There has been, I concede, that girl with her hair streaming in one of the getaway-people petrol ads on TV. The car, man-driven, goes fast, with roar and dust-trail, across a sort of idealised game reserve which of a sudden vanishes as they drop down to beach and breakers. There's a phallic symbol in every snap-happy gear change, every gesture.

She does not, nor ever did, exist, of course. "I have never," Stirling Moss once said, "found a woman who enjoyed speed for its own sake, either driving or being driven. I think it's a peculiarly male reaction."

Like me, he maybe exaggerates a little. But the point is valid, and I agree with him, as with his theory that the ultimate enjoyment of speed is for itself alone. Once the element of destination is brought in (and women tend to have destinations, as Moss well knows) the purity of the sheer enjoyment of speed is utterly besmirched.

The relationship men and women have with the motor-car is not the same. Men love cars after their fashion and I suspect that women do not. It is generally the man, by enshrined social custom, who looks after the cleaning of the car. This is not accidental. Men who would not be seen dead with rag and polish *inside* a house happily spend three hours of a Sunday in full view of the neighbours producing the gleam on the bonnet you can see your face in—and which can be destroyed thereafter by half an hour's flog in the rain. Women are less likely to do it. Their sense of possessiveness is as strong, but they are less interested in this particular possession: or, at least, interested in it for motives quite different from the man's—as an extension of home, perhaps, rather than as an escape from it.

It would be amusing to do some market research on male and female attitudes to the idea of the garage, which is, in effect, a car-house. One always seems to be meeting women who complain that their houses are too small—which in the average equation of 3/4 bedrooms, plus 2 ents., plus 2/3 kids is understandable. Yet here we are in the twentieth century—and especially in Britain, where land is scarce and often ludicrously expensive—happily giving over one large-sized room of our cramped living space to tucking up a piece of metal, which usually isn't there for most of the waking day anyway. It would be more sensible to turn the garage into a playroom (or whatever is our fancy) and leave the car at nights on that wasted approach-path to the garage which most houses possess. This suggestion, I suspect, would be favoured by many women and vigorously attacked by virtually all of the men.

Women's approach to cars is more utilitarian. There are, for instance, practically no women racing drivers. This is not only because women do not like speed for its own sake, but because a race lacks that tangible *destination* of which we have already talked. It is also because women do not possess that sense of personal, cut-throat competitiveness which men have. A car is an invitation to a man to compete, whether on a race-track or jostling in the pack to get round Hyde Park Corner. Into it he pours his desire to prove his virility, his superiority or whatever. Women do not feel the same compulsion.

There are, on the other hand, quite a number of women—like Pat Moss-Carlson—who have made a name as rally drivers. It is easy to argue here that rallying *does* involve some kind of destination in a way that the sport of motor-racing does not, and that rallying calls for participation in a welter of detail concerning navigation, speed-judgment and so forth. Women tend to like detail, are good at it.

This predilection for detail seems to me to emerge in the way a woman looks at a car. Because she does not *love* it, this is not to say she does not *enjoy* it. But she will enjoy different aspects from those which seize the male. Her eye, so far as the practical business of comfort and efficiency in a car is concerned, may well be more searching.

Men tend to be more dogmatic about *the* car they like to drive. There are those who will defend their choice against all reasons of logic. It may be indifferently designed inside, it may have well-known weaknesses in comfort or engineering. But there is something in it to which that particular man's fantasy self responds, and his loyalty, once given, is total. Men champion their chosen loves as fiercely, and irrationally, as they pick holes in those of their rivals (or have you never heard a Triumph 2000 man set upon a Rover 2000 man, and vice-versa, in disputation about what are, after all, two somewhat similar machines?).

There are also, incidentally, practically no women motoring correspondents —though occasionally women are asked to balance up what men write, as an indulgence to current fashion, or as a joke, by male editors—and this is probably because women would tend in writing regularly about cars to be a drag to men readers. They would concentrate overmuch on those aspects which would slowly corrode the image of the car as something glamorous, sexy, desirable, fulfilling. The love affair would be destroyed.

How many makers of cars, moreover, have women in their design departments? Precious few that I have been able to discover. There might usefully be more, for if there were it's likely that in many areas sensible car design would advance more quickly, and also that some of the myths which manufacturers (men, of course) cling to about female attitudes to cars would be more quickly destroyed. I mean things like colour. Manufacturers seem to have it as an article of faith that the one element in which women are *very* interested is the colour of their car. They may have market-researched this, and I have not, but in my experience women have far less of an obsession about colour in cars than the sellers believe.

Women are, though, likely to be interested in the genuine good looks of a car. Efficiency in a car comes first; but efficiency need be no barrier to prettiness. Good design will combine the two. This has without doubt sunk in as a principle at Cowley and Coventry in the last ten years.

The angular, clean-cut shape of the Italianate line which has swamped British car design since the late 1950s illustrates this. For years my eye was offended by the tubby car, like the Morris Minor. Testing one, there came the realisation that the reaction had more to it than some vague aesthetic prejudice. The boot on the Minor was curved, which sacrificed much of the space a square-cut boot gives. Since it opened from the ground-floor end, the Minor boot was also hard on one's back. Basic rule for cars: the less stooping and bending the better.

The unfussy, tight shape may now have become accepted in Britain (brilliantly executed, too, on a Japanese car like the Toyota Corona) but other lessons have been less quickly assimilated. Unpretty, and inefficient, adjuncts to cars persist. The chrome strips which (on 'de luxe' or 'super' versions of small cars especially) are so often stuck on the side panels are doubly grotesque. They are ugly, cutting the car in half

183

horizontally, suggesting that it ought to open like a mechanical Easter egg. They are also a practical menace; they act as water-traps, beneath which corrosion often starts its destructive work.

Manufacturers will doubtless say they know to whom they are selling. People *like* chrome strips. They will say the same about the wood or mock-wood facias on the posher British cars—an antique status symbol sadly perpetuated in that 1965 Rolls which was supposed to be bringing the marque's image up to date. Has no one a brighter and newer idea (stainless steel? leather? *anything*) than walnut for more expensive dashboards; or than chrome strips for side-panels? Why not let the panels stand as panels?

I remain unconvinced that you can't sell good design to people if you really want to. Automatic transmission, I bet, will be sold in the end even to those who claim they don't get the feel of *real* driving without manipulating a gear lever. It depends how badly you want to *sell* it, and *how* you sell it.

The sad thing is that though design has made marked advances in the last twenty years, the pace has not been fast enough. In safety, for instance. What man, buying a car, asks first if it is safe, or really demands that it is? It has, though, been encouraging recently to find safety beginning to emerge as a selling point: with the Rover 2000, with Mercedes-Benz and even, belatedly, in America.

Nor are advances discriminating enough. Look at the British small car which on its 'super' version sports a cigarette lighter but ignores a headlight flasher and wing mirrors. Wing, or outside, mirrors are a sore point. Five thousand pound jobs leave them off. Yet the offside wing mirror, at least, is crucial to safe driving on crowded roads—especially with British (and other nations') lane discipline what it is —and should be standard equipment. It's a question of priorities, and these aren't always got right.

So often, too, unco-ordinated design defeats even its own good points. Boots, for instance, are shaped sensibly and spaciously, then ruined by having wheel arches, petrol pipes and spare wheels crammed into them. Should not, in this day and age, all spare wheels be slung under?

One has to be sensible about this and not greedily expect too much. Only money *can* buy certain things on a car. It's a touch pointless to complain that the £600 small car has little leg-room for a 6-footer in the rear seats. It just isn't made that way, nor probably can be. You pay your money and take your choice. Yet there are basic points of good design which all cars *can* afford to follow. And the best cheap cars are those which incorporate most of them— maximum storage, easy-to-read instruments, quickly identifiable controls, efficiently-shaped seats and so on. Some specifics will fill in the outline.

Women are more interested in the detail of storage-room than men. They it is who have to worry about shopping, handbags, the kids' sweets, and packages of all shapes and sizes. Was it not astonishing that a big car like the Vauxhall Cresta of 1966 should have had no below-facia shelf? Don't tell me that knees are knocked on shelves, or that they can be dangerous in accidents. The designers' job is to make sure they aren't—by recessing or padding or whatever. A tray in almost any car meant for family use is essential—for handbags, biggish packages, boxes of tissues—and should have dividers in it, to stop things rolling about. It is much more useful than that dreary old 'glove compartment' which is never used for gloves and which can become a dire dumping ground for mouldering sweets, sticky papers, half-gnawed apples, forgotten parking tickets, fag-ends, or worse. And will no one design a built-in wastepaper container for cars, especially bigger ones?

There should also be a prize for the person who invents a car which can have wide, sensible storage compartments in car doors (as on Minis) while retaining the traditional up-and-down windows (*not* the dazzlingly inept sliding windows of the Mini). They could be as useful as a wide rear-window shelf and an uncluttered boot.

The list of things which, from a woman's point of view, make for efficiency, or mere usefulness, in a car is endless. Here is a start, important points jumbled with the not so important. They tend to come out that way.

Engines should be quiet.

Ashtrays need shields to avoid scrabbling fingers in filth when stubbing out.

Acceleration is more crucial, and more fun, than high top speed.

184

Gears should be flexible (like that joyous Cresta 3-litre-plus engine which managed 15 m.p.h. effortlessly in top gear).

Doors should be four, or very wide.

Clutches and steering should be light and not have too much play. Both items on the Ford Mustang were brutes; you felt you were winding the wheel for an eternity—though the answer, I admit, is probably to settle for power steering.

Bonnets should be openable from *inside* the car, with no need for grubby safety-catch fiddling down near the front bumper.

Dipsticks, and batteries, should be easy to get at.

Handles should be flush-fitting inside (e.g. the Triumph 1300) and outside too (e.g. more and more Italian cars). They should also be as large and obvious as possible; a plague on those nasty little finger-hurting press-buttons you still find on many quarter lights or 'ventilation panels'.

Cars should be ventilated properly, for demisting and heating, *without* those quarter lights being needed, in fact. It's the passengers who get the icy blast when the driver opens his quarter light; and women are often passengers. Fittings like the Rover 2000's cool-air-at-face-level ventilation, or the Ford

Above: *test day at the Brands Hatch, Kent, circuit for three contributors to this book— Stirling Moss, Maxwell Boyd and Elizabeth Benson. Cars shown overleaf are some of those Elizabeth Benson has tested; they form part of the background to her piece.*

185

Ford Mustang: with this car, Ford of America halted slumping sales around 1960. Their slogan was 'total performance'. Sales exceed 1 million.

Triumph 2000: middle-price-range British car appealing Elizabeth Benson in overall design and comfort and for help detail—like easy-to-operate 'piano key' switches.

Cortina's Aeroflow system, ought to be standard.

Rear reversing lights always—yes; childproof locks as standard fittings—yes; interior padding like the Jensen's as standard—yes; deep boots rather than long boots—yes; automatic chokes that don't choke properly—no.

Where did all the sun-roofs go? Very sad.

Make-up mirrors on sun visors or inside glove boxes are becoming more common—good.

The height of a car is interesting to a woman; most women don't like dislocating hips or providing a sideshow when getting in and out. Heights and angle of seats too. Women like to sit up when driving more than men. It's probably part of the fantasy bit for the male to like lying low in the Jim Clark manner.

Adjustable steering wheels are also nice for women; it's to do with the way we're shaped.

Lights that come on automatically inside glove boxes and boots (e.g. the Humber Sceptre) are O.K. Seats which are hard against the floor (i.e. almost all seats) and make the interior of cars even trickier to clean are not.

Press-button windows should be in more; so should knobs which do things to the outside of a car from the inside (e.g. many American cars have a device for adjusting the positioning of the outside mirror without having to stop and dismount to do it; the Jensen C-V8 introduced a knob similarly operating the petrol tank cap).

Automatic transmission should always retain the alternative of gear operation for non-traffic jam conditions.

And so on.

Yet even beyond all such random choices, there are general principles:

One—instruments should be dependable. Why can't speedometers give the right speed? Why don't fuel gauges tell the truth? One blurb for a British medium-size car actually made a point of saying that when the gauge registered empty there was really a gallon of gas left. How does that stop you forgetting to fill up once you've grown accustomed to the facia that's kidding you? It's helpful, though, if the facia bits and pieces do some of the thinking for you. Like the light that tells you when you've not let the handbrake off properly (e.g. the Porsche 1600 SC or Rover 2000) or that flickers when gas is running low (e.g. the Triumph 2000).

Two—if you can't do something well, don't do it at all. Ashtrays of poor plastic which swivel inefficiently, and which are ungettable-out when full (without cursing and finger-nail breaking) should be banned. So should tatty 'courtesy handles' on de luxe versions of small cars. They are offensive to the eye, add to the price, and are almost invariably useless; rear-seat passengers in cars this size are usually too tightly packed to need to hang on to anything. Hard, too small, and badly-positioned arm-rests (amazing how many fulfil that categorisation) are another modern bane of the indiscriminate tarting-up of cheaper cars to ape the posher marques.

Three—double-purpose, simplifying controls are good. Steering column switches which combine turn-indicators

186

*ensen C-V8: high performance, quality British
car. "Like sitting in a jewel box", says E.B.,
because of padding encasing front-seat riders.*

*Humber Sceptre: in 1966
form a snug car with a
G.T. feel in its drive.*

*Morris Minor 1000: virtually
unchanged design since 1948;
by mid-1960s 1,500,000 sold.*

and headlight flasher, or flasher-plus-dipswitch, are what I mean (e.g. Austin 1800 or Triumph 1300). So are knobs which combine windscreen wipers and washer—and which, even better (e.g. the Jaguar E-type 2+2, the Jensen C-V8 or Rover 2000), have variable speeds for the wiper as well. There ought to be more cars (combining the virtues of station-wagon and saloon, without the wagon's too frequent bleak look of utility) in which the rear seats fold flat when necessary, with access from the boot. Only sporty jobs, like the Mustang, the E-type 2+2, or the Porsche 1600 SC, seem to have gone in much for this—and their rear seats are scarcely seats at all, but supports for the smallish, and strictly on shortish trips. The Renault 16 approaches this ideal.

Four—are bumpers for bumping, or fenders for fending, or not? I wouldn't mind if they were. Aren't men more worried about retaining the bland undented look of the chrome prow than women? The final death blow for all hopes of rationality about bumpers was perhaps sounded by the Vauxhall designs which built sidelights and indicators vulnerably *into* the front bumper.

Five—when space in a car is anything like fully utilised, passengers outnumber the driver. Their comfort should more often be sought. Heaters which toast the driver and ignore the back-seat people are nasty. Vents for heating, and cooling, should always (e.g. Triumph 2000) be provided for the back seats.

The trouble with cars is not only that design doesn't move ahead fast enough, but that sometimes it goes into reverse.

A perfectly wonderful reclining seat on a pre-1965 Jensen C-V8 was turned into a tricky one when the car was revamped. On the early re-vamps you had darn near to open the driver's door to change the angle of the seat. It was, happily, corrected later.

P.R. prose that disguises rather than reveals is also a pest. Even one of the delicious extras I saw listed in a Mustang catalogue—the "Accent Paint Stripe and Rocker Panel Molding Package"—is preferable to the British brochure that says the seat covering "breathes like leather" (whatever that means) and talks of "sprung courtesy pulls", which sounds fiendishly, and I'm sure unintentionally, lavatorial. I'd be more interested in knowing how easy to clean the seats are and whether the straps for people to hang on to—which is English for 's.c.p.s'—are (a) needed, and (b) well-made.

But that's the hub of it, really. The trouble with women writing about cars is that (so far as men are concerned) they don't know enough about them. This piece proves it, of course. A couple of thousand words and not one mention of torque, compression ratios or even of braking distances. Is nothing, not even a love affair, sacred?

187

The most desirable cars

What (and this is fact, however much it's a mixture of the rational and irrational) do people look for in their cars? Which are the most desirable automobiles? Here are the answers, and the cars, which a few people in Europe came up with in mid-1966.

Bernard Braden
actor, comedian, commentator

I drive a convertible because if I could only put the top down one night a year it would still be worth while to me. I drive a Lincoln convertible because (a) it's the only convertible I know of that has four doors, and (b) it allows me to pull up beside the driver of a Rolls-Royce and say, "What's it like driving a small car?"

Jean Shrimpton
model

I don't worry particularly about what car I have, whether it's big or elegant or anything like that. I am interested in speed, though. I like a car that goes fast. But apart from that, all I want is something that gets me from place to place with no fuss. And because I use a car all the time in London, it can't be too big or difficult to park. That's why the desirable car for me at the moment is the Mini Cooper, which I've had especially sprayed Pacific Blue. It's the only car I've ever owned.

Peter Knapp
art director 'Elle'

I have driven many sports cars in my lifetime and my two favourites were the Fiat Abarth 1100, which held the road exceptionally well and was practically impossible to overturn, and then the 300 SL 1955. I am still attached to the look of its bodywork although it is now mechanically completely out of date. The car at present has its third motor, about 380,000 kilometres, its third gear box, its fifth clutch, and I had disc brakes put on in 1960.

Naturally I am now curious to know the latest Ford Mark II or the Ferrari that is being produced. But sentiment makes me keep my Mercedes.

As a visual artist one tends to like a car for its aesthetic qualities.

Jim Clark
racing driver

My ideal car has never been built. I'd want something small you could suddenly slide out into a big five-seater with lots of boot space, that sort of thing. I seem to live out of the boot of the car I have now at times. That's a Ford Galaxie 500, and it really is a desirable car to me. I've reached the stage where I want a car to be very easy to drive and one which does things quietly without any fuss. I like the comfort of the Galaxie, the ease of driving, the automatic transmission, the power steering, the electric window buttons, and all that. I really do feel so much less tired, even after driving it fast, that it means a lot. Off the track I'm just lazy about driving, I think. But for a town car, well, you can't beat a Lotus Elan. That's my other car. It has all the size advantages of a Mini, and it's fun to drive. Fibreglass construction is no bugbear to me. If it gets bumped, you just smooth it over and fill it in.

John Braine
novelist

My ideal car is always the car I drive at the moment. I now have a Mercedes 190. It comfortably accommodates the five of us and our luggage, but that isn't why I bought it. Nor did the desire to show off enter into it: I am my own status symbol. What I wanted was security. My ideal car goes exactly where I direct it under all conditions and in the event of a crash gives one a chance of survival. This sounds terribly prosaic—my ideal car is a sort of father-figure. But the Mercedes has glamour too—one not only feels safe in it but also on the verge of adventure.

Terence Stamp
actor

If I can't have a Rolls or an Aston I don't want a car at all. That's how I feel at the moment, which is the reason I'm walking these days. I prowl about in front of those showrooms in Berkeley Square looking at the Park Ward specials and waiting the day when I can smash down a cheque for £8,300 and drive away—listening blissfully to the ticking of the world's most expensive clock.

Malcolm Muggeridge
controversialist

The only car I've ever wanted—which thank God I've never owned—is the Mercedes convertible. The big convertible. With every gadget you can think of. The car that I use and like is the Triumph Herald convertible. I like cars that open. Often in quite bad weather I open them. I like air. I think the Mercedes is very elegant, very easy to

drive, *terribly* expensive and therefore I shall never have it. I think the car one doesn't own is more attractive, and when I see one driving along I think: "There's the most elegant car I've ever seen."

Paul McCartney
Beatle, composer, M.B.E.

My most desirable car is two cars. Well, is there any one car that's perfect for everything you want to do? I go for the shape of the car, and whether it will go fast or not, though I must admit that whenever I've been above 120 it scares me. Once on the M1 I was doing more than 120 and suddenly I noticed that all the little cars weren't paying as much attention to the road as I was. I broke out in a hot sweat and came down to 90. The thing about cars is that all the people who are doing 70 think they've got the fastest car in the world. My most desirable cars are the ones I'm driving now, whatever they are. At present I've got a Mini-Cooper with a Radford conversion. But that's much too noisy for long journeys. The engine won't stop engining and the heater won't stop heating. The other car's an Aston DB6. Before that it was a DB5. When I first bought an expensive car I hadn't even heard of the Ferrari or Maserati. I just naturally looked around for a British car. We make the best, don't we? And I took a fancy to the Aston. The truth is, though, I'm not a car addict. I feel embarrassed having to go into a garage and then pointing vaguely at the car and saying, er, I think it's the, er, you know, er, that's gone wrong. . . .

Ronnie Scott
jazz musician

In the first place it costs just over £11,500, which is a beautiful dream to begin with. It is, of course, Italian, and all Italian cars seem to have a glamour all their own.

It's the Ferrari 500 Superfast Pininfarina two-seater coupé. The maximum speed is 185 m.p.h. and it develops 400 b.h.p. at 6,500 r.p.m. by means of the traditional Ferrari all-aluminium V 12 engine with three twin-choke Weber carburettors. The lines of the car are superb in the accepted sleek workmanlike Ferrari tradition, and the interior is in impeccable taste. Very important as far as I'm concerned is the fact that it is a drophead coupé because in the dream I'm heading south in the sun, with a deep mahogany tan, at a comfortable 130 m.p.h. with the hood down, along one of those great French motorways, straight as an arrow, to keep an appointment in Barcelona with Vanessa Redgrave.

Professor Colin Buchanan town and traffic planner

There's no car on the market just now which I really pine for. At the moment I drive a Ford Zodiac Estate because it suits the sort of person I am. The pleasure of driving to me is to drive a big, powerful car slowly. I'm a strong believer in speed limits. I love this sensual feeling of gliding along in quiet. It's what I'd like about the Rolls—if I ever get to the state of driving a Rolls. But a car is very much a utility job; it's to get from A to B.

Hardy Amies fashion designer

I'm *mad* about the Jensen—well, it's so powerful. You can only do 70 miles an hour, but when you get to a crossroads and you're lined up for the lights, you're away—whoof, like that. It's not an ideal chauffeur's car—I *would* like them to do a Jensen with four doors because it's got to be used for lots of purposes and if you have two ladies in the back, they're not terribly

happy about clambering out of the front door. But I'm prepared to lump that. It's got a sunshine roof, and very often that's the only air I get during the day.

Peter Hall theatrical director

I don't have a favourite car, though I regret to say I'm obsessed by means of transport. My stable consists of an Aston Martin DB5 convertible, which I wouldn't trade for anything; a 1923 Rolls-Royce 20 open tourer; a Mini Traveller with basketwork sides, and a Shorrocks supercharger; a Volvo speedboat to go on the back of the Aston Martin; and a Raleigh collapsible bicycle to go in its boot.

I have in my time had intense love-affairs with a Jaguar XK150, an MGB and one of the first Jaguar E-types. I *think* I like the vintage Rolls the best, because of the deference that other drivers treat me with on the road. This is in sharp contrast with the Aston Martin which arouses jealousy, fury and suicidal tactics. I am, you see, fulfilled in my cars, if in little else in my life.

Barbara Castle transport minister

I cannot name my most desirable car. Unfortunately no such vehicle yet exists. If it did it would have *all* the following features:

Securely anchored seats (all fitted with safety belts); a padded facia; recessed instruments; collapsible steering wheel and column; burst-proof and child-proof locks; safety glass; bodywork built to absorb impact, especially at the front and back of

the car; good all-round vision; brakes designed to stop the car in any emergency without loss of control; stability at all speeds; easy but positive handling. And my ideal car would make the least possible noise and cause the least possible pollution of the atmosphere.

Donald Campbell land speed record-breaker

I think my *ideal* car is really Bluebird, but for everyday purposes I'd like Mr. David Brown's Aston Martin. You've got tremendous performance, wonderful roadholding and marvellous braking. The look of a car is like a woman, isn't it? A woman's got to be pretty easy on the eye, but if she's highly beautiful and hasn't got much on top, she'd be inclined to irritate you. It's very nice to have the Aston Martin with the electric windows and the fine coachwork. But on these archaic British roads, constipated as they are, you'd be better off with a flying machine.

The great bank robbery Grand Prix

by No. 93761 as told to No. 78904

Here's another fact about cars. Some men love them for one very special reason: crime. They drive them in a way that might make even some Grand Prix drivers tremble. And they have very firm ideas about which cars they love the most. There's one snag: the top talent too often gets prematurely retired. Like the authors of this piece, who were in the South Michigan state prison when they turned literary. It's all (one understands) fact; only the names were changed to protect the guilty.

In the more hip circles here at state prison it is generally held that the two top drivers of all time were Juan Fangio and Clarence Heatherton. There are probably a number of outsiders prepared to argue the point—with most of the disagreement centred on Clarence—but it's true all the same. You just have to judge by different standards, since Clarence made his reputation driving getaway on bank heists.

Clarence was a Londoner, and he looked every bit of it. When I first met him in 1945 he was a spry little old man, done up in baggy tweeds and wearing a pair of those steel-rimmed spectacles of the sort you see only on Englishmen and characters in old Charlie Chan movies. He also sported a toothbrush moustache that gave him a half-raffish air. Clarence had driven in British races and rallies for years before he was tempted into crime by a yen for an expensive Bugatti. After his first fling, which cost him a stretch in Wormwood Scrubs, he became a full-time wheelman and never went back to proper racing. Clarence was one of the oddballs who really liked the excitement of his work, but he always insisted that he drove only for love of that elusive Bugatti—or, as time went by, perhaps a 1,750-c.c. Alfa Romeo or a 300 SL Mercedes.

Clarence was as efficient as a computer behind the wheel, even though he nursed a quaint set of prejudices about cars. For instance, he never got over grousing about the disappearance of the running board, a very useful feature back in the Twenties when he started in the business. A standard technique on bank jobs in those days was to herd an assortment of cashiers and customers out to the getaway car and go tearing off with them stacked on the running boards. This show of togetherness usually kept the police from doing any careless shooting.

Another of Clarence's dislikes was the automatic transmission. I remember one time in 1960 we were parked outside a Chicago loan office, right in the middle of a job, and the old geezer decided to give me a lecture on the subject. He concluded it—after we had pulled away amidst a clanging din of alarm bells and shouts for help—with the determinedly pious observation that automatics were wicked. "An automobile," he declared, "should have a stick shift, as God intended."

In the early days of the profession, when Clarence was starting out on his career, there were more makes of cars to choose from than there are today. The main considerations were size and horsepower. There was the early Locomobile, some models of which boasted up to 120 h.p. There were the indestructible Cadillacs and the heavy, high-riding Buicks. Also popular for their speed all through the Thirties were such makes as Hudson, Terraplane and Ford.

John Dillinger was a great fancier of Fords. In fact, he was so partial to them that one time while he was on the run in Illinois, with every cop in the country trying to track him down, he took time to write a letter of appreciation to Henry Ford.

Hello Old Pal:

Arrived here at 10 a.m. today. Would like to drop in and see you.

You have a wonderful car. Been driving it for three weeks. It's a treat to drive one.

Your slogan should be:

"Drive a Ford and watch other cars fall behind you." I can make any other

car take a Ford's dust.
Bye-Bye
John Dillinger.

After volunteering this testimonial old John immediately ditched the Ford in favour of a freshly stolen Chevrolet coupé. Which proves, at least, that there is no brand loyalty among thieves.

Probably the most fondly remembered car among old wheelmen is the Cord. It was hard to come by but much esteemed by the cognoscenti, because it was remarkably nimble and because driving it demanded a certain deft touch which helped to weed out the amateurs.

By contrast, most cars on the road today make pretty crummy getaway vehicles. They are sprung and shocked for a nice spongy ride, which is comfortable only when you don't have a cruiser on your tail. So wheelmen look for specific characteristics when selecting a car for a job. The first thing they want is a good stiff suspension that will cut down the lean on fast turns. And if they can spot a model with disc brakes and anti-roll bars, all the better.

The ideal getaway car, under present-day conditions, would seem to be something like a Jaguar: fast, plenty of pick-up and easy to handle in our heavy traffic. A cinch to outrun anything the law might have. Unfortunately, a Jaguar is *not* the ideal getaway car. I used one a couple of years ago on a bar hold-up— and if you have never tried making it through the door of a Jaguar at a dead run with a sawed-off and a sack of money clutched to your bosom, you just don't know the meaning of limited headroom.

Important as the right car is to a getaway, nothing is more important than the man at the wheel, and at this, as I say, Clarence Heatherton was king. I liked to think that Clarence passed at least a part of his great skill on to me when he introduced me to the art of armed robbery and taught me the rudiments of git-driving. Not that I've ever had any illusions about my skill as a wheelman. The truly good drivers are specialists, and very often they are men with a proper racing background. I don't claim that race drivers are any more given to larceny than, say, jai alai players or pole-vaulters, but there is obviously a flaky fringe around the sport. When a driver does get into the rackets, he's more likely to stay behind the wheel than to take up pickpocketing.

I worked with a lot of these speedway drop-outs over the years, and they are the most off-beat group of characters you could ever hope to get arrested with. Some are just flat-out kooks. There was a wheelman in Detroit, for instance, who twitched. I mean *all* the time. He had nerve spasms in his fingers, and his left eyelid fluttered like the shutter of a 16-mm. Bell & Howell. It didn't seem to hang him up on his driving, but he had been barred for life from legitimate racing when it began to interfere with other drivers who developed sympathetic tics.

Another specimen was a big German who still, somehow or other, finds occasional employment around Cleveland. He looked like Charles de Gaulle and once worked as a pit man for the great Fangio—for about two hours. He was a perfect driver for hold-ups if you could keep him away from the engine, but if he so much as tweaked a spark plug the whole motor was good for a three-week lay-up.

A good git-man must have a knack for coaxing total performance out of middling machines. He has to be careful and deliberate, and it doesn't hurt if he's a little paranoid. The best wheelman in St. Louis right now, as a matter of fact, is a guy who quit racing when he became convinced that the rest of the drivers on the circuit were conspiring to put him through a rail. On a heist he is always certain that every stop sign, traffic light and speed limit is there just to trap him. He imagines prowl cars lurking in each alley, and he has this nutty idea that all women drivers are police molls. Working with this guy is harder on the nerves than a three-month stretch in solitary— but, man, is he ever careful.

The real wheel talent shows up less in aberrations than it does in proper cornering. On city streets it's impossible to cut down approach and exit angles, and in order not to lose speed the driver must have enough finesse to handle a power skid.

One of the oldest tricks in the profession is to let the cops get right on your tail on a gravel road, then suddenly swing the wheel hard over for a controlled, four-wheel slide, timed to dig out on to a side road. Any wheelman who can't do this with his eyes shut would be better off in a nice comfortable cell.

The variation on this—the 180° skid

—requires pure genius. The only wheel-man I ever knew who was really accomplished at this was a skinny little hillbilly named Beauregard Washburn who didn't look competent enough to drive a herd of pigs. Now Beauregard Washburn was all eyeballs and Adam's apple, with shaggy sideburns holding up the slack in his jaws. He'd learned to skid a car through 180°—with the help of a heavy load of moonshine in the rear end—down around Nashville while playing tag with revenue agents. The night he demonstrated the trick for me, we had a 500-pound safe in the trunk and a 3,000-pound police car on our tail trying to get right in there with it. We were heading east out of Kalamazoo on a mangy little dirt road, and things looked a lot better for the cops than they did for us. But suddenly Beauregard tromped on the brakes and spun the wheel over. We must have done a quarter of a mile sideways and then backwards before Beau finally dredged up enough power to get us moving forward again. For a few minutes I was completely unglued. And so, I imagine, were the cops when they found themselves still heading east with us going west.

Occasionally a driver like Beauregard, with no background of legitimate racing, will make the grade as a top git-man, but professional criminals prefer professional drivers—since wash-outs are generally disasters. Some friends of mine learned this the hard way last spring when they decided to make a driver out of an ex-bookie called Wimpy. They taught him everything they could and even packed him off to a school in California where they train race drivers. But Wimpy had neither the wit nor the co-ordination for driving. On his very first job he let a diagonal parking arrangement at a small-town supermarket job rattle him to shreds. He positioned the car in the parking slot backward, a technique made popular by an ex-road-racer who used a convertible and worked by himself, taking advantage of the diagonal parking for a Le Mans start. But it didn't work for Wimpy. When his pals came piling into the car with the loot, he immediately laid down a quarter inch of rubber screaming out of that slot—*backward*, through the market's plate-glass window and right into a soap display.

But Wimpy wasn't the worst. On the beef that earned me my current sentence

I came bursting out of a Detroit jewellery store with guns and hot necklaces hanging out of every pocket, only to find that my idiot driver had very carefully wedged our car into a parking space. He wasn't even behind the wheel, for all the good it would have done. He was, God preserve us, feeding coins into the meter.

And that's the sort of thing that is becoming more and more typical of the business. The real trouble is that there aren't enough men with racing experience coming into the profession—men like my old friend Clarence. I have a fond picture in my mind of Clarence today, a little older and with thicker lenses in his glasses, but still in tweeds and proper English to his larcenous core. He's sitting in a freshly stolen G.T. 350 Mustang, immediately in front of a

bank in some small eastern community —one of those quiet places off the main highway with miles of country road stretching out in all directions. Clarence has one eye cocked on the town constable and the other on his confederates in the bank (common criminals, of whom he doesn't really approve), but his mind is on that fine power plant in front of him, listening to it tick over and just waiting to let it out on the only kind of race that ever mattered to him.

That's not too unlikely a vision, but it's coming to be a very rare one. Git-driving is losing its colour, I'm afraid, and is becoming less specialised. It is being taken over by clods who pull jobs on the spur of the moment and drive off willy-nilly into the back bumpers of police cars or get hung up at toll booths with nothing smaller than a hot twenty.

It's enough to take the heart right out of you.

Crime will probably be with us for a long time, but the Grand Prix git-driver, I fear, is as outdated as Clarence's running board.

Above: *one of the classic crime-and-getaway cars. It looks like any other 1928 Cadillac which has seen better days. But it belonged to Al Capone, gangster, of Chicago, Illinois. Its sturdy exterior hides armour-plating. The windows are bullet-proof. The rear window was in effect a 'turret' through which a light machine-gun could be fired.*

195

First, hypnotise your driver
and then you'll find out what he really wants
by Stephen Black

Motorists say they want safer cars. But do they? To discover what they really want and enjoy in driving, Dr Black used hypnosis to probe their unconscious. He is a medical researcher, specialising in the nervous system and psychosomatic illnesses. His car project, in which he employed the new science of ergonomics —the biological study of design—was sponsored by the Harry Ferguson Research Organisation. This is something of what he found out.

It is no use making cars people will not buy—just as it is no use inventing safety harness people will not wear. The car of today is still a dangerous status symbol, studded inside and out with sharp points and blunt instruments. The ergonomic car would look very different from cars as we know them: but could it be sold? We can take a statistically significant sample of the population and ask questions, but the answers will indicate only what people 'think they think'— about a car that does not exist. And such techniques provide no indications as to the *reasons why*. If we are concerned with such a potentially lethal product as the car, it is the *reasons why* that are most important.

To discover what people think they think, the routine techniques of market research were employed. To discover the reasons why, hypnosis was used to obtain evidence from the unconscious mind. Almost by definition, what we say under hypnosis comes from the unconscious—Freud first realised the significance of the unconscious when watching Bernheim's experiments with hypnosis. But it is impossible to obtain a statistically significant sample of suitable deep-trance hypnotic subjects. We used only 25—mostly under 25 years of age.

We found that many conscious reactions to the car could be explained from the unconscious material obtained in this way. But we also found a considerable discrepancy between a good deal of what people said when awake and what they said when hypnotised—and that, to the unconscious mind, danger on the roads may often add to the excitements of motoring. On the evidence of this small sample, at least, it would seem that the root of all our trouble on the roads is the muddled, greedy and, above all, wildly aggressive unconscious mind of man.

Consciously, our group was well satisfied with the design of cars and tended to enthuse over the latest Motor Show models although they were thought "too expensive" and there was much criticism of the 'workmanship' on all makes except the most highly priced. Road safety was recognised as "an important question", and the wearing of safety harness was accepted sanctimoniously as a "good thing". Those who owned cars without safety harness were always about to have it fitted. Those with safety harness, however, admitted that they did not always use it. Road deaths were discussed as a source of anxiety. Most subjects believed that, apart from the roads, "fast driving" was the main cause of accident deaths. But the "pedestrians" were also blamed.

Under hypnosis at the unconscious level, these subjects all stressed the significance of "freedom" associated with car ownership. This was related to fantasies about driving in the country, which were often lyrically expressed. One subject, a medical student in his last year at hospital, said: "I see myself driving fast on a warm day with the windows open. It is not a busy road, but busy enough to make the driving interesting. . . . I have somebody with me to share my driving. . . . It is a wonderful sense of freedom: there is nothing between me and almost everything I really want . . . I like to feel she admires me and the way I handle the car. The sun, the sky and the road and that wonderful feeling of power: it's the feeling of power I suppose. . . ." (This is a summary of a long, rambling statement made under hypnosis.)

Another male subject said, under hypnosis: "The pleasure comes from moving. I have an impression of the world going by, but I don't belong to it any more. I'm on a journey, outside it all. I feel free. . . . I'm driving fast and enjoying it." Asked for the significance of "driving fast", this subject replied: "It's the power, a sense of superiority, a feeling of being master of it all."

The class war is evidently still going on. Our group was basically one with middle-class aspirations, although many of its members were of working-class origin. Consciously these origins had largely been set aside, but unconsciously they were still very much in evidence. The car, it seemed, was used by society to bolster the class structure of the past. The symbolism of the car had been used by "them" to set off "their" supposed superiority to "us". One young man under hypnosis said: "It's a bit like the cut of officers' gear in the Navy—a very subtle way of showing who's in command." Another said: "Even the police know who the roads are made for—I was done trailing a chauffeur-driven Princess. We were both doing 50, but nobody stopped them . . . and I said so. It cost me five pounds." Said a nursing sister: "I keep my old car a secret. It's just not Matron's idea of a nurse."

Questioning under hypnosis about road dangers indicated that fear of road accidents is a *conscious* reaction to mortality figures in the papers. But unconsciously it is always "the other fellow" who has the accident—and the greatest cause of accidents was the frustrating *slow* driver who blocks a narrow road. Moreover, the wearing of safety harness was thought to be "cissy" or "composty".

"Accidents happen all the time . . ." said one subject. "I think we're pretty used to accidents now. You expect accidents to happen, to other people of course." Said a woman: "You see some terrible things on the roads sometimes. It's probably the first time most people see a corpse, but you never really worry about it afterwards. Anyway I don't."

Most revealing of all was the following: "I can't pretend I really mind it when I see a car accident. In a funny way it makes a journey interesting. You pull out, try to pass and have to pull back—you look such a fool when that happens.

And then you see some monumental pile-up and the police and all that, but it kind of justifies you for not having tried to make it after all. We saw eight big car accidents last year when we went to Devon. . . ."

Such findings may seem surprising to those who think of the unconscious as seething with unexpressed anxieties about life in general. But these results correspond with our unconscious attitudes to nuclear weapons. *Consciously* we all claim to be anxious about the threat of nuclear annihilation, but *unconsciously*, as revealed by hypnosis, we do not really live in fear—which is why we so rarely dream about it.

An attempt was made to analyse in more detail the significance of motoring "freedom". This "freedom" had warm, homely associations, connected with the countryside or with the sea, also with the family. Said one subject: "To me a car has always meant going to the seaside, holidays, Mum and Dad."

But the freedom of motoring also implied an element of excitement. It is known in psychiatry that the car is a symbol of sexual prowess, supplying as it does both strength and power and a rhythmic response. And the idea of "freedom" quickly led at the unconscious level to ideas of licence.

The car is linked to the idea of "a journey" and on this journey—under hypnosis—our subjects soon found themselves at first alone without "the family", and then "alone with the right person". The transition was very easy. Said one man: "It's a journey on which you can very well end up by becoming a father yourself."

Asked under hypnosis why owner-drivers insist on bringing their cars into town, most subjects became indignant. The roads were there to be used by everyone; it was everyone's "right" and attempts by "the Government" to stop people using cars were all part of the same trouble: "In this country they don't really want ordinary people to have cars, whatever the advertisements say." The use of a car in town meant that you were "free", you did not have to depend on "buses and trains" and most significantly you could "*escape*".

Eight separate subjects, five women and three men, used the word "escape" in connection with motoring. Said one man: "In town you are surrounded by people; that's why public lavatories become important—you can be alone for a few minutes. And that's the point of a car in town: once behind the wheel you are alone and yet the world still goes by outside. Sometimes I drive down Oxford Street singing at the top of my voice to the radio. I have the windows shut: nobody can hear me. You can cuss and blind as much as you like in a car. You can do anything you want. . . ."

An electrician said: "I think best in a car, going along that is. You see things very clearly. When I was worried over Mary, I felt much better in the car than at home. With the wireless going and the heater on, it's a bit like home anyway. And you can be sure of being alone." Said another subject: "I get into the car after work and I'm free until I get home. It's my only really free time in the whole day. I suppose if the house was bigger I could be alone at home, but I can't."

The greatest value of the material elicited under hypnosis lay in the constructive ideas produced by the subjects when invited to imagine the ideal car. The unconscious is largely unhampered by frustrating reality. The resulting fantasies were experienced either under hypnosis during the session, or were later reported under hypnosis as dreams experienced during normal sleep.

At the seaside, the subjects would have done better with a caravan. The car of their dreams would go "anywhere" on or off the road—it would even float, like the German Amphicar. It was also fitted out with all the amenities of a cosy annexe to Mon Repos: the kettle was boiled on a gas stove and tea was taken inside the car on folding tables. The seats turned round to accommodate the tea party and when it rained several subjects were discovered playing cards. The seats also folded down to make a bed—they could sleep in the car, make love in the car and take their holidays in the car. Fittings included hanging cupboards for clothes, drawers and shelves and a litter-bin.

Challenged, however, that what they really wanted was a Dormobile or other motorised caravan no subject accepted this as quite equivalent to the ideal. Paradoxically, their dream car was still very much a modern status symbol, but it was also a car fitted with all the amenities of a caravan. Illogically, it still looked like an ordinary car and it still handled well on the open road at speeds of 100 m.p.h. or more.

Introduced to a four-wheel-drive car, several subjects argued *consciously* that they could see no virtue in its ability to travel freely off the road. And in this they were supported by the results of market research. Yet when hypnotised these same subjects apparently forgot their own arguments, and listed all kinds of advantages to be found in off-road motoring—picnics, romantic interludes, parking at point-to-point meetings, following motor-cycle scrambles and shooting rabbits in the fields at night. A number of subjects reached out in the unconscious to include African safaris and desert travel on overland trips to the Far East.

There is also, it appeared from the subjects, a deep unconscious fear of "getting stuck" if you leave the road in a normal car. A country lane may be "unpatrolled", and if "disaster" overtakes you, there may be "no one close at hand to help". You might find yourself "in a dead-end" and a dead-end, it transpired, meant "turning in a muddy farmyard or a narrow lane".

To our younger subjects, it is true, off-road motoring offered "adventure", even the possibility of "getting stuck with the right person". But the vision of a car wallowing in "impotence with spinning wheels and nothing happening" was still highly disturbing to these subjects. There were dark fears of bumping the "precious sump", or damaging what one subject called "the shrouded privacy of my differential". Yet the risk of damage to their precious cars from road accidents was barely considered.

Consciously, we deserve to survive; unconsciously we have only ourselves to blame if we are killed. Clearly, we should limit respect for the unconscious to contributions on details of design. The ergonomist's problem is to design a car which is safe, but which will also sell. And it might sell if the car fulfils some of the more respectable dreams of the unconscious.

To summarise, the three basic demands of our Ideal Car in order of their significance to the engineer are:

It must be safe

It must be able to go "anywhere"

It must be a home-from-home.

Left: *Stephen Black has just taken the mind of the driver to pieces: this is what you'd find if you took a modern racing car to pieces. The machine is the Ford-powered Lotus which Colin Chapman designed specially for the Indianapolis 500 of 1965. In it Jim Clark became the first Briton ever to win this greatest of American races.*

The unlovers

The feeling has been growing during this last section. Now it must be stated frankly. There are some people who do not love cars; and there are some machines that seem to hate them. Even at that, the people we are talking of usually know all about the loving. It's just that they rarely subscribe to it.

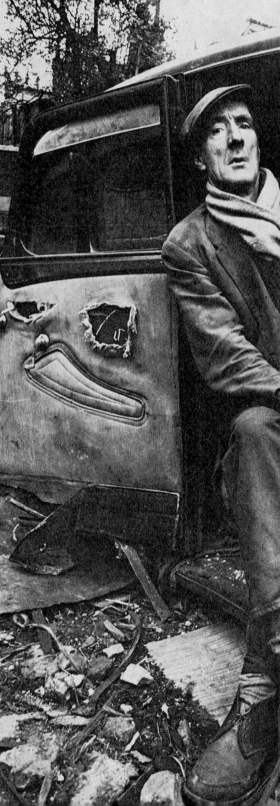

Left: *these are three people who have a rather different relationship to cars from the rest of us. David Aggio (far left) is a second-hand car dealer in Warren Street, London; in this wheeler-dealing world men can't afford to be in love with cars. Ted Brailey (centre) is a car-breaker, and Tony Bird (near left) operates a car-crusher, which is seen swallowing the last remains of somebody's one-time loved one. For more about their worlds, and about a fourth category of people who aren't notably in love with cars, turn over.*

Wheeler-dealers: Warren Street, London W.1, has been the undisputed Mecca of the British second-hand car trade for years. The inhabitants live and breathe our obsession with cars without the smallest emotional contact. A man calling a car 'she' here is almost certainly an outsider.

"You can't afford to fall in love with a car here," said a trader. "It's fatal." What he meant was that Warren Street men are born dealers, who happen to have landed in the car trade, and poker-players don't form attachments to the Queen of Spades.

The private owner has no place in this game, and many Warren Street men more or less won't deal with him at all. "The man in the street is very quick to condemn the Warren Street trader, but it's the public that are the villains. It's they who try to sell us cars with H.P. on them. They're a menace." Selling to the public is only slightly less unpopular than buying from them. "They take up half an hour of your time and then buzz off saying, 'I'll have to think about it'. I've no time for messers."

Both buying and selling are firmly based on the notion that whatever fast ones you think you're pulling, the one you don't pull, ever, is to neglect to mention even the smallest fault in your car. A very large part of the buying is done on the phone, either from hire fleets or garages disposing of their 'choppers' (cars taken in part exchange). The trader 'borrows' the car, which means he buys it 'as described', and if it later turns out to be otherwise it can be 'snowballed'—that is, returned to the original seller. The same trust applies on the money side—"you can only do a bloke once". Only with 'buying as seen' is there any room for deception: a buyer is assumed to have good eyesight and to know the rules, like "save your cheque for the morning when the light's not fading".

If an ordinary car stands for a week without a suitor it begins to look like a 'bottler' (non-seller) and the trader may eventually be driven to 'knocking' it (accepting a bid that means a loss). Penury, however, is not exactly round the corner: a man making less than £100 a week over the last few years was definitely not doing well.

There are, though, two schools of thought in the Street, old and new—the new being largely those prepared to be orthodox salesmen and deal with the public if necessary. For the old school, Mark Harris: "Salesmanship has no place here. Both sides know what they want. If a man makes a bid, he's bought it. And if I'm buying on the phone and it takes me more than two minutes, I don't buy." For the new, David Aggio, curly-haired, 36, with brocade tie, cigar, and a typical new-school office—built-in washbasin and leaded-glass drinks cabinet: "Believe in salesmanship? We thrive on it."

Here are the two schools operating. Old, buying: "Ridiculous, you're miles away. How much is that? Monkey? It's not everybody's colour, is it?" Again: "I'd be a lousy buyer of it, John. I'd be merciless. I wouldn't get there. You've tried hard enough. . . . About a month? Do I send for it? Four-eighty. O.K."

New, buying and selling: David Aggio says he will buy anything, and cites as evidence a 1947 Rover he has outside. His office, unlike the others, is full of breathless messengers saying things like, "My punter's going cold"—a punter is a dealer-buyer—while Aggio haggles endlessly on the phone with people he doesn't know over cars he hasn't seen. "I'd want some change out of that. Can't you chip me a tenner back? We're not going to get fat out of it, I assure you . . . I'll come down and we'll deal."
Anthony Cowdy.

Breakers: Ted Brailey of Islington, London, started as a car-breaker in 1937. A one-man business, usually: just a yard with maybe one or two helpers. The idea is to buy very broken-down cars very cheaply. Then you break them up and sell the bits which have value: dynamo, distributor, tyres. People often have to pay the breaker to take their car away. Ted Brailey says he doesn't feel anything for cars himself. But his customers often do.

"A lady came here once, she had an old '35 Austin, and she spent, oh she spent untold money on it, and she got pulled with the police with it and she asked me whether I'd take it away. She'd give it for nothing. She nearly broke her heart when she give it to me. I put the hammer through it and she started crying out here.

"Another woman, she lived round the corner. Her husband died—Charlie his name was—he had an old Austin too. He used to come round and ask me if I had a dynamo or something, but I never charged nothing because he was an old man. And after he died his wife asked me would I take the car away. Well, when I put the cutter through it there was so much paint on it, she said he used to paint it up every month, it was about half an inch thick, and with all the cutting it blew back in my face. I had to burn it off. Set the car alight to burn it. He loved it. Here, he even painted his exhaust box aluminium. Painted all the wheels aluminium. He had more paint . . . well, he spent a hundred pounds in paint on it.''

Crushers: There is a faster, more mechanised, and somehow more final way of getting rid of your old car than giving it to a breaker. Feed it to a crusher. The machine must be the most potent unlover symbol of the age. The Bird-Crusher (page 201) is the largest mobile crusher in Europe. With only two men operating it, it can swallow between 1,000 and 2,000 cars a week, reducing each to the biggish-suitcase-sized metal bundle shown here. The firm operating it offer the crusher's services free to local councils in Britain, providing they collect car carcases at one site, ready for destruction. The crusher-men sell the scrap to steel plants. It takes three minutes for a car to be digested by the crusher, which cost

£65,000 and exerts pressure of 4,800 lbs. per square inch on its victims. The unloving embrace of the crusher seems to be needed by society: it's been estimated that in Britain 400,000 vehicles a year must be scrapped if roads are not to be clogged or landscape defaced. Strangely, it's out of love for their car that some people have called upon the Bird-Crusher. Tony Bird says that a one-

family 1934 Buick once went into the crusher. Its owners were so enamoured of it that they opted to have it destroyed rather than sold.

Derek Jewell.

Workers: Mass-production factories which make cars can be very bleak, ugly, dirty, noisy and deadly monotonous for many of the men and women who work in them. The words below were recorded at one of Britain's biggest car plants for a B.B.C. programme, *Factory*, by Alasdair Clayre, a writer and fellow of All Souls College, Oxford. They are typical of many other car factories and of many other factories of every kind:

"There's one department there which they call Trip Hammers, and you can't even hear yourself think, let alone speak. It's terrible. One trip hammer is about twice as bad as a pneumatic drill, and you've got at least six of those all going at once.

"You can show a man how to do a job that's going to take him three minutes. Well, he becomes proficient at that job and he's probably interested in it for a day, perhaps three days. But at the end of three months he hates the sight of it.

"After a very little while you could do it without even thinking about it. It's terrible, the monotony. As I say, to break the monotony people start, well, not exactly fighting but ribbing one another. If you can take the ribbing, O.K. If you can't take the ribbing you get a lot more of it. But as I say, the monotony is the biggest thing they've got to fight against.

"You see perhaps two hundred men spread out at about four feet apart and all of them perhaps just going as hard as they can go. This was the thing that impressed me. I said to myself, well, I don't know, you've got twenty more years left in you of work: are you going to carry on like this for the rest of your life?

"Over in the cleansing department, they're the lowest paid men in the works, and yet they've got the dirtiest and filthiest jobs. Because everything's got to be cleaned, you see. It must be clean and tidy. To clean out a pit, a sludge pit you see—that's where all the dross is going off—the smell's enough to drive a man insane."

The car as killer by George Perry

The final fact of loving is inescapable. Cars kill. It is a measure of their fascination for us that society seems to accept this. No matter what palliatives are tried, the slaughter on the roads continues. In Britain around 8,000 die each year, and 280,000 are injured; in America 48,000 die, 1,700,000 are hurt. Usually the people who are killed are not widely known. They make no headlines, only statistics. But sometimes the victims are the famous. These were some of them.

E. R. Sewell and **Major Nitrobe** owe their place in this gloomy gallery because they were the first motorists in Britain to be killed. The date was February 25, 1899. Queen Victoria still reigned; the notorious 'Red Flag' Act—making it compulsory for a man on foot to precede every automobile—had been repealed less than three years before. The place was Grove Hill, Harrow, Middlesex. Both passenger and driver were thrown out of their wrecked vehicle.

Jack Jones was the aggressive Labour M.P. for Rotherham. A month after the 1959 General Election he was fined £5 for assaulting another driver who had obstructed him. He was killed near Woodhead on the Sheffield-Manchester road on the night of October 31, 1962, on his way home from a dinner dance. The car plunged down a 100-ft slope into a ravine. The inquest revealed that the 68-year-old M.P. had had an acute haemorrhage of the pancreas.

Driving back to London from the Edinburgh Festival, **Dennis Brain**, the horn-player, died near Barnet on September 1, 1957. The Concertgebouw at Edinburgh played Schubert's *Unfinished Symphony* in tribute and Poulenc composed *Elegy for Horn and Piano* in his memory.

The five-times-married Dominican diplomat **Porfirio Rubirosa** was the legendary millionaire playboy of all time. He got off to an early start as a polo-playing army captain who, in his twenties, married the daughter of Trujillo, the Dominican dictator. Later brides included the French movie star Danielle Darrieux and the heiresses Doris Duke and Barbara Hutton. He died in his Ferrari on a road cutting through the Bois de Boulogne, in the early morning hours of July 5, 1965. He was nearing the age of 60 and was out shopping for his last wife.

Gone With the Wind, published in 1936, was **Margaret Mitchell's** only book. An all-time best-seller, the film from it made more money than any other. The author of this epic novel of the American Civil War lived quietly on its proceeds in Atlanta, Georgia. On the evening of August 11, 1949, she was hit by a taxi in Peachtree Street—through which her heroine, Scarlett O'Hara, had forced her buggy when Atlanta was surrounded by Union soldiers. She died a few days later.

Wilfred Fienburgh first entered Parliament as Labour member for North Islington in 1951. He is remembered mainly for his fine, posthumously published novel, *No Love for Johnny*, a bitter study of political life which was later successfully filmed. He died on February 3, 1958, after crashing into a lamp post at Mill Hill, in North London.

Albert Camus, born in Algeria in 1913, was one of the most influential literary figures in post-war France, first as editor of the left-wing daily *Combat* and later as novelist, playwright and philosopher. In 1957 he was awarded the Nobel Prize for Literature. On January 4, 1960, the car in which he was travelling ran off the road near Sens and struck a tree. "All youth grieves for him," said fellow Nobel winner François Mauriac.

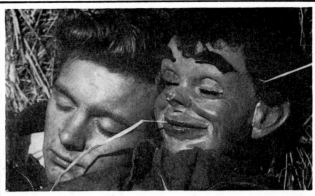

Dennis Spicer, 29, was in the Royal Variety Performance with his ventriloquist act. Two weeks later, on November 16, 1964, he was killed in a head-on collision on the A.1 near Stamford, Lincolnshire, returning from a Harrogate charity show. In London the night before his agent had signed a Palladium contract on his behalf. He never knew.

In 1958 **Mike Hawthorn** crowned a seven-year career in Grand Prix racing when he beat Stirling Moss at Casablanca. He thus became World Champion—by one point. Four months later, on January 22, 1959, having retired from racing, he crashed on a public road. It was the Guildford by-pass, near the Hog's Back in Surrey—the same stretch of road where he had learned to drive eleven years earlier.

Prince Aly Khan bettered his father's obsession with horses by becoming a gentleman jockey with over 100 winners. His second wife was Rita Hayworth, the film star. After their divorce his constant companion was the Paris model, Bettina, who was with the 48-year-old playboy on the night of May 14, 1960. His Lancia ploughed into another car on the Boulevard Henri Cellier, St. Cloud, near Paris, killing him and injuring her. The chauffeur was in the back seat—unhurt.

On August 29, 1935, King Leopold of the Belgians was driving with his wife, the 29-year-old **Queen Astrid** along the shores of Lake Lucerne. Suddenly the car went out of control, struck a tree, ploughed through a wall and dropped into the lake. Astrid, thrown out with great force, died in the King's arms. The tragedy, only 18 months after King Albert's death in a climbing accident, plunged Belgian morale into a morbid state of depression.

James Dean made only three films, *East of Eden, Rebel Without A Cause* and *Giant.* He was first a symbol for the non-conforming youth of the mid-Fifties; later he was the inspiration of a morbid death cult. He died in a Porsche, near Salinas, California, on September 30, 1955, aged 24.

Belinda Lee, daughter of a Devon hotel proprietor, was the most promising student of her year at the Royal Academy of Dramatic Art. Although tipped for big stardom, her career in British films fizzled. An unhappy marriage, entanglements with Italian nobility, sleeping drug overdoses and Garbo-esque behaviour produced bad publicity. Her last films were made on the Continent and usually featured her as a *femme fatale*. On March 14, 1961, she was killed in a 100 m.p.h. blow-out at San Bernardino, California, returning from Las Vegas. The Vatican newspaper commented on the "empty vanity" of films and the dangers of irresponsible speeding.

Isadora Duncan was a revivalist of Greek classical dancing and an advocate of free love. In 1913 her two children were drowned when a car they were in went out of control into the Seine. On September 14, 1927, practically broke after her failure to found a dance school in Russia, she was trying out a Bugatti along the Promenade des Anglais in Nice. Her trailing scarf caught in the rear wheel, jerking her back and breaking the spinal column.

Bonar Colleano, born in New York in 1924, first appeared on the English stage in 1933. He was in many British films after the war and his biggest stage triumph was as Kowalski in the London production of *A Streetcar Named Desire*. In 1958 a bankruptcy examination revealed that he owed £8,000 income tax. Three months later, on August 17, he was killed at the wheel when his Jaguar hit a fence a mile from the Birkenhead exit of the Mersey Tunnel.

Ernie Kovacs was a satirical comedian who wore a large black moustache and chewed cigars. He became famous on New York television and then went to Hollywood where he mixed screwball comedy (*Operation Madball*) with sinister character acting (*Our Man in Havana*). A hell-raising founder-member of 'The Clan', he died after a party on the night of January 13, 1962, when his station wagon skidded off the rain-wet Santa Monica Boulevard and hit a light pole.

Acknowledgements

The idea of this book originated in conversations about cars with my wife, Elizabeth. She has, alias Elizabeth Benson, also written a section of it, but she has contributed far more towards it than this. She, and my family, bore the brunt of my preoccupation with it.

To the team whose names appear with mine on the title page I am obviously indebted. No one could have had more enthusiastic, inspiring and efficient colleagues. The tolerance and encouragement of Denis Hamilton, Editor of *The Sunday Times*, has also been very important to me, as has the helpfulness of Godfrey Smith, Editor of *The Sunday Times Magazine*, who is a fount of ideas and good humour about virtually everything, cars included.

Others, too, have helped with this book. First, on the research and secretarial front, Doris Bryen, Janey Burland, Mirabel Moir and my wife did a great deal, while Susan Raven meticulously read the proofs. Second, there were those who contributed ideas. Notions which I incorporated in one way or another came from Bill Boddy, Roger Bolam, Stanley Daw, Graham Finlayson, Felice Gordon, George Greenfield, David King, Roger Law, James Leasor, Meriel McCooey, Beryl Moir, Muriel Theobald, Oscar Turnill and Ian Yeomans.

Around half the material in this book was specially commissioned for it, and I am grateful to the writers, illustrators and photographers who produced it. This original work includes the articles by Elizabeth Benson, Bill Boddy, Maxwell Boyd, Pete Brock and John Bentley, John Dankworth, Peter Dunn, Henry Longhurst, Lord Montagu of Beaulieu, Peter Sellers, David Sylvester and Elisabeth Woolley; photographs by Christopher Angeloglou, Duffy, Graham Finlayson, Lord Snowdon, Michael Ward, Bryan Wharton and Ian Yeomans; drawings by David Frankland, Peter Sullivan and Roger Law; and the model made by Deirdre Amsden.

The remainder of the book is drawn from material created during the last three-quarters of a century. That material has a very wide variety of origins. The following specific sources should be mentioned:—

Photographs have been provided by, among others, *The Sunday Times*, the Montagu Motor Museum, the Hulton-Radio Times Library, the Temple Press Library, Associated Iliffe Press Ltd., and the Ford Motor Company, who also helped with the commentaries to the drawings by David Frankland and Peter Sullivan. To all these pictorial sources, and many more not individually mentioned, I am grateful.

The articles by Hunter Davies, Maurice Wiggin and my own on the Cooper Car Company appeared in their original versions in *The Sunday Times*. They have been considerably revised, updated and expanded for this book. I have also made use of the description of 'Automania' as it was coined in *The Sunday Times Magazine*, from which also came the basic idea for *The Car As Killer* and the shortened version of Anthony Cowdy's *Wheeler-dealers*.

The Great Bank Robbery Grand Prix first appeared in *Sports Illustrated* © 1966 Time Inc. The Henry Groshinsky photograph first appeared in *Life* © 1966 Time Inc. *A Simple Little Three-car Trick* © 1958 by Ken Purdy, first appeared in *This Week*.

The statements by John Surtees (page 46) originally appeared in interviews with Brian Glanville (*The Sunday Times*), Godfrey Winn (London *Evening News*) and Ken Hawkes (*World Sports*); those by the Graham Hills (page 44) in interviews with Hunter Davies (*The Sunday Times*) and me; those by Peter Arundell (page 42) in an interview with me (*Ford Times*); those by Jim Clark (page 40) in his book *Jim Clark at the Wheel*, reproduced by permission of Jim Clark and Coward McCann Inc.; those by Stirling Moss (pages 34–38) in *All But My Life: Stirling Moss Face to Face with Ken Purdy*, reproduced by permission of E. P. Dutton and Co. Inc.; and those by Phil Hill (page 39) in Robert Daley's *The Cruel Sport* © 1963 by Robert Daley, reproduced by permission of Prentice-Hall Inc.

Acknowledgements for permission to reproduce text and other extracts are also due as follows:—

William Collins and Co. and David Higham Associates for the extract from *The Green Hat* by Michael Arlen;

The Golden Press Inc. for the extract on the Model T Ford from *The Treasury of the Automobile* by Ralph Stein;

Prentice-Hall Inc. for the extract on Ferrari from *The Cruel Sport* by Robert Daley © 1963 by Robert Daley;

The executors of the Ian Fleming Estate and Jonathan Cape Ltd. for the extract from *Live and Let Die* by Ian Fleming;

Charles Scribner's Sons for the extracts from *The Forsyte Saga* by John Galsworthy and *The Diamond As Big As The Ritz* by F. Scott Fitzgerald;

Farrar, Strauss and Giroux, Inc. for the extract from *The Kandy-Kolored Tangerine Flake Streamline Baby* by Tom Wolfe;

A. Watkins Inc. and David Higham Associates for the extract from *Busman's Honeymoon* by Dorothy L. Sayers;

J. B. Lipincott Co. for the extract from *Passport to Peril* by James Leasor;

Mrs. Laura Huxley and Harper and Row Inc. for the extract from *Those Barren Leaves* by Aldous Huxley;

The Estate of the late Nevil Shute Norway and A. P. Watt and Son for the extract from *Marazan* by Nevil Shute;

Jonathan Cape Ltd. for the extract from *Poets' Pub* by Eric Linklater;

Mrs. George Bambridge and Doubleday and Co. Inc. and the Macmillan Co. of Canada for the extracts from *Steam Tactics* by Rudyard Kipling;

Methuen & Co. Ltd. for the extract from *The Lightning Conductor* by C. N. & A. M. Williamson;

Chapman & Hall Ltd. for the extract from *The Lightning Conductor Comes Back* by C. N. & A. M. Williamson;

G. R. N. Minchin and Arthur H. Stockwell Ltd. for the extract from *N.7: A Novel* by G. R. N. Minchin;

Little, Brown and Co. for the extracts from *A Singular Man* by J. P. Donleavy and *Great Morning* by Sir Osbert Sitwell;

New Directions Publishing Corporation for the extracts from *Automotive Passacaglia*, contained in *The Air-Conditioned Nightmare* by Henry Miller © 1945 by New Directions;

Macdonald & Co. for the extract from *Peter Jackson— Cigar Merchant* by Gilbert Frankau;

Macmillan & Co. and David Higham Associates for the extract from *Great Morning* by Sir Osbert Sitwell;

Professor A. W. Lawrence and Jonathan Cape Ltd. for the extract from *The Mint* by T. E. Lawrence;

Harcourt, Brace and World Inc. for *she being Brand* from *Selected Poems* 1923–58 by e. e. cummings;

Curtis Brown Ltd. for *Detroit, Spare That Wheel*, from *You Can't Get There From Here* by Ogden Nash;

John Murray Ltd. for the extracts from *A Subaltern's Love Song* and *Hertfordshire*, contained in *Collected Poems* by John Betjeman;

The New Yorker Magazine Inc. for *Ambition* by Morris Bishop © 1950 The New Yorker Magazine Inc.;

Edward Arnold Ltd. for *Inconvenience*, from *Ruthless Rhymes for Heartless Homes* by Harry Graham;

The Macmillan Company and Dr. John Masefield O.M. for the extract from *The Long Drive* by John Masefield;

Villiers Publications Ltd. for the extracts from *The Collected Motor Verses* of W. H. Charnock;

Patrick Campbell and Penguin Books Ltd. for *Reverie in Low Gear*, from *The P-P-Penguin Patrick Campbell*;

Edgar Leslie Inc. and Mills Music Inc. for the extract from the lyrics of *Get Out and Get Under* by Grant Clarke and Edgar Leslie;

Robert Mellin Ltd. for the extract from the lyrics of *Shut Down* by Brian Wilson and Roger Christian;

Secker and Warburg Ltd. for the extract from *Man and Motor-Cars (Ergonomic Study)* by Stephen Black;

Saul Steinberg and Hamish Hamilton Ltd. for the drawing from *The Passport*;

Giles and Beaverbrook Newspapers Ltd. for the cartoon by Giles;

The Viking Press Inc. for the drawing from *The Underground Sketchbook of Tomi Ungerer* © 1964 by Tomi Ungerer;

Punch for the cartoon by Thelwell;

Osbert Lancaster and John Murray Ltd. for the cartoon from *A Few Quick Tricks* by Osbert Lancaster;

Ronald Searle and Perpetua Ltd. for the cartoon from *Merry England Etcetera*;

The articles by Bill Boddy, Peter Dunn, Elisabeth Woolley, Peter Sullivan, Pete Brock and John Bentley, David Sylvester, John Dankworth, Peter Sellers, Lord Montagu of Beaulieu, Maurice Wiggin, Maxwell Boyd, Elizabeth Benson, and George Perry are, in each case, © 1966 by the respective author and Derek Jewell. *How I Found The Lost Cord* is © 1966 James Leasor and *Progress to the Mustang* is © 1966 Henry Longhurst. The Introduction and other material by the editor is © 1966 Derek Jewell.

Printed and bound in Great Britain. First published in the United States of America in 1967 by Walker and Company, 720 Fifth Avenue, New York, N.W. 10019.

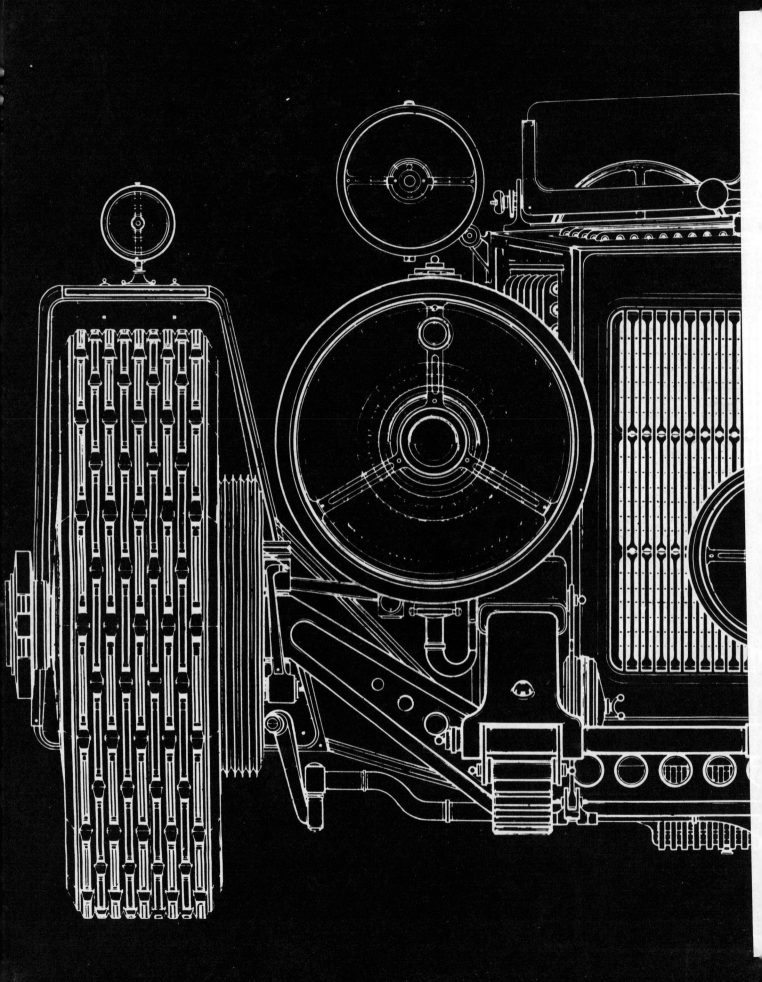